Targeted Tracks

The Cumberland Valley Railroad in the Civil War, 1861-1865

Scott L. Mingus Sr.
and Cooper H. Wingert

Savas Beatie
California

Library of Congress Cataloging-in-Publication Data

Names: Mingus, Scott L., author. | Wingert, Cooper H., author.

Title: Targeted Tracks: The Cumberland Valley Railroad in the Civil War, 1861-1865 / by Scott L. Mingus, Sr. and Cooper H. Wingert.

Other titles: Cumberland Valley Railroad in the Civil War, 1861-1865

Description: First edition. | El Dorado Hills, California: Savas Beatie, [2019] | Includes bibliographical references.

Identifiers: LCCN 2019007961| ISBN 9781611214611 (hardcover: alk. paper) | ISBN 9781611214628 (ebk)

Subjects: LCSH: Cumberland Valley Railroad Company—History. | Cumberland Valley (Md. and Pa.)—History—Civil War, 1861-1865. | Pennsylvania—History—Civil War, 1861-1865—Transportation. | Maryland—History—Civil War, 1861-1865—Transportation. | Railroads—Maryland—History—19th century. | Railroads—Pennsylvania—History—19th century. | United States—History—Civil War, 1861-1865—Transportation.

Classification: LCC F157.C9 M56 2019 | DDC 975.2/03—dc23

LC record available at https://lccn.loc.gov/2019007961

First Paper Edition, First Printing

Trade paper ISBN-13: 978-1-61121-543-4

SB

Savas Beatie
989 Governor Drive, Suite 102
El Dorado Hills, CA 95762
Phone: 916-941-6896 / E-mail: sales@savasbeatie.com
Web: www.savasbeatie.com

Our titles are available at special discounts for bulk purchases. For more details, contact us at sales@savasbeatie.com.

Proudly printed in the United States of America.

Scott dedicates it to his wife, Debi,
and Cooper dedicates it to his parents,

*   *   *

In Memoriam

Lila Fourhman-Shaull,
Director of Library and Archives, York County History Center

Table of Contents

List of Maps

List of Photos and Illustrations

List of Photos and Illustrations (continued)

List of Abbreviations Used in Text and Notes

B&O: Baltimore and Ohio Railroad
CCHS: Cumberland County Historical Society
CVRR: Cumberland Valley Railroad
FCHS: Franklin County Historical Society
FRR: Franklin Railroad
GNMP: Gettysburg National Military Park
JCCW: Joint Committee on the Conduct of the War
LC: Library of Congress
LSU: Louisiana State University
MMA: Mechanicsburg Museum Association
NCRY: Northern Central Railway
NYSNG: New York State National Guard
PHMC: Pennsylvania Historical and Museum Commission
PMTD: Pennsylvania Military Telegraph Department
PRR: Pennsylvania Railroad
PSA: Pennsylvania State Archives
PVM: Pennsylvania Volunteer Militia
UNC: University of North Carolina
USHEC: United States Army Heritage and Education Center
USMRR: United States Military Railroad
USSC: United States Sanitary Commission
UVA: University of Virginia

Foreword

$\mathcal{D}espite$ the critical role played by railroads during the Civil War, very little has been written about one particular railroad that operated in Pennsylvania. Thankfully, that oversight has been rectified in fine fashion by Scott Mingus and Cooper Wingert in *Targeted Tracks: The Cumberland Valley Railroad in the Civil War, 1861-1865*, a fast-paced and exciting study that combines industrial, economic, social, and military history in narrating the fascinating story of this line.

Railroads in America came of age with the coming of the Civil War. By 1861, the country boasted more than 200 different railroads, with two-thirds of the track miles crisscrossing northern states. This modern technology would play a major role in the conflict from its very start. The North had a distinct advantage in this regard, and used railroads to ship hundreds of thousands of men and untold tons of supplies when and where they were needed throughout the war. Despite the multitude of problems plaguing the Confederacy, the South managed to use its railroads to strategic advantage on several occasions. Railroads played an important role during the Southern victory at First Manassas during the war's first summer, for example, when Confederate troops were transported via rail to reinforce Gen. P. G. T. Beauregard's army. Another classic use of railroads unfolded in 1863 when most of James Longstreet's First Corps rode the rails from Virginia to North Georgia to reinforce Gen. Braxton Bragg's Army of Tennessee. Bragg used the troops to help win at Chickamauga—the only major Southern victory in the Western Theater during the entire war.

Targeted Tracks covers much more than rails, boxcars, and steam engines. Here, for the first time, is the complete study of not only the Cumberland Valley Railroad, but the region it traversed and served and the men responsible for running and maintaining the line. The authors reach back more than 150 years to give readers a capsule history of the 85-mile Cumberland Valley. Before European settlement, the major transportation networks consisted of nothing more than Indian paths crisscrossing the entire Eastern Seaboard. The authors discuss the development of roads in the area, the formation of the CVRR in 1837, how it was built, the obstacles it faced, and the men who faced them.

By the late 1850s, the CVRR was a prosperous line. John Brown and his associates used the railroad in 1859 to secretly ship weapons (listed as "hardware" on shipping manifests) to Chambersburg, where they planned much of the failed raid on Harpers Ferry. In late spring 1861, the CVRR was involved in the first extensive strategic use of a railroad during the war when a small Union army under Maj. Gen. Robert Patterson staged at Chambersburg for a failed foray to contain Confederate forces operating in the Shenandoah Valley. Several thousand men from Patterson's command were transported south to Hagerstown, Maryland, via the CVRR and the Franklin Railroad. Patterson, however, failed to contain the small Confederate army under Gen. Joseph E. Johnston, which slipped away (partly by rail) to reinforce Beauregard at Manassas. The Southern victory changed the course and scope of the war.

The CVRR played a little-known but important role during the 1862 Maryland Campaign. After the battle of Antietam, Maj. Gen. George B. McClellan faced significant logistical problems, partly because of the disrupted Baltimore and Ohio Railroad. McClellan turned to the CVRR for help transporting badly needed supplies, ammunition in particular, to the railhead at Hagerstown, where it was shipped to the nearby Antietam battlefield. The railroad also played a role in transporting more than 400 wounded Union soldiers to Chambersburg, Pennsylvania, where hospitals had been established to care for them. Around this time, the CVRR transported Pennsylvania volunteer militia to the region as a bulwark against further Confederate incursions. A few weeks after Antietam, the railroad suffered its first major wartime loss when Maj. Gen. Jeb Stuart led around 1,800 Confederate cavalrymen on a raid around McClellan's Army of the Potomac.

On October 11, Stuart occupied Chambersburg and destroyed the round house and shops of the CVRR.

Devout students of the Gettysburg campaign and battle will thank Mingus and Wingert for their vivid account of that campaign in the Cumberland Valley. During this period the railroad suffered more damage from Confederate raiders, and learn about other aspects of Lee's invasion, including the abduction of free blacks for shipment back into the South. After the battle, the CVRR helped transport Confederate prisoners north to Union prisons. The entire book is outstanding, but I found this section, in particular, to be one of the highlights of Targeted Tracks.

The authors also include a detailed account of McCausland's Raid and the burning of Chambersburg in July 1864, when the entire inner core of the town was destroyed and the Confederates engaged in a drunken orgy of looting. Ironically, the CVRR suffered less damage in that raid than earlier Confederate incursions. At the war's end, the CVRR brought the soldiers home from the war. A third daily train was added to carry the many thousands home. On a sadder note, a special train traversed the Cumberland Valley north to Harrisburg on Saturday, April 22, jammed with people determined to view President Lincoln's funeral train, which had stopped at Harrisburg while taking the martyred president to his final resting place in Springfield, Illinois. Mingus and Wingert conclude their study with an overview of the postwar operations of the CVRR, how they repaired wartime damage, and role it played hauling veterans to their numerous reunions.

The engaging narrative is supported by impressive firsthand research and exceptional scholarship that will have great appeal to students of railroads during the war, and to anyone who wishes a fuller and richer appreciation of how Confederate incursions north affected key logistical lifelines. I commend the authors for taking the time and going to the trouble of researching and writing such a valuable contribution to Civil War studies. Their effort proves once again that there is still much to learn about our favorite subject.

Ted Alexander
Chief Historian (ret)
Antietam National Battlefield

Acknowledgments

Cooper and I are extremely grateful that our mutual good friend Ted Alexander wrote the foreword to this book and kindly offered to share materials from his fine book, When War Passed This Way. His active participation in this project enriched the manuscript multiple times along the way. We are in your debt, Ted.

Due special consideration is long-time Cumberland Valley chronicler and collector M. L. "Mike" Marotte III. He graciously responded to emails and then met with me in person to discuss items in his extensive files. As we broke bread together in Gettysburg, we found much in common, and his enthusiasm and support for our project was simply outstanding. Thank you, Mike!

We also appreciate the fine efforts of Michele Wade of the Franklin County Historical Society, who graciously made available to us the library's collection of articles on the Civil War and the Cumberland Valley Railroad. Lila Fourhman-Shaull of the York County History Center did the same from their archives, including making available reference books and other useful materials. Robert L. Williams, my co-author on our book on the Philadelphia, Wilmington & Baltimore Railroad in the Civil War, offered many useful suggestions. Elizabeth Howe and John Frye of the Western Maryland Room of the Washington County (Maryland) Free Library searched through their records of the railroad and Civil War in Hagerstown.

Long-time Pennsylvania Railroad historians/collectors John Frantz and his father, Ivan Frantz, Jr., offered guidance and direction, including offering several useful suggestions on source materials. Christopher T. Baer of the Hagley Museum in Wilmington, Delaware, gave us ideas on materials in the museum's collection, as well as the location of many of the CVRR's old minute books and other reference documents. Railroad historian/archivist Kurt R. Bell and Jonathan Stayer, Supervisor of Reference Services, helped suggest files from the collection of the Pennsylvania State Archives in Harrisburg. We are deeply grateful for their assistance, as well as Megan Rentschler and Mary Fenton, who helped pull key files for us. Dr. Iren Snavely, the rare collections librarian at the State Library of Pennsylvania, looked for copies of the Cumberland Valley Journal for us.

Richard Tritt, the photo curator at the Cumberland County Historical Society in Carlisle, prepared several images for us to use in the book. The staff of Dickinson College graciously gave us permission to use an image of the burning of the Scotland Bridge from their collection. John Heiser of the National Park Service searched through the holdings of the library of Gettysburg National Military Park for references to the Cumberland Valley Railroad or Franklin Railroad.

Jim Cassatt gave us advice, as well as providing an image of a postcard showing the CVRR station in Newville, Pennsylvania, late in the 19th century. The Washington County (Maryland) Free Library has a useful collection of Civil War-era Hagerstown newspapers, most notably the *Herald of Freedom and Torch Light* and the *Hagerstown Mail*. Well-known author and educator Dr. Matthew Pinsker of Dickinson College in Carlisle, PA, gave us permission to use images and documents from their collection.

Several people took time to review the manuscript at various stages of its development and offer advice and suggestions. They included Craig Breneiser, Ted Alexander, Roger Cutter, Barry Larkin, Mike Marotte, and Robert L. Williams.

Cooper and I also want to acknowledge and thank our publisher Savas Beatie, its managing director Theodore P. Savas, and Ted's entire team, including Sarah Keeney, Renee Morehouse, Sarah Closson, Lisa Murphy, and Stephanie Ferro. Fellow author Larry Tagg did the final proofreading and light editing. This is my fifth book with Savas Beatie, and, again, I commend them for their excellence and passion for the books they have published on my behalf. To this talented group of dedicated professionals who go out of their way to support their stable of authors, all I can humbly say is a heartfelt "Thank you!"

*   *   *

Note: Several images appear here courtesy of M. L. "Mike" Marotte III, author/historian, www.vintagefranklincounty.com.

Chapter 1

The Antebellum CVRR

Thick clouds of acrid, oily smoke hung in the crisp morning air. Under the dark canopy, angry orange-colored flames crackled as a massive warehouse filled with mountains of Federal military uniforms, weapons and military accouterments quickly became engulfed in the roaring inferno. Nearby, Confederate cavalrymen scurried about, ripping down the remaining telegraph wires of the Cumberland Valley Railroad yard.

The Southern horsemen were hoping to wreck the railroad for a considerable period to deny its use to the Yankees. The roundhouse and extensive machine shops soon met the torch. As the roof collapsed on the engine house, three steam locomotives sustained significant damage. Boxes of ammunition began exploding, adding to the growing tumult. Other soldiers loaded piles of supplies previously pilfered from the warehouses into heavy freight wagons. Horrified citizens watched from a distance, hoping the deliberate destruction did not extend to their homes or businesses. Some of their fellow Franklin County residents were in Confederate custody, facing a grim trip to military prison in Richmond, Virginia, to be used as future political pawns. Others, including the town's telegrapher and postmaster, had fled to safety before the Rebels arrived.

The date was October 11, 1862; the place was Chambersburg, Pennsylvania. Famed Confederate Brig. Gen. James Ewell Brown "Jeb" Stuart had led 1,800 veteran troopers north from Darkesville, in western Virginia, through Maryland and into south-central Pennsylvania, targeting the CVRR. The small but strategically important railroad ran southwest from Harrisburg, Pennsylvania, through the verdant Cumberland Valley to Hagerstown, Maryland. It was a vital supply route for Union Maj. Gen. George B. McClellan's Army of the Potomac, which was spread out between Harpers Ferry and Bakersville, Maryland, following the battle of Antietam the previous month. On their way north, Stuart's men had procured fresh horses from the bountiful farms of the Cumberland Valley and looted the village of Mercersburg in southwestern Franklin County. The lead elements of Stuart's column had reached Chambersburg, the county seat, about 8:00 p.m. the previous evening, when their bugles bleated their unwelcome arrival to the startled townspeople. Soon, a trio of concerned civic leaders had met the Rebel leaders to seek terms for the peaceful surrender of the town of 5,200 people. In a pouring rain, a detachment of the 2nd Virginia Cavalry headed five miles north to Scotland to burn the sturdy CVRR bridge over the Conococheague Creek—its loss, if the mission was successful, would sever McClellan's heavily used supply line. The rest of Stuart's command had occupied Chambersburg and vicinity, and were now smashing the railroad infrastructure before leaving and heading eastward toward Gettysburg.[1]

War had come to the Cumberland Valley and its most important economic link to the outside world, the railroad. Long before the advent of the "iron horse," the broad valley in south-central Pennsylvania and northern Maryland had been a major trade route and portage between the Susquehanna River and Potomac River, first for Native American tribes such as the Susquehannock and Iroquois and later for pioneer explorers and settlers, many of which were Scots-Irish or English. Part of what is today known as the Great Appalachian Valley, the Blue Mountain and Bear Pond ranges of the Appalachians constituted the western and northern boundaries of the Cumberland Valley, with the South Mountain range forming the southern and eastern perimeter. Narrow gaps gave access and egress for travelers and settlers. The valley, typically about 10 to 12 miles wide in most places, runs 73 miles from a point near the Susquehanna's West Shore near Harrisburg in a general southwesterly direction to the Potomac near Hagerstown, Maryland. In between those towns, in Franklin and Cumberland counties, lay a plethora of smaller Keystone communities, including Bridgeport (now Lemoyne), White Hall (now Camp Hill), Mechanicsburg, Carlisle, Newville, Shippensburg, Chambersburg, and Greencastle. The highest point, "the summit" at 783 feet

---

1 Adapted from W. P. Conrad and Ted Alexander, *When War Passed This Way* (Greencastle Bicentennial Publication/Lilian S. Besore Memorial Library, 1982).

above sea level, is in the central part of the Valley between Shippensburg and Chambersburg along the line of the Cumberland Valley Railroad.[2]

Origins

The early Native Americans referred to the densely timbered North Mountain range as Kau-ta-tin-chunk (later anglicized as Kittochtinny), meaning "endless mountains" or "main mountains." The setting sun cast shadows into the fertile, well-watered valley, teaming with wildlife and thick vegetation, mostly field grasses, low shrubs such as juniper and laurel, and a variety of stately oak, walnut, hickory, and maple trees. Berries and fruit abounded, as did rich deposits of iron ore and limestone. "It is said that the white men that first came to the valley were greatly impressed with its beauty and the natural productions of the soil," a 19th-century historian penned. "The grass was rich and luxuriant, wild fruits were abundant, and there was a great variety of trees in places… while in the open country the strawberry, dewberry and wintergreen made a luscious carpeting and furnished the Indians in their season a tempting and welcome partial supply of food." Game was abundant, providing food and pelts. In 1720, French fur trader James LeTort established a small outpost along what is now known as LeTort Spring Run near the later settlement of Carlisle. Over the next three decades, additional trappers and traders arrived, as did later waves of colonial settlers, their sturdy Conestoga wagons brimming with household goods. Most had moved westward across the Susquehanna River from the Philadelphia area, and trains of eager settlers headed deep into the rural interior of Pennsylvania. Many now called the Cumberland Valley home, while others passed through the gaps in the North Mountain range and headed for the Ohio River and beyond.[3]

By 1750, enough people lived in the Valley to allow the creation of a separate county, Cumberland, to be carved from Lancaster County. It stretched the length of the Cumberland Valley. The largest town, Carlisle, located near the site of James LeTort's fur trading post, became the seat. The Cumberland Valley played a key role in the French & Indian War from 1754 to 1763. Trade routes, control of the entry points to the Ohio Country, alliances with the Native Americans, and

---

2 Harriet Wylie Stewart, *History of the Cumberland Valley, Pennsylvania* (n.p., 1918), 1-10. See also, George P. Donehoo, *A History of the Cumberland Valley in Pennsylvania* (Susquehanna History Association, 1930).

3 Ibid.; Samuel D. Bates, *History of Cumberland and Adams Counties, Pennsylvania* (Warner, Beers & Co., 1886), 4-6.

national pride were all at stake for the British and French as the Seven Years' War spread from its European origins across the ocean to North America. Several small engagements were fought in the valley. Settlers constructed five small wooden forts at key points in the valley, including sites near what became Carlisle and Shippensburg. Inspired by the French, Native American warriors occasionally attacked the outposts and isolated settlements. The Treaty of Paris in 1763 finally brought an end to the global war, although strife remained for years in the Cumberland Valley between the natives and the ever-increasing population of whites, free blacks, and occasional slaves. During the American Revolution, several local farms provided food, forage, and supplies to the Continental Army, and ironworks produced cannonballs and other military equipment.[4]

To the south in Maryland, Washington County was carved out of Frederick County in 1776, largely through the efforts of German immigrant Jonathan Hager. He had founded Elizabethtown, named for his wife, in 1762. After that town became the county seat, people began referring to it as Hagerstown, a name that became official in 1814 when the Maryland State Assembly approved the change.

Industry and agriculture in the Cumberland Valley flourished, offering steady employment and fueling the growing prosperity of the region. By 1784, enough people lived in the southern part of the Valley in Pennsylvania to justify the creation of a new county, Franklin, to be split off from Cumberland County. Chambersburg became the county seat. Massive freight wagons hauled cargo on well-maintained paved turnpikes down through Hagerstown and on to Baltimore, or west toward Pittsburgh or east across South Mountain to Gettysburg and on through York and Lancaster to Philadelphia. Secondary roads, mostly well-packed dirt, connected the valley's communities to markets in Hanover and Frederick. The burgeoning economy gave rise to the need to move even larger quantities of freight and passengers quickly. Leading merchants in Baltimore considered several alternatives. In August 1827, they began discussing constructing railroads into the Susquehanna and Cumberland valleys. Investors in Massachusetts were operating a freight line to haul granite from mines to a riverport for subsequent transportation to Boston for use in the new Bunker Hill Monument. Several horse-drawn railroads were in service in Great Britain, and steam power loomed on the horizon.[5]

4 Ibid.

5 The Granite Railway is generally considered the first commercially successful US railroad company.

At the time, Baltimore and Philadelphia interests were competing to tap into the riches of the Cumberland Valley and the interior of Pennsylvania. In March 1828, the Canal Commission met in downtown Harrisburg to discuss connecting a railroad to the canal and portage system. Surveyor William R. Hopkins surveyed two possible routes from the Susquehanna River to Chambersburg, dismissing a possible route from Wrightsville in eastern York County west through Gettysburg and on to Chambersburg because of the difficulty of crossing South Mountain. He recommended a route from Harrisburg through Carlisle, but the state legislature took no action.[6]

Baltimore was closer to Chambersburg than Philadelphia, and thus suggested itself as the opposite terminus of a likely less expensive route for hauling freight, but in both coastal cities, investors were formulating their own plans to construct railroad lines. In 1828, the Baltimore & Susquehanna Railroad received its organizational charter in Maryland, with a goal of running track from Baltimore north to York and then on to the Susquehanna River. Plans were being developed to connect the B&S with additional lines that ran west through Hanover to Gettysburg, and then through the South Mountain gaps to Chambersburg in the Cumberland Valley. However, opposition to the plan in the Pennsylvania legislature stalled the project, and by 1832 the tracks were only completed from a few miles north from Baltimore through the countryside to Timonium. Pennsylvania legislators did not authorize the northward expansion into the Keystone State until 1834.[7]

Meanwhile, several prominent Philadelphia businessmen also sought access to the riches of the Cumberland Valley and began planning their own railroad through Harrisburg to Chambersburg. In January 1831, in Carlisle, Cumberland Valley civic leaders Frederick Watts, Dr. J. David Mahon, Charles McClure, John Harper, and James Woodburn were named to a committee to write a petition that would be forwarded to the Pennsylvania state legislature urging them to charter a railroad for the good of the valley's residents. "Its citizens have a right to expect," they wrote, "that they will be allowed, at least to participate in the advantages of those improvements which promise to enrich the state in its eastern and western borders." On April 2, Pennsylvania Governor George Wolf signed an act to

6 Paul J. Westhaeffer, *History of the Cumberland Valley Railroad 1835-1919* (National Railway Historical Society, 1979), 5.

7 For more on the early history of the B&S and its successor the Northern Central Railway, see Scott Mingus, *Soldiers, Spies & Steam: A History of the Northern Central Railway in the Civil War* (Amazon CreateSpace, 2016).

incorporate the Cumberland Valley Railroad to run initially from Carlisle to the Susquehanna River at or near Harrisburg. Several appointed commissioners began selling 4,000 shares of stock in the new railroad at $50 per share, with the expectation that a minimum of 1,500 shares had to be sold before the state would issue a charter to the new company. The merchants and farmers, however, did not support the initiative and the deadline for raising the start-up capital expired.[8]

The CVRR Finally Begins Construction

That sentiment changed over the next few years as the economy continued to expand and freight needs increased. Supporters of the proposed railroad continued their efforts to shore up funding. On April 15, 1835, Governor Wolf signed a bill reviving the railroad company, giving it six years to commence and finish the construction. The line was also to connect with the Main Line Works, most notably the canal system. This supplement expanded the railroad into Shippensburg and Chambersburg, and this time there was more enthusiasm for the ambitious project. "If a railroad is made from Harrisburg to this place [Carlisle], we can leave Carlisle at nine o'clock in the morning and reach Philadelphia at six o'clock in the evening," a reporter mentioned. "A farmer can put his produce into a railroad car in the morning and the same evening have it on Broad street, Philadelphia, and that, too, at *one-half of the expense* it would have cost him to have it taken by wagons." He urged that "our wealthy citizens (and we have many such amongst us) will step forward and subscribe liberally towards making 'Cumberland Valley Railroad.'"[9]

Starting in mid-May of 1835, sufficient stock was sold in three weeks, through subscription plans, to raise $642,000, and on June 2 Wolf signed the necessary paperwork to authorize the formation of the state-chartered Cumberland Valley Railroad Company. Stockholders met in Carlisle on June 27 and elected long-time Chambersburg attorney and former Federalist congressman Thomas Grubb McCulloh, a War of 1812 veteran and former U. S. congressman, as the first president. The board consisted of twelve appointed directors who would serve staggered terms. They included early railroad supporters Frederick Watts and

---

8 Frederick D. Brumbaugh, "A History of the Cumberland Valley Railroad Company, 1831-1837," in *Kittochtinny Historical Society Papers*, Kittochtinny Historical Society, vol. 16, 176.

9 *American Volunteer* (Carlisle, PA), May 14, 1835.

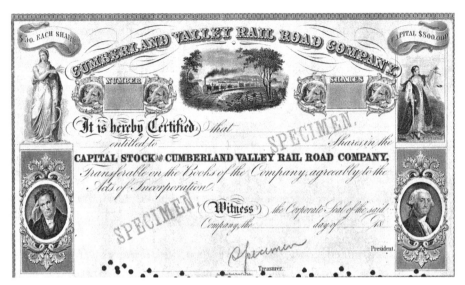

A specimen of an early $50 share of stock in the Cumberland Valley Rail Road Company that belonged to T. B. Kennedy, an early investor and company legal counsel who became the president of the CVRR. *Mike Marotte*

David Mahon, the latter a prominent Carlisle physician. Philadelphia, Carlisle, Chambersburg, and Shippensburg were all represented on the board.[10]

The directors set the compensation packages for the officers in the charter. President McCulloh received an initial salary of $1,500 a year plus travel and office expenses. The secretary, Abraham Hendel, received $300. Each of the directors would get two dollars a day plus ten cents per mile when traveling on company business. Surveyors, civil engineers, and anyone else needed to plan and construct the line would also receive compensation determined by the company officers. William Milnor Roberts came on board as chief engineer in early August 1835 at an annual salary of $2,000. Roberts was only 25 years old, but the Quaker-educated Philadelphian already had considerable practical field experience to augment his formal education in mathematics, architectural drafting, and engineering.[11]

10 Ibid., 179; *Laws of the General Assembly of the Commonwealth of Pennsylvania* (State Printer, 1836), 28-30. McCulloh, spelled McCullough in several accounts, served in the US House of Representatives from 1820-1821.

11 Brumbaugh, "A History of the Cumberland Valley Railroad," 180. Roberts's papers, including an extensive autobiography, are held in the Montana State University Library, Merrill G. Burlingame Special Collections.

Roberts soon began surveying possible routes for the proposed railroad. He soon focused on the two most promising, one that ran closer to North Mountain and one closer to South Mountain. A key was to locate the tracks close to as many potential customers as possible. Cumberland and Franklin counties contained 152 grist mills (with an annual total output of 340,000 barrels of flour), 80 distilleries making more than a million gallons of whiskey each year, nine iron furnaces and 14 associated forges and a rolling mill, three paper mills, 132 sawmills, 25 clover mills, and 45 factories making coarse cotton and woolen goods, as well as other assorted products. More than 250 retail merchants supplied the residents with sundries and other merchandise. He estimated that the new railroad had the potential to carry up to 86,000 tons a year of freight, produce, and general trade goods.[12]

Roberts recommended the southern route, but the directors were concerned that this path bypassed Newville, an agricultural center in Cumberland County about eleven miles west of Carlisle. In the end they compromised, using the southern route except for the section between Carlisle and Shippensburg, which would follow the northern route to include Newville and vicinity. In exchange, the borough and citizens of Newville would be required to pay the railroad $2,500 for the extra distance. Roberts and his associates began planning the right of way and obtaining the necessary five-rod-wide contiguous strips of land. The charter documents allowed the railroad to seize, for a fair price, any property it needed to complete its surveyed right of way, with the exception that it could not obtain burial grounds, churches, or dwellings (or any major outbuilding valued at more than $500) without the owner's consent.[13]

Roberts began advertising for contractors to submit proposals by sunset on November 14, 1835, to grade about 25 miles of the new line. "It is expected that the proposals of those who are not personally known to the Engineer will be accompanied by proper references," he advised in several newspaper notices. Dozens of potential bidders traveled to Carlisle to present their proposals in person before the deadline, thronging the hotels and restaurants of the suddenly bustling town. After careful consideration, Roberts selected Joseph S. Snowden of

---

12 Samuel Hazard, "Cumberland Valley Railroad," in *Hazard's Register of Pennsylvania*, vol. XVII, no. 20, November 14, 1835, 306-308, citing the *Harrisburg Chronicle*. Clover mills used rough grindstones to crush the flowered heads of clover to extract and clean the seeds, which were important in the rudimentary crop rotation system then practiced.

13 Ibid.; Brumbaugh, "A History of the Cumberland Valley Railroad," 177-78; *Carlisle Weekly Herald*, November 25, 1863.

Philadelphia as the general contractor for the project. Construction of the CVRR roadbed, graded wide enough for eventual double-tracking, began in January 1836, but it soon became evident that additional funding would be needed to complete the entire 52-mile length, acquire rolling stock, and begin operations. The board of directors agreed to augment the company's capital with additional cash from their own pockets to complete the line.[14]

Railroad officials contracted with William Norris's manufacturing firm in Philadelphia for the delivery of three new locomotives by the spring of 1837 at not more than $6,800 apiece. While the CVRR and Norris planned its initial engines, progress on the railbed through the valley slowed considerably. Many of the temporary construction workers were also farmers, and most of them needed to return home to bring in the summer harvest. They returned to work in August. A year later, the work was progressing, although costs were higher than expected.[15]

In his annual report to the board in December 1836, Roberts was more optimistic about the company's financial picture, although the cost to finish the line would still exceed the available capital. He now estimated the cost to begin operations, including acquiring engines and rolling stock, would be $681,400. He had re-worked the numbers based upon the work in progress and recent technical advances. As the roadbed progressed, crews needed to excavate much less rock than anticipated. He also now believed that he had underestimated the amount of freight and passengers that the railroad would carry, and had overestimated the cost of maintaining and repairing the line. Raw material increases, however, mitigated some of the cost savings.[16]

CVRR management petitioned the state legislature for aid, but it was not forthcoming. By April 1837, the board agreed that it needed to take out a loan for $200,000 to ensure the completion of the line within the original deadlines. However, a financial crisis leading to a depression, known as the Panic of 1837, soon gripped the country, and the banks and private investors were unwilling to take the risk of lending money to the struggling railroad company. The board sent

14 "Cumberland Valley Railroad: To Contractors for Grading," *Daily Pittsburgh Gazette*, October 17, 1835; "Cumberland Valley Railroad," *Carlisle Weekly Herald*, November 18, 1835.

15 W. Williams, *Appleton's Railroad and Steamboat Companion, Being a Travellers' Guide through the United States of America, Canada, New Brunswick, and Nova Scotia* (D. Appleton & Company, 1848), 254; Brumbaugh, "A History of the Cumberland Valley Railroad," 180-81.

16 *Second Report of William Milnor Roberts, Chief Engineer of the Cumberland Valley Rail Road Company, Made to the Board, on the 29th of December 1836* (Chambersburg, PA: Hickok & Blood, 1836), 6-9. Copy in the William Milnor Roberts Papers, Montana State University Library, Bozeman.

A so-called CVRR "shinplaster," an early promissory note that dates from 1837. *Mike Marotte*

a representative to Europe to seek funding, but he came back empty-handed. They managed, however, to obtain $50,000 from the Franklin Railroad Company to help keep the construction moving forward. When those funds dried up, the railroad began issuing promissory notes, known colloquially as "shinplasters," to its creditors and suppliers. They were redeemable in one year at six percent interest. Even so, the CVRR had to suspend construction on a bridge in July to keep the scrip in good credit, and the board members issued a public notice they would individually and collectively guarantee future redemption of the specie.[17]

The fledgling railroad received a license as a freight forwarder, but all the available capital was being put into construction, building the infrastructure, and acquiring locomotives, tenders, and passenger cars. Nothing was left to purchase freight cars (also known then as "burthen" or "burden" cars). As a result, several Valley firms already in the freight-forwarding business, over time, purchased their own cars that operated from their private warehouses. These companies hired their own conductors who accompanied their cars to supervise loading and unloading. Some of the more enterprising freight companies also sold tickets to passengers across different forms of transportation, including various railroads. The inability to control its own freight and the loss of associated revenue would plague the Cumberland line for several decades and limit its earnings.[18]

---

17 "House of Representatives," *The Keystone* (Harrisburg, PA), December 17, 1836; Brumbaugh, "A History of the Cumberland Valley Railroad," 182-85.

18 Mechanicsburg (PA) Museum Association, "The Cumberland Valley Railroad & Mechanicsburg," www.mechanicsburgmuseum.org/cvrr.html. Accessed January 7, 2018.

The plan was to connect the CVRR at Chambersburg to the Franklin Railroad, an independent company chartered in Pennsylvania in March 1832 and then in Maryland in January 1837. Early investors envisioned a connection with the Baltimore & Ohio Railroad and/or the Chesapeake & Ohio Canal system, but neither would be accomplished for several decades. The FRR, when completed at a projected capital cost of $300,000, would run 22 miles from Chambersburg south through Greencastle to Hagerstown, Maryland, where it would connect with the heavy freight and passenger traffic on the National Road. Civic officials in Hagerstown pledged $20,000 to the project, which would have its terminus on Walnut Street. Danish-born Hother Hage served as the chief engineer of the FRR; the Royal University of Copenhagen graduate would go on to a long career with various Pennsylvania canals and railroads. He finished the Chambersburg-Greencastle section in April 1837, with teams of draft horses providing the motive power on rather crude, strap-iron-capped wooden sills.[19]

Meanwhile, work continued throughout 1837 on the CVRR line from the Susquehanna River south toward Chambersburg. Soon, preparations were made to begin commercial operations. Much of the track was laid, using light flat rails made of bar iron. Crews constructed a fuel and water stop, along with platforms for passengers and freight, in Mechanicsburg. With capital still a at a premium, the only station buildings would be in Chambersburg and Carlisle. CVRR agents purchased a plot of flat land on the north side of Chambersburg near a tannery. The company erected an engine house with a turntable and a freight forwarding business soon constructed a warehouse nearby.[20]

Crews built a depot along the west side of Chambersburg's North Second Street, beyond the Falling Spring Creek, not far from the engine house. Its ground floor was planned to be level with the platforms of the passenger cars. Riders could get into and off of the cars without stepping up or down, unlike many other railroads of the day. A long, covered platform extended along the west side to give passengers some protection from the sun and rain. For refreshments, a bar room occupied the southwestern corner of the station. The CVRR erected its machine

---

19 *Appleton's Railroad and Steamboat Companion*, 1848, 254-55; *Commemorative Biographical Encyclopedia of Dauphin County, Containing Sketches of Representative Citizens, and Many of the Early Scotch-Irish and German Settlers* (J. M. Runk & Company, 1896), 224. The line from Greencastle to Hagerstown was finished in Feb. 1841, well after Hage left in 1838 for other opportunities.

20 John M. Cooper, *Recollections of Chambersburg, Pa., Chiefly Between the Years 1830-1850* (A. Nevin Pomeroy, 1900), 11, 59.

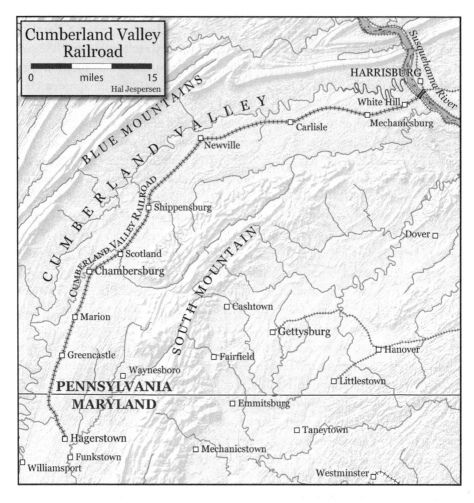

shops along a nearby alley, in the shadow of an impressive stone Catholic church. Hotels and other services for the passengers began to be constructed.[21]

The railroad soon took delivery of the shiny new locomotive *Cumberland Valley*, which arrived from William Norris's factory in Philadelphia after being hauled to Carlisle through Harrisburg by canal boats and hay wagons. The other two contracted engines were still under construction and would be delivered later that summer. At 8:00 a.m. on Saturday, August 19, 1837, the 16-mile First Division of the railroad from the new depot in Carlisle on High Street to White Hill on the west shore of the river opened when the *Cumberland Valley* steamed

---

21 Ibid., 60-61. The station, at 229 N. Second Street, served the CVRR from 1837 to 1876. Two other depots were later erected on the same site.

northeast on its initial run. Fifty-seven minutes later, the gaily decorated train reached the eastern terminus at White Hill without incident; it only took 47 minutes for the return trip. Work continued throughout the autumn southwest from Carlisle to Chambersburg, although construction had not yet resumed on the expensive covered bridge into Harrisburg.[22]

The CVRR held its formal grand opening on November 16, 1837, when two heavy locomotives pulled a seven-car train filled with dignitaries and invited guests from White Hill down to the new Chambersburg depot at North Second Street. "The cars left Harrisburg early on Thursday morning filled with guests, among whom were some of the most prominent in the state," the *Carlisle Herald and Expositor* reported. "Stopping at Carlisle another engine and cars were attached crowded to overflowing." Soon, the whistle sounded and the train, filled with more than 500 passengers, slowly pulled out for Chambersburg to the thunderous acclamation of the crowd of onlookers and well-wishers. At Newville, almost the entire populace was on hand to greet the novelty of the train. From there, the line ran through the most populous portion of the Cumberland Valley down to Shippensburg. There were few curves in this section of the road, and the locomotives made good time, despite frequent stops for wood and water. Just before the train arrived in Shippensburg, a delegation of local officials boarded it. A band gaily played "Hail Columbia" as the train steamed into downtown before throngs of flag-waving spectators. More cars were added there, increasing the passenger count to nearly a thousand. "When they arrived at Chambersburg [at 3:00 p.m.]," a Harrisburg newspaperman noted, "the cars, both inside and outside, presented a solid mass of heads, being loaded as thick as they could sit or stand." The dignitaries enjoyed a sumptuous banquet, replete with several toasts, at Culbertson's Hotel on the town square (known as "the Diamond"). Railroad president T. G. McCulloh praised the board and Chief Engineer Roberts for completing the project. Financier Thomas Biddle of Philadelphia and other prominent men, including Thaddeus Stevens, also spoke. After the festivities concluded, they crowded back into the cars and took an overnight trip back to the state capital, arriving at 6:00 a.m.[23]

22 *Daily Pittsburgh Gazette*, August 26, 1837; S. P. Bates, *History of Franklin County, Pennsylvania: History of Pennsylvania* (Chicago: Warner, Beers & Company, 1887), 231; Brumbaugh, "A History of the Cumberland Valley Railroad," 185. The locomotive had two driving wheels with wooden spokes.

23 *Carlisle Herald and Expositor*, November 21, 1837; "Opening of the Cumberland Valley Rail Road," *Harrisburg Telegraph*, November 20, 1837.

Cumberland Valley
Rail Road.

ON THE FIRST DAY OF FEBRUARY NEXT, the regular train of **PASSENGER CARS** will commence running daily as follows :

Leave Chambersburg at Four o'clock in the morning, arrive at Harrisburg at 8—at Lancaster at 12—and at Philadelphia before 6 P. M.

Returning it will leave Harrisburg as soon as the Cars from Philadelphia arrive, *about five o'clock* in the evening, and arrive at Chambersburg *at ten P. M.*

☞ It is expected that this Train will in a short time leave Philadelphia *at six* instead of *eight o'clock* in the morning, and then arrive at Chambersburg *before dark* of the same day.

There will also be a daily line of **FREIGHT CARS** from Chambersburg to Harrisburg and back, which will carry produce & Merchandize to and from those places in the most safe, cheap and expeditious way.

T. G. M'Culloh,

Pres't Cumb. V R R Co

25th January, 1838.

This early commercial advertisement for the new Cumberland Valley line shows the initial timetable. *Mike Marotte*

The CVRR soon initiated a regular schedule of two trains per day carrying through the broad valley between Chambersburg and the Susquehanna River. With the railroad bridge over the river still unfinished, freight wagons and stagecoaches carried the passengers and cargo from White Hill into downtown Harrisburg. Two sections of track in the state capital still needed to be completed by the end of the year. Fortunately, the state legislature finally released the necessary funding, beginning with the first installment in June. Those tracks would eventually connect the CVRR to William Milnor Roberts's concurrent construction project, the Harrisburg, Portsmouth, Mount Joy and Lancaster Railroad. Roberts reported to the CVRR board that he had expended $406,831.50 in the little less than two years of construction at a "cost less per mile than almost any other railroad of equal importance in the world." Fortunately, the route was largely straight, without any mountains or high hills, featuring a level grade and few major water crossings other than the Susquehanna.[24]

In his third, and what proved to his final, annual report as chief engineer of the CVRR, Roberts congratulated the board and stockholders for the "signal success which has thus far attended this important undertaking." He also thanked the board members for pledging their individual fortunes to finish the job, especially in light of "this most trying crisis"—that is, the financial panic in 1837 that had threatened to suspend construction after the board had exhausted nearly all available funds. Now, however, the railroad was a reality, at least from Chambersburg to the West Shore.[25]

Former CVRR supporter Thaddeus Stevens soon became a potential rival. In 1838, he asked the commonwealth to build a railroad, at government expense, from his iron mines and furnaces in Franklin and Adams counties to the Baltimore & Ohio Railroad. That, of course, would help line his own pockets and likely divert much-needed freight hauls from the CVRR. A transportation-focused committee of the state senate eventually ruled in favor of the CVRR, and Stevens' project was abandoned.[26]

24 *Minute Book of the Cumberland Valley Railroad, 1837*, as quoted by Brumbaugh, "A History of the Cumberland Valley Railroad," 185; *Philadelphia Public Ledger*, June 21, 1838.

25 *Third Annual Report of William Milnor Roberts, Chief Engineer of the Cumberland Valley Rail Road Company, Made to the Board, on the 28th of December, 1837*, 2-3. Copy in the William Milnor Roberts Papers, Montana State University Library, Bozeman. Roberts, his work completed, soon resigned and moved on to other projects.

26 "James Weston Livingood, *The Philadelphia-Baltimore Trade Rivalry, 1780-1860* (Pennsylvania Historical and Museum Commission, 1947), 146-47.

Perhaps the most expensive engineering challenge on the CVRR was the planned 4,000-foot-long covered bridge over the Susquehanna River between Bridgeport and Harrisburg. Estimated to cost at least $95,000 to construct, it would have 23 spans (averaging 173 feet in length) with two arched viaducts, one 53 feet long and the other 84 feet. The design of the wooden lattice bridge featured two carriageways, with the second pair of railroad tracks laid on top of the flat roof. Draft horses would pull the cars across the span.[27]

In mid-January 1839, the latticed bridge over the Susquehanna River finally opened to the cheers of throngs of onlookers as the first train rumbled across the rooftop tracks. The "splendid structure," almost a mile long, enabled continuous service from Chambersburg through the state capital to Philadelphia via the Harrisburg, Portsmouth, Mount Joy and Lancaster Railroad and the connecting Philadelphia and Columbia Railroad. Stagecoaches took passengers west from Chambersburg to Pittsburgh, offering passengers a cost-effective alternative to the Pennsylvania Main Line of Public Works, a state-owned enterprise of canals, inclines, and the Allegheny Portage Railroad to travel between Philadelphia and Pittsburgh. Civil engineer Hother Hage studied the possibility of building a continuous railroad from Chambersburg over Cove Mountain and the Alleghenies and on to Pittsburgh, but this was deemed too expensive at the time and was soon discounted.[28]

CVRR President T. G. McCulloh issued a broadsheet with an illustration of the locomotive and the stagecoach-like passenger cars and announcing that "on the first day of February the regular train of passenger cars would commence running as follows: Leave Chambersburg at 4 o'clock in the morning; arrive at Harrisburg at 8, at Lancaster at 12, and at Philadelphia before 6 P.M. Returning, it will leave Harrisburg as soon as the cars from Philadelphia arrived, about 5 o'clock in the evening, and arrive at Chambersburg at 10 P.M."[29]

The early cars, as well as the unusual engine design, attracted attention. Some fifty years later, a commentator recalled them: "The crude and simple beginnings;

27 W. Williams, *Appleton's Railroad and Steamboat Companion, Being a Travellers' Guide through the United States of America, Canada, New Brunswick, and Nova Scotia* (D. Appleton & Company, 1848), 254; Brumbaugh, "A History of the Cumberland Valley Railroad," 180-81.

28 *Adams Sentinel*, January 21, 1839; Albert J. Churella, *The Pennsylvania Railroad, Volume 1: Building an Empire, 1846-1917* (University of Pennsylvania Press, 2012), 59, 75; Randy Watts, *Mainline Railroads:1828 to 1993, Railroads of the Cumberland Valley, Book 5* (Keystone Computer Services, 1993), 37-38.

29 Bates, *History of Franklin County*, 231-32.

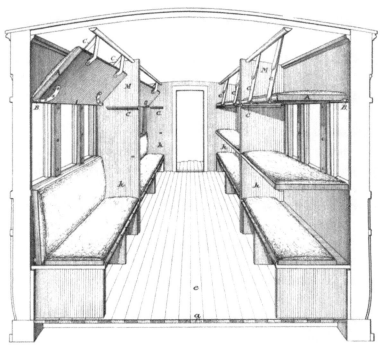

Schematic interior end view of the Chambersburg—the CVRR's first sleeper car. *History of the CVRR, from an image from Pullam vs. Wagner, 1887*

the old strap rails that would so playfully curl up through the car and sometimes through a passenger; the quaint, little, old engines that the passengers had to shoulder the wheels on an up-grade, where they would 'stall' so often with five of the little cars attached to them; the still more curious coaches, built and finished inside after the style of the olden-time stage coaches, where passengers sat face to face, creeping along the country—what a wonder and marvel they were then to the world and now in the swift half century what a curiosity they are as relics of the past."[30]

McCulloh and Managing Director Philip Berlin oversaw one of the railroad's earliest innovations—the dedicated sleeping car, reportedly a first in the world. It would facilitate passengers who were traveling from Philadelphia to Pittsburgh, using the CVRR before transferring to westbound stagecoach. Berlin contracted Philip Imlay of Philadelphia to construct the special car, named the *Chambersburg*.

30 Durant, Pliny A., *History of Cumberland and Adams Counties, Pennsylvania* (Warner, Beers & Co., 1886), 75.

It featured three rows of upholstered wooden berths stacked one above another, held by leather straps which provided a degree of comfort as the car swayed during the overnight journey over the rough rails and stringers. In the daytime, the berths folded back against the walls for seating. A wall separated the men's section from the women's. The railroad provided a round pillow and a blanket at no extra charge. Two years later, workers in the Chambersburg car shops converted a day coach into a second sleeper car, the *Carlisle*.[31]

One contemporary observer complained, "Obviously, the sleeper was for men only; no woman would have ventured inside that foul-smelling, candle-lit dormitory with its creaking wood floors, its row of brass spittoons, and its tiers of grumbling male bodies, laid out with their boots on like cadavers in a morgue." Ignoring such naysayers, the Philadelphia, Wilmington & Baltimore Railroad inaugurated its own sleeping cars in October 1838. It was a few years before the idea caught on with other railroads, with the Baltimore and Ohio using more luxurious, custom-built sleepers between Baltimore and Wheeling, Virginia, in 1848.[32]

Despite the continuing national depression, the Cumberland Valley Railroad soon contracted for three additional locomotives at a purchase price of $21,250 and two new passenger cars at $4,175. The board was pleased that, to date, the CVRR had operated without any injuries to its riders, a rarity for start-up railroads in that day. The *Robert Morris*, *Nicholas Biddle*, and a dedicated freight engine became the main locomotives in use from 1840 through the next ten years.[33]

At the time, the CVRR did not have formal ticket offices at most of its stops. "Passengers paid their fare to the conductor after they got on the train," elderly Shippensburg resident James P. Matthews recalled in the late 1890s. "There were no baggage checks. Trunks were put on the street as near the baggage car as practical, and were lifted into the car either by the owners, or the hotel porters. Chalk marks answered very well for checks." He noted, "The trains coming up from the east stopped at the Black Bear Hotel, and those coming down from Chambersburg stopped in front of the Union Hotel... The was aboundant [sic] time for the passengers to get on and off as the trains waited for the changing of

---

31 Bates, *History of Franklin County*, 232. The exact date the car entered service varies from account to account, but it was likely sometime after February 1838 when regular service began between Harrisburg and Chambersburg.

32 Richard Reinhart, ed. *Workin' on the Railroad: Reminiscences from the Age of Steam* (The University of Nebraska Press, 1970).

33 Bates, *History of Franklin County*, 232.

the mails… The engineers and other trainsmen gossiped with the bystanders and gave them such choice bits of news as they picked up along the route, and there was no rule against entering the neighborhood bar-rooms and toning up for the run to the next station."[34]

Believing he had accomplished his goals with the railroad and seeking new opportunities, Thomas McCulloh submitted his resignation as president in April 1840 to take over management of the Bank of Chambersburg. His replacement was Charles B. Penrose, a long-time CVRR board member from Carlisle and an early advocate in getting the railroad chartered and constructed. Penrose, an attorney and prominent Whig politician who was the speaker of the state senate, only filled the leadership role for a year. Under his capable but brief leadership, the railroad turned a profit of $77,000 which the directors applied to the payment of interest and reducing the principle of the outstanding debt. Penrose resigned on April 26, 1841, to accept a Federal government position as solicitor of the treasury under President William Henry Harrison. The CVRR board that same day named Frederick Watts as president of the company.[35]

Effective New Leadership

No one would have as much impact on the affairs of the Cumberland Valley Railroad Company as Frederick Watts. He would serve capably for the next 26 years, presiding over a period that saw sustained profitability and growth. Watts was born in Carlisle on May 9, 1801, to one of the valley's leading families. His father, David Watts, was one of the region's most influential and distinguished attorneys, "a large and athletic gentleman" and "a man of very positive character, of great grasp and vigour of mind." His mother Julia Ann was a daughter of General Henry Miller, a career military officer who served with distinction in the American Revolution and later commanded U. S. forces at Baltimore during the War of 1812. His namesake grandfather, the first Frederick Watts, a Welsh immigrant who had served on the twelve-man Supreme Executive Council of colonial Pennsylvania, was also a general during the Revolutionary War, leading

---

34 "Recollections of James Peebles Matthews," *The News-Chronicle* (Shippensburg, PA), June 18, 1954. Ticket sales would be initiated in Shippensburg in 1850 at a local drugstore. Several smaller communities along the route of the CVRR did not have ticket offices until after the Civil War.

35 CVRR Annual Report for 1840, in *Journal of the Senate of the Commonwealth of Pennsylvania*, Volume 2 (State Printer, 1841), 92-95; Bates, *History of Franklin County*, 232.

Pennsylvania's "Minute Men." The younger Frederick was a member of the Dickinson College class of 1819, but did not graduate because of the school's financial woes. He later moved in with an uncle, William Miles, who operated a successful farm in Erie County in the northwestern part of the commonwealth. Watts returned to Carlisle in 1821 and studied law, passing the bar exam and building a lucrative, extensive practice on East High Street. He owned a prosperous farm outside of town, and was an early advocate of mechanical reapers, once bringing in inventor Cyrus McCormick for a demonstration. In July 1838, with his law partner Charles B. Penrose, Watts bought the Pine Grove Furnace at a sheriff's sale for $52,500. The ardent Whig later became the reporter of the Pennsylvania Supreme Court for several years, resigning the prestigious post in 1841 to assume the leadership of the CVRR.[36]

Watts inherited an undercapitalized company deeply in debt and facing serious cash flow issues that limited its ability to invest in much-needed repairs. The road was "out of repair, unproductive, and in a dilapidated condition" when Watts took over. Rolling stock needed replacement or upgrading, and several locomotives were in disrepair. He applied his high energy, strong organizational skills, and keen judgment to tackle the most pressing problems first.[37]

Watts arranged with the Franklin Railroad Company, which connected with the CVRR at Chambersburg, to take over day-to-day operations of its line, and he began using his extensive machine shops in Chambersburg to repair and improve the rolling stock and locomotives. His crews constructed the first enclosed cab ever put on an American locomotive, the Franklin Railroad's *Washington*, in 1841. Over time, Watts sold the line's engines and replaced them with the CVRR's heavier and more reliable motive power. The FRR, however, never demonstrated a sustainable profit, so after a short time, the CVRR withdrew its engines and turned over operations of the FRR to D. O. Gehr, a businessman from Chambersburg, who switched to horse power to pull the railcars. The Franklin Railroad underwent several ownership changes over the next decade due to its persistent unprofitability.[38]

36 Frederick Watts files, Archives & Special Collections, Waidner-Spahr Library, Dickinson College, Carlisle, PA; Thornton Osmond, "Hon. Frederick Watts," (A paper read before the Hamilton Library and Historical Association of Cumberland County, February 28, 1930), Cumberland County Historical Society (CCHS), Carlisle, PA.

37 Alfred Nevin, *Centennial Biography: Men of Mark of Cumberland Valley, Pa. 1776-1876* (Fulton Publishing Company, 1876), 94-95, 204, 214, 307-309.

38 Bates, *History of Franklin County*, 232-33.

Despite its struggles, the survival of the Franklin line also appeared to hold importance for the CVRR's future. Only through the Franklin Railroad, Watts explained, did the CVRR connect to the famed National Road that ran through Hagerstown, through which the line gained "a considerable amount of trade and travel." If the Franklin Railroad had stopped service, he argued, the result would have proved "injurious" to the CVRR's own interests.[39]

The brief financial partnership with the Franklin Railroad, however, was one of Watts' few regrettable business decisions after taking the presidency of the Cumberland Valley Railroad. Among his many early accomplishments was to balance the CVRR's expenses with its revenues, including setting new rates for travel between the communities the railroad served: 50 cents to ride the 12 miles from Harrisburg to Mechanicsburg; 87½ cents for the 22 miles to Carlisle; $1.25 for the 34 miles from the state capital to Newville; $1.50 for the 45-mile one-way trip from Harrisburg to Shippensburg; and $2.00 for the passengers who went the 56 miles from the riverside city to Chambersburg. By the end of 1842, he reported total earnings of $70,116.82 to the board of directors and publicly expressed his optimism that "prosperity will again bless the county," despite the ongoing national recession. If it did, he affirmed that the railroad would make money for its shareholders.[40]

And Frederick Watts proved true to his word. The CVRR, over time, began paying dividends to Long and its other investors, despite setbacks such as in December 1844, when a disastrous fire consumed the Susquehanna River bridge, and again the following year when spring flooding in mid-March claimed most of the replacement bridge then under construction. (It was finally reopened in 1846.) Because of fears that sparks from passing locomotives might again ignite the superstructure, engines were banned from crossing the bridge under power. Railroad workers at Bridgeport disconnected the locomotives and allowed the force of gravity to propel the cars on the slight downhill grade across the bridge into Harrisburg. Teams of draft horses and mules pulled the cars in the opposite direction.[41]

39 *Annual Report of the Cumberland Valley Rail Road Company, With their Receipts and Expenditures From the 1st January, 1842, to the 1st January, 1843* (E. Beatty, 1843), 3-5.

40 *Appleton's Railroad and Steamboat Companion*, 1848, 254.

41 "Spring Freshet of 1846," in *Niles' National Register*, March 1846, 34; Mechanicsburg (PA) Museum Association, "The Cumberland Valley Railroad & Mechanicsburg," www.mechanics burgmuseum.org/cvrr.html. Accessed January 7, 2018.

The CVRR bridge across the Susquehanna River was engulfed in flames and badly damaged in December 1844. The bridge was repaired and reopened in 1846. The fear of a future fire resulted in the ban of engines from crossing the structure under power, relying instead on a downhill grade and gravity to cross the roughly mile-wide river. *Davis Collection, Cumberland County Historical Society*

By the end of fiscal 1849, revenues had risen to more than $100,000. Freight, first reported that year in the annual report, totaled 74,877,924 pounds, the leading quantities consisting of 15,627,530 pounds of flour, 10,252,782 pounds of iron ore and 8,494,260 pounds of coal. The agricultural bounty of the Cumberland Valley was regularly hauled over the road, with 2,109,088 pounds of livestock, and over 1,500,000 pounds each of bacon, salt and various "agricultural productions." Significant amounts of leather, lard, whiskey, hardware, stone, fish, furniture, oysters, and paper were also freighted along the CVRR, rewarding a range of livelihoods in the company's namesake valley. However, the tonnage was a fraction of what it could have been, had the railroad been better capitalized in its early years before the network of private freight forwarders gained a dominant position along the line.[42]

42 Bates, *History of Franklin County*, 232; *Report of the President and Directors of the Cumberland Valley Rail Road Company, to the Stockholders, January 18th, 1850* (Herald Office, 1850), 14.

In 1849, the same year that he entertained President Zachary Taylor at his home in Carlisle, Watts accepted an appointment to become the presiding judge of Pennsylvania's Ninth Judicial District. Knowing that he needed to leave the day-to-day administration of the CVRR in capable hands, he brought in several new men who soon proved themselves to be capable, trusted subordinates. They included Ormond N. Lull, a Vermont native who joined the railroad to take charge of the mechanical department. Watts, valuing Lull's leadership ability, later named him as the superintendent of the road in 1856, a position that Lull capably filled for the next 18 years before becoming the chief engineer and supervisor of motive power.[43]

Watts also hired Daniel Tyler, an 1819 West Point graduate and former army officer, to supervise the gradual replacement of the CVRR's outdated rails to heavy iron T-rails, which were much sturdier and less prone to breakage and lifting than the existing ones. Tyler was also tasked with reducing the grades and curves. At his recommendation, Watts hired young Alba F. Smith to modernize the motive power, rolling stock, and other equipment. Two years later, after carefully studying the railroad's operations and comparing it with other lines, Smith recommended obtaining lighter engines for passenger service, dedicating the heavier ones strictly to haul freight. The normal passenger train at that time normally consisted of two passenger cars and a baggage car, rarely more. Smith expected the lighter engines would "effect a great saving both in point of fuel and road repairs."[44]

Watts and the board of directors adopted Smith's suggestion, and the company soon contracted two light-weight 2-2-2 tank engines, the *Pioneer* (CVRR engine number 13) and *Jenny Lind* (engine number 14) from Seth Wilmarth's Union Works of South Boston, Massachusetts, at a stated cost of $7,642 apiece (the railroad eventually purchased the Pioneer for $6,200 in gold.) Both were damaged in transit when another train ran into them near Middletown, Pennsylvania. After repairs and slight modifications in the Chambersburg shops, the two engines were placed in service. They proved to be able to pull a four-car passenger train at speeds up to 40 miles per hour, enabling the CVRR to achieve its desired cost reduction goals. In his annual report to the board for fiscal 1851,

---

43 Civic Club of Carlisle, *Carlisle Old and New* (J Horace McFarland Company, 1907), 119.

44 *New York Tribune*, September 11, 1850; John H. White, "The 'Pioneer': Light Passenger Locomotive of 1851 in the Museum of History and Technology," Smithsonian Institution, United States National Museum, Bulletin 240, Contributions from the Museum of History and Technology, Paper 42, 1966.

The *Pioneer* (circa 1880), photographed by George M. Primrose.
Cumberland County Historical Society

Watts noted that the lighter locomotives were "admirably adapted to our business." Two more of somewhat similar design, the *Boston* and the *Enterprise*, would join the CVRR fleet in 1855. These four engines would form the backbone of the regular passenger service through the early years of the Civil War.[45]

Ridership saw a surge in 1850 after Capt. Henry H. Etter purchased a defunct hotel and warm springs on Blue Mountain in Perry County. He expanded the main lodge with a 75-foot extension and reopened the facility to the public. "The springs are situated on the banks of and empty into Sherman's Creek, a stream associated with the thrilling scenes between the early settlers of that part of Pennsylvania and the aborigines, whose hunting grounds lay in its margin," Etter advertised in several newspapers. "They are 11 miles from Carlisle (through which the Cumberland Valley Railroad passes from Chambersburg to Harrisburg) from which place visitors can at all times procure excellent conveyances." He went on

---

45 White, "The 'Pioneer.'" Tank engines did not require a separate tender; they carried their own on-board water supply.

An 1853 drawing of Harrisburg, the capital of Pennsylvania and the starting point for the Cumberland Valley Railroad. Note the train crossing the CVRR bridge over the Susquehanna River on the right. *House Divided Project at Dickinson College*

to attest that "the qualities of the water at these springs are most extraordinary indeed for the speedy and permanent cure of scrofula, tetter, eruptions of the skin, in fact every species of Cutaneous Diseases." The CVRR enjoyed the free advertising and resulting spike in ticket sales. The Warm Springs Hotel soon gained a widespread reputation as a leading summer resort.[46]

In the meantime, the CVRR bridge at Harrisburg was emerging as an unwelcome competitor to the nearby Camelback Bridge, an iconic covered toll bridge privately owned and operated by the Harrisburg Bridge Company. The directors of the Camelback—who included some of Harrisburg's leading citizens—complained that the CVRR was cutting into their business, which thrived on charging passengers who came by foot, horse, and carriage, in addition to farmers driving their livestock to market. In November 1850, they signed an agreement with the CVRR, which secured the Camelback's monopoly on non-rail traffic. The CVRR pledged to no longer "permit passengers on foot, horseback, wheels or… carriages… or live stock of any description to pass over their bridge"

46 The *Lewistown* (PA) *Gazette*, June 7, 1850, and the *Carlisle Weekly Herald*, June 12, 1850, offer two examples of the frequent ads that Etter ran in newspapers across south-central and central Pennsylvania.

during a period of 10 years, extending until 1860. In return, the Harrisburg Bridge Company would pay a fee of $5,000 annually to the CVRR.[47]

By April 1851, the railroad was healthy enough for the board of directors to declare a four percent semi-annual dividend on its preferred stock based upon having a surplus from the previous six months' earnings. "The road is now free of debt," reported the *Baltimore Sun*, "its stock divided into $700,000 preferred and $400,000 common stock." Watts continued to pursue cost savings, increases in operating efficiency, and additional sources of revenue while stressing safety.[48]

That October saw another short-term surge in ridership and corresponding windfall profit for the CVRR. Promoters in Harrisburg organized a heavily advertised Pennsylvania Agricultural Fair that proved to be highly popular. On October 30 alone, "the Cumberland Valley Railroad brought down this morning twenty-three cars, and one thousand two hundred passengers in one train," according to newspaper reports.[49]

The enterprising Frederick Watts also formed convenient working relationships with neighboring railroads, including in 1851 with the York and Cumberland Railroad, which connected with the CVRR's tracks near Bridgeport. This finally fulfilled the decades-long idea of continuous rail service between the Cumberland Valley and Baltimore. However, Watts began to lose passengers and mail service a year later when the Pennsylvania Railroad completed its line from Harrisburg west to Pittsburgh, enabling riders to bypass the longer route on the CVRR to Chambersburg and the subsequent stagecoach trip by turnpike through the mountain passes. The CVRR became a regional railroad serving Harrisburg and the valley. He did accomplish a key milestone: strengthening the Susquehanna River bridge to allow the passage of a small locomotive to replace horsepower to pull railcars across the structure. The CVRR purchased a specially designed engine, the *Utility*, specifically to use for bridge duty. It would enter service in 1854.[50]

A Lebanon newspaperman marveled in early 1853 that the CVRR could make money, given its limited reach. "[I]f the Cumberland Valley Railroad," he penned,

47 Minutes of the Harrisburg Bridge Company, November, 6, 1850, MG 112, HSDC.

48 *Baltimore Sun*, May 2, 1851; *Carlisle Weekly Herald*, May 21, 1851.

49 *Baltimore Sun*, October 31, 1851. Daily attendance at the state fair averaged more than 20,000 people.

50 Watts, *Mainline Railroads*, 39-40. Watts, an ardent Whig, lost the district-wide election in 1851 to remain as judge. He returned to Carlisle to resume his legal practice, while retaining his leadership of the railroad company and of the Pennsylvania Agricultural Society.

"which begins nowhere and ends nowhere could last year earn 8 per cent on its large capital, from a purely local business, this road running through one of the richest Valleys in the State..." would prove "infinitely more profitable" with a rail connection to the West and the Great Lakes.[51]

Efforts continued for some time to connect the CVRR with Pittsburgh to compete with the PRR's popular new route, but insufficient capital and a lack of sponsorship at the state level kept the project on the drawing board. "The Cumberland Valley road would gain immensely by an extension to Pittsburg[h]," the *Valley Spirit* opined in February 1853. An informant in Harrisburg, who supposedly was "rubbing elbows with the members of the Legislature," believed the long-dreamed-of connection would be made. "[Watts] may be right about it," the newsman added. "We hope he is. But we will have more faith in what he says, when he informs us where the money is to come from. If Capt. [Daniel] Tyler and others of the Cumberland Valley Road would put their shoulders to the wheel, something might be done." Alas, it was not to be.[52]

The CVRR board put the company's modest profits, after paying a dividend to investors, back into railroad operations, including ordering nine new locomotives from Seth Wilmarth's Union Works between 1850 and 1855. A new 4-4-0 freight engine, the *William Penn*, enabled the company to deploy longer and heavier freight trains. Judge Watts leased most of the older, undersized 4-2-0 engines to the York and Cumberland Railroad, but they proved to be underpowered and unable to handle the grades on the latter line. The agreement was soon voided, and the engines were sold in 1852. He also ordered the construction of passenger/baggage combination cars, designed to allow people and their personal bags to ride together in the same car. In 1856, the CVRR modernized the Susquehanna Bridge by adding two 90-foot iron spans in the middle.[53]

51 "Reading's Subscription to the Lebanon Valley Railroad," *Lebanon Courier and Semi-Weekly Report*, May 13, 1853.

52 *Valley Spirit*, February 24, 1853.

53 CVRR vertical files of the Franklin County Historical Society, Chambersburg, PA. In 1855, Watts, as the leader of the Pennsylvania State Agricultural Society, had spearheaded efforts to establish a school where the sons of farmers could learn science and agriculture. He helped select a suitable site in rural Centre County. Farmers' High School would eventually evolve into Pennsylvania State University, and Judge Watts is often considered as the "Father of Penn State." For more details, see Mark W. Podvia, "The Honorable Frederick Watts: Carlisle's Agricultural Reformer," *Penn State Environmental Law Review*, 299, 2009.

Starting in 1857, passengers embarking on a train in Chambersburg, Carlisle, or elsewhere in the valley could connect with the Philadelphia & Reading Railroad via the new Lebanon Valley Railroad's terminus in Harrisburg. A new regional competitor emerged that same year when the Western Maryland Railway began service from Westminster, a relatively short freight haul via wagons from Chambersburg, directly to Baltimore. Until then, merchants and shippers in the valley typically sent their goods via the CVRR to Harrisburg and then down to Baltimore on the Northern Central Railway. Now, increasingly, goods were loaded into wagons headed east on the busy turnpike through the gaps in South Mountain to Gettysburg. From there, the freight was loaded into burden cars and sent to Hanover Junction for relay down to Baltimore on the Northern Central. George P. Worcester, the engineer and surveyor for the Western Maryland, estimated that his line might draw more than $145,000 annually from farmers and businessmen in the Cumberland Valley's Washington County, Maryland, and Franklin County, Pennsylvania, if the tracks could be extended from Westminster west to Hagerstown.[54]

That same year, in July, the CVRR took possession of a gleaming new 4-4-0 steam locomotive from the Lancaster Locomotive Works in Lancaster, Pennsylvania. "The driving wheels are nearly five feet," a Carlisle newsman related, "and the cylinders fourteen inches in diameter, with a stroke of twenty-two inches. Colorful drawings on the engine recalled events from the country's history and "the tank is ornamented with sketches of western life." The 48,000-pound engine was "splendid" in his opinion. "This Locomotive is used for freight trains alone, and she sometimes brings up so many cars that if the road had any short curves, the engineer might be afraid of running into the hind end of his own train." The engine was christened *Judge Watts*.[55]

An investment group headed by New York financier Jay Cooke purchased the Franklin Railroad (by now known as the Chambersburg, Greencastle & Hagerstown Railroad Company) in August 1857 and partnered with the CVRR to operate the line again. In March 1859, work accelerated on replacing the antiquated and inadequate rails of the FRR from Chambersburg to Hagerstown with modern T-rails. Over a period of several days, eighteen rail cars full of new

---

54 Harold A. Williams, *The Western Maryland Railway Story: A Chronicle of the First Century—1852-1952* (Western Maryland Railway Company, 1952). 16-23.

55 "New Locomotive," *Carlisle Weekly Herald*, July 22, 1857. The term 4-4-0 refers to the postwar Whyte notation: the number of leading wheels, the number of driving wheels, and the number of trailing wheels.

iron arrived at the depot in Chambersburg. "The iron is the best quality being first class T rail," the *Valley Spirit* informed its readership. "The workmen have commenced operations on the first section of the road, and along the entire line the timber is being delivered as fast as it can be produced." Lumber procured under local contracts was also arriving in large quantities to be transformed into ties.

The CVRR offered competent leadership for the project. "We are gratified to learn that the road is to be constructed under the Superintendency of Col. O. N. Lull," the newsman added. "No better man could have been selected for the purpose. He is thoroughly conversant with railroad matters, and understands how to make as well as manage a road, equal to any other man in the country. We have no doubt whatever that this road will be completed and put in running order in a very few months." The FRR's president, A. J. Jones of Harrisburg, received praise for overcoming many difficulties to get the project moving forward. "We are well satisfied in our mind that he will find it a safe and good investment," the paper believed, "and one from which he will realize a handsome remuneration."[56]

John Brown and the Cumberland Valley Railroad

In the mid-1850s, while Frederick Watts was busy modernizing the Cumberland Valley Railroad with new locomotives, rolling stock, and T-iron, the spotlight of national events narrowed on the bitter issue of the western expansion of slavery. Before the end of the decade, that spotlight would shine directly on the Cumberland Valley.

John Brown was a Connecticut native whose vicious ambush of pro-slavery men in "Bloody Kansas" had gained him national attention and made him a lightning rod in the slavery debate. In 1856, he returned with three of his sons to the East, where he spent time collecting funds and support for his anti-slavery militancy and a possible return to anti-slavery combat in Kansas. Over the next few years, he met with many of the country's leading abolitionists, including Frederick Douglass, Gerrit Smith, and Harriet Tubman. His fervor led him to plan a daring raid in 1859 on Harpers Ferry, Virginia, where he hoped to spark a slave

56 "The Franklin Railroad," *Valley Spirit*, March 16, 1859. The FRR following Walnut Street into downtown Hagerstown, stopping at the intersection with Washington Street. The depot was diagonal across the street from St. Mary's Catholic Church. For more, see Stephen R. Bockmiller, *Hagerstown in the Civil War* (Arcadia, 2011), 18.

revolt. Obtaining the financial backing of a small group later known as the "Secret Six," Brown contracted for 200 Sharps rifles and 1,000 pikes.

In the late spring of 1859, Brown and an Ohio-born trusted lieutenant, John Henri Kagi, arrived in Chambersburg to prepare for the raid. He would stay, on and off, for four months. Having grown a long beard to avoid recognition, Brown used the alias Dr. Isaac Smith, claiming to be a mining expert looking for iron ore. They took upstairs rooms in the widow Mary Ritner's boarding house on East King Street a half-block from the Cumberland Valley Railroad station. "Dr. Smith" quietly blended into the community, including teaching Sunday School at a nearby church and drifting in and out of town, at times taking CVRR cars to Harrisburg to connect with trains heading to destinations such as Philadelphia.[57]

At the time, Chambersburg residents were evenly split in their sentiments on the slavery question. "The community of which Chambersburg was the centre of business and sentiment was nearly equally divided on the political issues of that day;" newsman and prominent landowner Alexander K. McClure wrote, "but the undertow of anti-slavery conviction was stronger than the partisan dogmas which made one-half the people declare slavery a lawful and therefore a defensible institution."[58]

Brown, with his sons Oliver and Owen and his friend Jeremiah Anderson, left Chambersburg on June 30, 1859, for Hagerstown. In early July, he rented a vacant farm near Sandy Hook, Maryland, for $35 in gold from the estate of the late Dr. Robert F. Kennedy, saying he needed the property for nine months. It would serve as a secret staging area for the planned raid on Harpers Ferry, less than five miles away. Under the guise of transporting farm or mining implements, Brown's accomplices, including another son, began shipping double-boxed loads of weapons to "Isaac Smith & Sons" in Chambersburg. Several mysterious shipments arrived on the trains from Harrisburg. The duo stored these implements of war, as well as locally purchased tools, in a sizeable warehouse situated at the northern end of town. "The railroad from Harrisburg here does no freight business itself," Kagi noted, "that all being done by a number of forwarding houses, which run private cars. I have requested each of these (there are six to eight of them) to give me notice of the arrival of anything for you." The

---

57 Cumberland Railroad vertical files, FCHS; James W. Cree, "John Brown at Chambersburg," *Kittochtinny Historical Society*, 1906, vol. XIV, 59-73. Mary Ritner's late husband was the son of an anti-slavery former governor of Pennsylvania, Joseph Ritner.

58 A. K. McClure, "An Episode of John Brown's Raid," *Lippincott's Magazine of Popular Literature and Science*, vol. 32, September 1883, 279-81.

rifles arrived in batches on July 22, 25, and 27, having earlier been transported from West Andover, Ohio, via river and canal.[59]

Showing more caution the closer he came to the Mason-Dixon Line, Brown often personally drove wagonloads of "hardware" from the Chambersburg warehouse some 50 miles south to the farm, removing them from the rail lines where they might attract more scrutiny. Emma Jane Ritner, the young daughter of Brown's Chambersburg boarding house matron, recalled riding "for a mile or two" with the amiable "Dr. Smith" as he drove "farm tools" down to his new farm. Throughout the summer and into the early fall, Brown returned at intervals, hauling more weapons.[60]

Brown and Kagi met with Frederick Douglass in mid-August at an abandoned stone quarry outside of Chambersburg. Douglass did not approve of the planned raid and discouraged free blacks from joining Brown's proposed militia force, although his associate, former slave Shields Green, did so. Over the next few weeks, a handful of Brown's supporters continued to arrive in Chambersburg; several of the whites stayed at the Ritner boarding house while the black men found other lodging in town. The late arrivals included Osborne Perry Anderson, a free black man born in Chester County, Pennsylvania. He arrived on a CVRR train on the morning of September 16. "Dr. Smith" and his assorted friends did not arouse any suspicion while in Chambersburg. No one apparently knew that this was the famed revolutionary who had stirred up so much trouble in Kansas. "While residing here," the editor of the *Valley Spirit* later wrote, "they kept to themselves—expressed no insurrectionary opinions to any one—paid their bills regularly, and in every respect behaved themselves in such a correct and orderly manner as to attract little attention."[61]

Unknown to the townspeople, Brown continued to amass weapons for his planned slave insurrection. Railroad officials were equally unaware of the false manifests. On September 15, John Kagi, calling himself "John Henrie," informed

---

59 John Brown vertical file, FCHS; F. B. Sanborn, ed., *John Brown: Liberator of Kansas and Martyr of Virginia, Life and Letters* (The Torch Press, 1910), 533.

60 Emma Ritner Robert, "Recollections of John Brown," Ritner File, FCHS; Louis A. DeCaro, Jr., *"Fire from the Midst of You": A Religious Life of John Brown*, (New York University Press, 2002), 261; Osborne P. Anderson, *A Voice from Harpers Ferry: A Narrative of Events at Harpers Ferry; with Incidents Prior and Subsequent to its Capture by Captain Brown and His Men* (Printed for the Author, 1861), 22.

61 Richard J. Hinton, *John Brown and His Men* (Funk & Wagnalls, 1894), 259, 507; "Insurrection at Harpers Ferry," *Valley Spirit*, October 26, 1859.

another conspirator, "A quantity of freight has to-day arrived for you in care of Oaks & Caufman. The amount is somewhere between 2,600 and 3,000 lbs. Charges in full, $25.98. The character is, according to manifest, 33 bundles and 4 boxes." With a few of his band still in Chambersburg in the early autumn, Brown and more than a dozen other followers, black and white, secluded themselves on the remote Kennedy farm. There, they planned the final details of the operation to seize the U. S. Armory in Harpers Ferry and use the thousands of muskets stored there to arm the expected force of rebellious slaves.[62]

On October 16, Brown finally launched his long-planned attack with 18 followers, leaving three conspirators behind at the farm as a rear guard. The hoped-for uprising of area blacks failed to materialize. The Harpers Ferry raid quickly devolved into a disaster over the next few days, and ten of Brown's band, including his "secretary of war" John Kagi and a few citizens died. The victims included the mayor of the town. Brown—along with many of his surviving compatriots—was later captured. U. S. military forces under the command of Col. Robert E. Lee forced him to surrender on the 19th after a brief siege of the town's firehouse where Brown and some of his men had holed up. Brown's supporters who could escape scattered throughout the countryside. Several men, led by one of Brown's sons, managed a circuitous escape route to the north and west.

Two other accomplices, Albert E. Hazlett and Osborne Perry Anderson, again found themselves approaching Chambersburg, now as fugitives from the law. A native Pennsylvanian in his early 20s, Hazlett was having a hard time of it, slowed down considerably by painfully blistered feet. Unable to keep pace, he urged Anderson to go on without him. Hazlett staggered northward through poor weather, following the bed of the Cumberland Valley Railroad, a familiar line which he knew led north towards Harrisburg. It also made him easily visible. Given his condition and the rewards placed on his capture, Hazlett made it surprisingly far—almost to Newville—before he was apprehended on October 22. Another escapee, Francis J. Merriam, made it independently to the obscure station at Scotland, where he boarded a northbound CVRR train to Harrisburg. From there, he went on to Philadelphia. Fugitive slave bounty hunters from

---

62 Anderson, *A Voice from Harpers Ferry*, 22; "Important Documents—Giddings Clearly Implicated," *Valley Spirit*, November 2, 1859. The owners of the warehouse, at the time, were David S. Oaks and Alfred D. Caufman.

Waynesboro, who were well acquainted with the back roads of the Cumberland Valley, captured other members of Brown's fleeing band.[63]

The sheriff of Cumberland County brought the sullen Hazlett to the courthouse in Carlisle, where on October 29 local authorities complied with Virginia's request for his extradition. Judge Frederick Watts presented the court with a warrant signed by Pennsylvania Governor William F. Packer. Witnesses from Harpers Ferry had travelled to Carlisle, where they "testified positively that the prisoner was one of the persons who invaded Harpers Ferry[.]" The court was satisfied that a "monstrous crime" had occurred, and "that the prisoner was there and participated in it." Hazlett would later hang, alongside many of his fellow combatants, including John Brown and Shields Green. Osborn Perry Anderson managed to escape eastward, where he found comfort and aid in downtown York. He stayed for several weeks with prominent merchant and railroad entrepreneur William C. Goodridge, a former slave who was the town's leading conductor on the Underground Railroad in the 1850s. When the coast was clear, Goodridge secreted Anderson in one of his Reliance Line freight cars and sent him to Philadelphia. Anderson later made it to Canada and safety. He was the only survivor of the handful of free blacks who assisted John Brown in the ill-fated raid on Harpers Ferry.[64]

The Eve of War

Judge Frederick Watts and his Cumberland Valley Railroad had played only an incidental role in the explosive Harpers Ferry affair. Most of the conspirators had purchased tickets (some, like "Dr. Isaac Smith," on multiple occasions) and took the CVRR cars to Chambersburg, but the rifles and pikes had all arrived in private rail cars (albeit pulled by Cumberland Valley locomotives over the company's tracks). The railroad, and Watts, faced no recrimination.

Major changes were on the horizon for the Cumberland Valley Railroad. In 1859, the Pennsylvania Railroad purchased enough outstanding stock to take a

63 Ibid., 517-518.

64 "The Harpers Ferry Insurgent at Carlisle," Chicago *Press and Tribune*, November 1, 1859; Anderson, *A Voice from Harpers Ferry*, 53-54, 56; McClure, "An Episode of John Brown's Raid," 279-280; David S. Reynolds, *John Brown, Abolitionist: The Man Who Killed Slavery, Sparked the Civil War, and Seeded Civil Rights* (Alfred A. Knopf, 2005), 371. For more on Anderson and Goodridge, see Scott Mingus, *The Ground Swallowed Them Up: Slavery and the Underground Railroad in York County, Pa.* (York County History Center, 2016).

controlling interest in the CVRR, which continued to operate as an independent company although the PRR appointed its own nominees to the board of directors. The PRR wanted to prevent the Reading Railroad from partnering with the CVRR to connect with the Baltimore and Ohio Railroad. That proposed line would have been a significant rival to the PRR's freight and passenger business.[65]

Under Judge Watts' firm hand, the railroad had steadily improved its gross revenues, which had risen from $108,000 in 1849 to more than $180,000 in 1859. The cost of replacing the flimsy early rails with sturdier T-iron and of rebuilding the bridges had tempered profits in some years but, overall, the CVRR was on the right track. The company's preferred stock did well for its investors.[66]

Judge Watts and his ridership were keeping a wary eye on political events that threated to tear apart the nation. The westward expansion of slavery, the very continuation of its presence in the South, ardent abolitionist feelings in sectors of the North, lingering regional partisanship over numerous economic and social issues, Federal versus state and local power—all had contributed to the tension that had risen for years between the slave states and free states. John Brown's ill-fated raid on Harpers Ferry sparked fresh, often vitriolic dialogue over the issue of slavery, and some in the South talked openly of secession and independence from the Federal government.

Even the country's railroad firms became embroiled in the simmering sectional split. Harrisburg's *Daily Telegraph* responded to reports that Southern rail companies "are displaying their . . . devotion to the slaveholding interest by passing resolutions, in effect, that they will not buy anything of us Northern sinners which they can obtain on better terms elsewhere. [I]f they were sensible financiers," the Republican editors of the *Telegraph* cackled in retort, "[t]hey should have done so always[.]"[67]

The Cumberland Valley Railroad was entirely a Pennsylvania road, but it connected at Chambersburg to the Franklin Railroad, which ran into a slave state, Maryland. Hagerstown, however, at least on the surface, was mostly pro-Union. Other southern Pennsylvania lines, including the Northern Central Railway and the Philadelphia, Wilmington & Baltimore Railroad, also had their termini in

65 Watts, *Mainline Railroads*, 40-41; Mechanicsburg (PA) Museum Association, "The Cumberland Valley Railroad & Mechanicsburg," www.mechanicsburgmuseum.org/cvrr.html. Accessed January 7, 2018.

66 John Majewski, *A House Dividing: Economic Development in Pennsylvania and Virginia Before the Civil War* (Cambridge University Press, 2000), 77.

67 "Southern Railroad Companies," *Harrisburg Daily Telegraph*, December 20, 1859.

Maryland, but they ended in Baltimore, a hotbed of growing anti-government feelings.

As the 1859-60 fiscal year drew to a conclusion, Watts could look back on his tenure as president of the Cumberland Valley Railroad with considerable satisfaction. He and his team of hand-selected senior leaders had rescued the ailing company, restored its profitability, satisfied its debts and creditors, and positioned it for future growth. Safety and reliability were now the railroad's hallmarks. In the past year alone, 118 tons of iron T-rails and 7,000 new white oak sills (ties) had been laid to improve operating efficiency and make for a smoother ride. A newly installed iron roof over the Susquehanna River bridge had been completed within budget and was now meeting all expectations. All motive power was in good condition and well maintained. Newer, more powerful freight engines such as *Tiger* and *Leopard* had been added to the fleet.

Watts planned to "withhold no expense necessary to keep our road and rolling stock at all times in the best possible order," he penned in the October 1860 annual report to the stockholders. "Our entire freedom from accident, the perfect regularity with which our train are run, and the satisfaction which the public evince, in the manner in which the business is done, satisfactorily attest the care and solicitude of our superintendent, and all those who are employed in its transaction."[68]

With the PRR's cash infusion, the CVRR leased the Franklin Railroad on January 26, 1860, formally extending its service from Harrisburg down to Hagerstown, Maryland. After being operated in 1842-43 by the CVRR, the Franklin Railroad Company had since resumed independent operations but had again fallen on hard times. The recent modernization of the ties and rails pleased Watts, but for the FRR, "like all local roads, it will require time to develop the business of the country through which it passes." He expected that "it will amply remunerate its enterprising owners."[69]

Little did the former judge, nor his railroad clientele, know how tumultuous the next few years would be for the Cumberland Valley Railroad. War clouds loomed as the November 1860 presidential election neared. Four men vied for the coveted position. The Democrats had failed to unite around a single candidate at their quadrennial convention and had split, with two regional candidates

---

68 *Twenty-Sixth Annual Report of the Cumberland Valley Railroad Company, to the Stockholders, Made October 1, 1860* (Printed by the Herald Office, 1860), 7.

69 Ibid., Watts, *Mainline Railroads*, 42-43.

emerging—Illinois Senator Stephen A. Douglas in the North and Vice President John C. Breckinridge in the South. In the middle of the country, where conciliatory feelings ran strongest, the Constitutional Union Party emerged, with Tennessee Senator John Bell as its choice. Finally, the Republican Party, less than a decade old but enjoying a surge of popularity with its stance against the westward expansion of slavery, named former Illinois congressman Abraham Lincoln as its candidate at its convention in Chicago. In an often bitterly contested election, Lincoln won the Electoral College and became the president-elect. In local and state elections held at other points in the year, Republicans had won many other key positions throughout the North, including the governorship of Pennsylvania.

Reacting to the results, seven slaveholding states in the largely Democratic Lower South within a short time seceded from the Union. Over the winter, they formed the Confederate States of America, with its initial capital in Montgomery, Alabama, and quickly began organizing a new government. Mississippian Jefferson Davis, formerly the U. S. secretary of war in Franklin Pierce's administration, was inaugurated as the Confederacy's first president. The Confederacy soon began establishing a provisional army.

Decades of festering political, social, and economic disagreements between the North and South, often fueled by heated arguments in Congress and in the newspapers over the westward expansion and, indeed, the very existence of the "peculiar institution" of slavery, were about to come to a tragic head.

Chapter 2

1861: The War Begins

1861 began, Cumberland Valley residents little suspected how momentous the year would be. Reaction along the route of the Cumberland Valley Railroad to secession and the subsequent formation of the Confederacy was split. Most towns had both Democratic and Republican newspapers. In Harrisburg, German-born George Bergner, an ardent Republican whom Lincoln would reward with the capital's postmastership, published the *Pennsylvania Telegraph*. He frequently targeted his Democratic foils, editors Oramel Barrett and Thomas C. MacDowell of the *Patriot and Union*. Their political sparring often was vitriolic and uncompromising.[1]

Similar fiery partisan rhetoric filled the pages of newspapers throughout the Valley. In an incendiary editorial, Edward W. Curriden of the pro-Republican *Shippensburg News* blatantly accused the *Carlisle Volunteer* of falsehood and treason. He claimed, "Not one word was to be found in that sheet which was not intended to strengthen the hands of the traitors, and involve the country in difficulty and disaster." Curriden likened *Volunteer* editor John B. Bratton's false support of Abraham Lincoln to the serpent's scheming in the Garden of Eden and to Marc Antony supporting Brutus while orating over Julius Caesar's body. He urged area Democrats of good standing to repudiate Bratton. Curriden's strong pro-Union

---

1 Richard L. Dahlen, "Harrisburg's Civil War Patriot and Union: Its Conciliatory Viewpoint Collapses," *Cumberland County History* (Winter, 1998), vol. 15, no. 2, 115-17.

principles incurred the wrath of many of Shippensburg's residents, some of whom threatened mob violence. However, when he strongly condemned the ransacking of the rival paper by angry Republicans, Curriden won the respect of enough local Democrats that no retaliation came to his office.[2]

In Chambersburg, home to more than 5,200 people, the *Franklin Repository* charged lame-duck President James Buchanan with failing to act decisively to preserve the Union. In response, the staunchly pro-Democratic *Valley Spirit* asserted that while Republicans blamed Buchanan for the perilous state of the country, they were the cause of the division by deliberately antagonizing and provoking the South.[3]

In Hagerstown, the southern terminus of the railroad, William D. Bell's *Herald of Freedom and Torch Light* was decidedly anti-secession and pro-Union, while archrival *Hagerstown Mail* generally sympathized with the South. The two papers quarreled frequently. The 4,500 residents included a few who believed the *Mail* did not go far enough with its pro-South sentiment; soon, another paper would emerge with even stronger anti-Lincoln opinions.[4]

The political debate raged throughout the Valley, at times even dividing families. In Carlisle on Monday evening, January 14, 1861, several residents from all over Cumberland County met at the courthouse to discuss a resolution favoring the Crittenden Compromise, a proposed congressional act that would, among other provisions, protect slavery in the South and extend it westward, following the line of the Missouri Compromise. The goal of the proposed legislation was to resolve the secession crisis and bring the Confederate states back into the Union. Judge Frederick Watts "addressed the meeting with his usual clearness and ability," according to a reporter, in support of the resolution. He believed that some parts of the proposed compromise would strengthen the hand of the Union men in the border states and thereby arrest the secession movement. To his dismay, his son William was among the leading opposition speakers. After a spirited discussion, the local resolution passed but the Crittenden Compromise

2 "A Filthy, Treasonable Sheet," *Shippensburg News*, April 20, 1861; G. O. Seilhamer, ed., *Biographical Annals of Franklin County* (Genealogical Publishing Company, 1905), vol. 1, 182. Curriden doubled as the postmaster of Shippensburg, as well as a newspaper editor. He sold the newspaper early in the war and, with a partner, purchased the *Herald of Freedom and Torch Light*.

3 "Cursing Mr. Buchanan," *Valley Spirit*, January 2, 1861. The U. S. Census of 1860 listed 5,273 people in Chambersburg, out of 42,121 in Franklin County.

4 "Chronicling America: Historic American Newspapers" website, Library of Congress. https://chroniclingamerica.loc.gov/lccn/sn84026707/.

was doomed to failure in Congress. Opponents on the national level included President-elect Abraham Lincoln.[5]

Judge Watts, like so many other former Whigs who had become Republicans, was pleased that Pennsylvanians had elected Andrew Gregg Curtin as the commonwealth's first Republican governor. He had the Cumberland Valley Railroad issue special excursion tickets for all residents who wished to attend Curtin's inauguration in Harrisburg. On January 15, crowds of interested people flocked to the CVRR station at the southwest corner of Pitt and High streets in Carlisle to board the trains for the capital. Business was brisk.[6]

While arguments over the blame for disunion filled the papers in the Valley, the Cumberland Valley Railroad also was in the news. For years, officials in Harrisburg had been angry with the company for repeatedly failing to obey a June 1857 act of the city council that ordered the railroad to station flagmen at the crossings at Second and Third streets on Mulberry Street. However, watchmen were never on duty. Pedestrians, horses, carriages, and wagons remained in danger that passing trains might strike them. Frustrated, the mayor finally cited Judge Watts and leading railroad officials. Several witnesses appeared at a special hearing in early March and corroborated the accusation. A reporter believed the evidence proved the company officers had willingly violated the law. "Judgement will no doubt be entered against them," he wrote, "and they will be compelled to pay the fine of eighty dollars, the amount of the penalty."[7]

Soon, another CVRR employee also made the papers, this time on a more positive note. At the time, Federal government positions such as a town's postmaster were filled by appointment based on political patronage. A change in national political fortunes usually resulted in a change in the office holder. With the inauguration of Lincoln and the rise of the Republicans, Chambersburg residents had wondered for some time who would receive the coveted post in their town. Several veteran local politicians clamored for the appointment, but, instead, it went to a popular railroad conductor, as the papers announced on April

5 Merkel Landis, "Civil War Times in Carlisle: An Address Delivered at Hamilton Library, Carlisle, Pa., February 12th, 1931," in Carlisle in the Civil War (Hamilton Library and Historical Association, n. d.), 3; "The County Meeting," *Carlisle Weekly Herald*, January 18, 1861. Both the Senate and the House rejected the proposal, which was raised by Kentucky Senator John J. Crittenden, a Constitutional Unionist who supported John Bell of Tennessee in the presidential election of 1860. Kentucky was considered a border state, in that it was a slave state that abutted free states. Other border states included Delaware, Maryland, Virginia, and Missouri.

6 "The Inauguration," *Carlisle Weekly Herald*, January 11, 1861.

7 "The Cumberland Valley Railroad," *Harrisburg Daily Patriot and Union*, March 7, 1861.

10. "The long suspense as to who would get the Post Office appointment, at this place, has at length been relieved," began the report,

> and the lucky individual turns up to be Mr. J. W. Deal, of the Cumberland Valley Railroad. Some persons have honors thrust upon them while others are eagerly seeking them without success in these Lincoln times. Mr. Deal . . . belongs to the former class—he was not an applicant for the position and did not ask the appointment from anyone. It was simply a spontaneous outpouring of gratitude—a free-will offering in consideration for his distinguished services in the Wide-Awakes! The Hon. Edward McPherson who had this gift in his keeping—through his position Congressman of the District—it would appear had no confidence in the rag, tag and bobtail politicians of Chambersburg, and, therefore, bestowed the appointment on one who is not much identified with the place, and could not be supposed to have imbibed much of its political heresy. At all events the appointment is a good one, and about the best course that Mr. McPherson could have adopted to get himself out of the tight place into which he was driven by the horde of hungry applicants howling around him for the position. All honor to McPherson for this appointment! It suits the Democracy first-rate in every particular, although we must hold him responsible for a great deal of profanity in regard to it in his own party.[8]

Just two days later, local partisan politics again took a back seat to national affairs. Early on the morning of April 12, telegraphic messages received at the CVRR's depots brought the news that secessionists had fired on Federal-held Fort Sumter in the harbor of Charleston, South Carolina. Updates came with regularity. The next day, reports indicated that, after a lengthy Confederate bombardment, Union Major Robert Anderson had surrendered the beleaguered garrison and a Rebel flag now waved over the bastion. The divided nation was now at war; the decades-long antagonistic verbiage had escalated into open hostilities. Throughout the Cumberland Valley, residents began preparing for war. "Another exciting time for our citizens," a Shippensburg resident scrawled in his diary on the night of April 16. "An effigy, a stuffed man, hung by the neck on the telegraph wire over the street with the inscription 'Beware, Traitor's Doom.' The stars and stripes floating from all private and public homes in the town."[9]

8 "Post Office Appointment," *Valley Spirit*, April 10, 1861. McPherson owned a tenant farm near Gettysburg. In July 1863, Union troops on McPherson's ridge played a key defensive role during the first day of the battle.

9 "Effects of War News," *Shippensburg Chronicle*, June 12, 1913. The paper ran the unidentified resident's entire diary for 1861-1865 over a two-month period in the summer of 1913.

"THE WAR BEGUN," the *Valley Spirit* blared in capital letters in its April 17 weekly edition, while placing the blame squarely on Lincoln and the Republicans. The new *Semi-Weekly Dispatch*, Chambersburg's second Republican paper, lambasted the "vacillating and effeminate" administration of former Democratic President James Buchanan, a native of Cove Gap in western Franklin County. "Traitors and perjured thieves" had captured Fort Sumter. However, the secessionists had made a major miscalculation, in the editor's opinion; news of the bombardment had "roused the spirit of Northern Patriots."[10]

Those patriots included Judge Frederick Watts. On April 20 in Carlisle, scores of men gathered at the Cumberland County courthouse to pass a series of resolutions pledging their loyalty to the government and to protect the families of men going off to war by giving them financial aid. Watts and the other signatories declared their "undying attachment to the Stars and Stripes of the Union," as well as their "firm determination to live or die under its folds, as the emblem of our Constitution and our laws." They repeated a pledge given by their forefathers during the Revolutionary War, committing their lives, fortunes, and sacred honor.[11]

In the trackside communities scattered along the line of the Cumberland Valley Railroad, anxious crowds gathered to discuss the import of the stunning news that America was now at war with itself. One thing was clear: the interconnected network of railroads would play a key role in moving Federal troops into position to put down the rebellion.

Railroads at the Time of the Civil War

The Cumberland Valley Railroad was a small part of the vast railroad system that the Federal government could use to move supplies, food, medicine, and soldiers into position to implement Lincoln's decision to preserve the Union by force. More than 21,000 miles of track (and more than 45,000 miles of telegraph lines) spread across the North, with the heaviest concentration in the East. Pennsylvania boasted the most total miles of any state, with 2,600 miles of track laid by 1860. The major western cities—Chicago, St. Louis, Minneapolis, Cincinnati, and Indianapolis—offered good assembly points for fledgling armies

---

10 "The War Begun," *Valley Spirit*, April 17, 1861; *Chambersburg Semi-Weekly Dispatch*, April 19, 1861.

11 "The War! Meeting of Citizens," *Carlisle Weekly Herald*, April 26, 1861.

to organize, draw supplies, and stage military expeditions into Tennessee and the Mississippi River region. Likewise, in the East, armies could converge at any number of places, but Harrisburg, Pittsburgh, and Philadelphia figured prominently in early War Department planning. Several former West Point graduates and other army officers were pre-war railroad executives and employees, and they well understood the opportunities that trains offered for military transportation.[12]

However, the Northern rail network largely consisted of many small, regional lines such as the Cumberland Valley Railroad and several mid-sized companies. While fifteen firms each had more than 200 miles of track, in some cases they were of different gauges or had other factors such as bridge limits, steep grades, or radii of curves that precluded the easy transmission of locomotives and rolling stock from one line to another. The army itself had no significant railroad presence at the time; the United States Military Railroad was still well in the future. Logistically, railroads had seen limited military use in North America during the Mexican War. Overseas, trains had played roles in the Crimean War and the Second Italian War of Independence. The onset of the Civil War offered a unique opportunity to prove both the strategic and tactical value of rail transportation on a scale never before seen.

There were several other challenges in moving mass quantities of troops over railroads designed for peace-time business. Most passenger trains were only five to ten cars in length, while freight trains often were much longer and more frequent. The result was, as the war began, many of the new troops had to ride in improvised freight cars or coal cars, often with rudimentary wooden benches installed and no heat or ventilation. Most of the lines were single track, meaning potentially lengthy delays at sidings while awaiting the passage of trains going in the opposite direction. Head-on collisions were not uncommon, especially in places with limited or inefficient telegraphic communications. Few railroads had enough machinists and other trained employees to keep the engines and rolling stock in top condition under the stress of a major military mobilization. Many experienced railroad men left their positions and joined the army with the early calls for soldiers, adding to the shortfall of skilled employees.

---

12 A detailed analysis of American railroads in the 1860s is beyond the scope of this book, but the authors recommend several important reference works, including John E. Clark, Jr., *Railroads in the Civil War: The Impact of Management on Victory and Defeat* (LSU Press, 2004); Thomas Weber, *The Northern Railroads in the Civil War, 1861-1865* (Columbia University Press, 1952), and others listed in the bibliography.

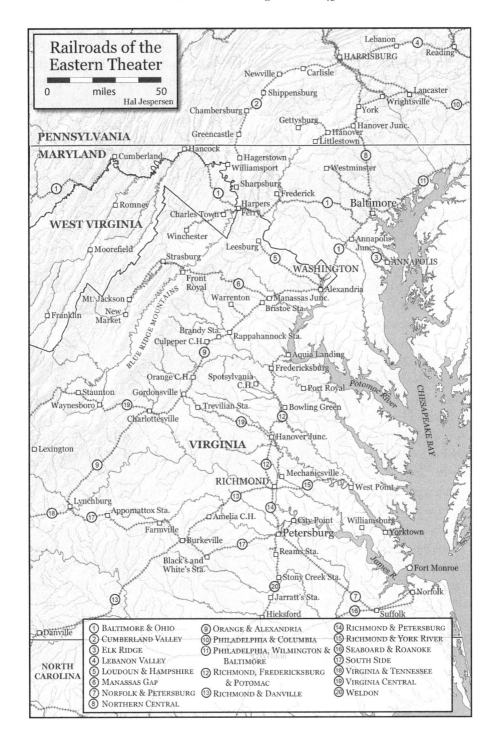

Railroads of the
Eastern Theater

0   miles   50

Hal Jespersen

PENNSYLVANIA

MARYLAND

WEST VIRGINIA

VIRGINIA

NORTH
CAROLINA

CHESAPEAKE BAY

Lebanon ④ Reading
HARRISBURG
Newville Carlisle
Shippensburg
Chambersburg ②   Lancaster
Wrightsville
York ⑩
Greencastle Gettysburg
Hanover Junc.
Hancock Hanover
Littlestown
Cumberland Hagerstown Westminster ⑧
Williamsport ⑪
① Sharpsburg
Romney Frederick
Charles Town Harpers ① Baltimore
Ferry
Winchester Annapolis
Leesburg Junc.
Moorefield Strasburg ⑤ ① ③ ANNAPOLIS
WASHINGTON
Front ⑥
Mt. Jackson Royal Alexandria
Warrenton Manassas Junc.
Franklin New Bristoe Sta.
Market
Brandy Sta.
Culpeper C.H. Rappahannock Sta.
⑨
Aquia Landing
Orange C.H. Spotsylvania Fredericksburg
Staunton Gordonsville C.H. Port Royal
Waynesboro ⑲ Trevilian Sta. Bowling Green
Charlottesville ⑲ ⑫
Hanover Junc.
Lexington
⑨ ⑫
RICHMOND Mechanicsville
⑬ ⑮ West Point
Lynchburg ⑭
⑱ Appomattox Sta. Amelia C.H. City Point Williamsburg
⑰ Farmville Petersburg Yorktown
Burkeville ⑰
Reams Sta.
Black's and Fort Monroe
White's Sta.
Stony Creek Sta.
⑬ ⑳ Norfolk
Jarratt's Sta. ⑦
Hicksford ⑯ Suffolk

Danville

BLUE RIDGE MOUNTAINS

Potomac River

James R.

① BALTIMORE & OHIO	⑨ ORANGE & ALEXANDRIA	⑭ RICHMOND & PETERSBURG
② CUMBERLAND VALLEY	⑩ PHILADELPHIA & COLUMBIA	⑮ RICHMOND & YORK RIVER
③ ELK RIDGE	⑪ PHILADELPHIA, WILMINGTON &	⑯ SEABOARD & ROANOKE
④ LEBANON VALLEY	BALTIMORE	⑰ SOUTH SIDE
⑤ LOUDOUN & HAMPSHIRE	⑫ RICHMOND, FREDERICKSBURG	⑱ VIRGINIA & TENNESSEE
⑥ MANASSAS GAP	& POTOMAC	⑲ VIRGINIA CENTRAL
⑦ NORFOLK & PETERSBURG	⑬ RICHMOND & DANVILLE	⑳ WELDON
⑧ NORTHERN CENTRAL		

The South was in much worse shape, railroad-wise, than the North. The new Confederacy had significantly fewer miles of track (only about 9,000 miles) and vast sections (particularly in the Deep South and the west, such as Texas and Arkansas) had little or no railroad coverage. Track gauges varied more, with a higher percentage of narrow-gauge lines and less inter-connectivity. Virginia led the way in terms of net mileage at 1,800 and in dollars of railroad capitalization, but, as the war began, the Old Dominion had not yet seceded. A number of railroads were still unfinished, with no connectivity to other lines, particularly in central Mississippi. Others connected to waterways or canals for intermodal transportation, particularly of cotton, but that network was not conducive to moving troops speedily. Richmond, along with nearby Petersburg, was the most important rail center, with other key hubs in Atlanta and Chattanooga. However, in many cases, the rail lines did not intersect. For example, six different railroads entered Petersburg, but they did not have direct connections to one another.[13]

The early Union blockade of the South's key ports (known as the "Anaconda Plan," like the snake in squeezing the life out of its prey) would, over time, begin to choke off the supply of railroad iron, making repairs to the tracks and locomotives more difficult as the war progressed. There were substantially fewer coal-burning engines in the South. The majority were wood-burners, requiring a continual replenishment at the depots. Manpower shortages caused by the war would eventually plague several Southern railroads. The limited network of telegraph lines (about 4,500 miles) was not nearly as extensive in the South as in the North, and some companies relied strictly on old-fashioned flag signals and other means to communicate to the next station about passing trains.

One advantage the Confederacy did enjoy was that most Southern railroads were constructed in the 1850s (often using slave labor), meaning the rails, ties, bridges, and infrastructure were often newer than their Northern counterparts. Complicating the matter was the fact that, at least early in the war, some companies valued civilian passenger and freight service above military use. The Confederate government maintained a "hands-off" policy with the civilian railroads. By contrast, by the end of the first year of the war, the U. S. Department of War had taken an active role in the management of railroads and the associated telegraph network.[14]

13 Robert C. Black, *The Railroads of the Confederacy* (Univ. of North Carolina Press, 1952), 3- 5.

14 For more, see William G. Thomas, *The Iron Way: Railroads, the Civil War, and the Making of Modern America* (Yale University Press, 2013).

The South sorely lacked the massive industrial infrastructure of the North, particularly critical for the manufacturing of new steam engines. The most notable locomotive producer in the antebellum slave states was Ross Winans, whose extensive Baltimore works constructed a large number of engines for the Baltimore and Ohio Railroad and the Northern Central Railway, as well as for export markets. At its peak in the 1850s, the Winans Locomotive Works employed more than 350 people. Although dormant at the start of the Civil War, the equipment was still in place to produce engines. Winans, a Democrat and outspoken member of the Maryland state legislature, entertained strong secessionist sympathies despite his New Jersey roots. He was twice arrested early in the war for his virulent anti-Federal speeches and suspected supplying of the Confederates with arms and ammunition.[15]

With war now at hand, Confederate authorities early on put a premium on capturing Federal locomotives and converting them for Southern use where possible, and in destroying railroad facilities that that could be of use to the Yankees (for example, the Rebels would, early on, destroy the Baltimore and Ohio's extensive facilities in Martinsburg, western Virginia). During the war, not a single new locomotive would be produced in the Confederacy. In contrast, many major Northern manufacturers such as Rogers, Baldwin, Norris, Taunton, and several others increased their workforce and output as the war deepened, enabling the United States armed forces to capitalize on rail transportation. At the start of the war, factories in the Confederate States had the capacity to produce only a tenth of the number of new rails as in the North. Still, the South, if it stood alone, boasted the third largest railroad enterprise in the world, behind only the Northern United States and Great Britain.[16]

The Cumberland Valley Mobilizes for War

For Judge Frederick Watts and the board of the Cumberland Valley Railroad, the Civil War brought unique challenges. The company only had a handful of modern locomotives, and few were designed for the type of repetitive, heavy duty service that the government would require. Warehousing along the line was

---

15 For details on Winans' prolific locomotive production, see J. Snowden Bell, "The 'Camel' Engine of Ross Winans," *Journal of the Franklin Institute*, vol. 106, issue 4, October 1878, 246-48. During the war, the facility reopened as Hayward-Bartlett Locomotive Works.

16 John P. Hankey, "The Railroad War: How the Iron Road Changed the American Civil War," in *Trains* (March 2011).

limited to civilian enterprises; the company had contemplated setting up its own network but, when the war began, its storage facilities were limited. The machine shops in Chambersburg did not have the capacity to maintain engines properly in case of a sudden expansion of service. Several miles of track still needed new iron T-rails installed. Telegraph service was rather limited, with only a few stations along the route and few trained operators in case round-the-clock operations would be needed. Watts would need to rely on the assistance of other railroads and the government should the CVRR be pressed into service.

But there was good news, too. The road of the CVRR was generally straight, with few major curves or any serious grades. There were only a few bridges to maintain (and protect, in case of potential Rebel forays), most notably those major spans over the Conococheague Creek at Scotland and the Susquehanna River at Bridgeport. With its connectivity to the railroad network in Harrisburg and to the Franklin Railroad that ran down to Hagerstown, Maryland, the CVRR was well positioned to be a feeder for any Union incursion into the Shenandoah Valley should Virginia secede. However, if Maryland joined the Confederacy, the Harrisburg-to-Hagerstown route likely would be severed. There was also the possibility that Rebel forces might occupy Maryland if the slave state stayed loyal to the Union. Chambersburg thus emerged as the chief staging area in the Cumberland Valley for Federal troops in War Department plans.

On April 15, President Lincoln issued a proclamation calling for 75,000 volunteers to put down the rebellion. The news spread rapidly across the North.

Secretary of War Simon Cameron, a native of Lancaster County, Pennsylvania, and a major stockholder in the Pennsylvania Railroad Company, sent a telegram to the commonwealth's Republican governor, Andrew G. Curtin, requesting 16 regiments of infantry for immediate service. The governor, who would emerge as a staunch supporter of Lincoln's war policies, complied and had his aides

Judge Frederick Watts

House Divided Project at Dickinson College

Col. Thomas A. Scott served the Union as assistant secretary of war and also as a special advisor to Pennsylvania Governor Andrew G. Curtin. Scott had administrative control of the commonwealth's network of railroads during much of the Civil War. *Library of Congress*

begin the process of filling the requisition. Curtin planned to mobilize local prewar militia and home guard units, as well as recruit other volunteers to fill out the regiments. Over the next several days, scores of military officers from across the Keystone State wired their affirmations to the governor's office. President Lincoln would get his requested troops.

The string of communiques was made possible by the joint efforts of Col. Thomas A. Scott (Curtin's military adviser and an executive with the Pennsylvania Railroad) and William Bender Wilson, a long-time telegrapher who had set up the first commercial line between Harrisburg and Lancaster well before the war. Wilson and Scott went to Governor Curtin's chambers in the state capitol on April 17 and installed a relay magnet, with a telegraph key set on a window sill. It was "the first military telegraph office on this continent," in Wilson's assessment.[17]

Soon, the Republican governor of Ohio, William Dennison, Jr., began sending trainloads of Buckeye troops eastward toward Pennsylvania. In Pittsburgh, industrialist Andrew Carnegie acted as a go-between Dennison and Colonel Scott. A train of nine cars arrived in Pittsburgh on April 19, bound for

17 William Bender Wilson, *From the Hudson to the Ohio* (Kensington Press, 1902), 38-39. On April 25, four other experienced Pennsylvania telegraph operators met in Curtin's office before heading down to Washington. Two days later, they became the first operators to be employed by the new U. S. government telegraph system. That organization would soon evolve into the Military Telegraph Corps. Wilson traveled to Washington on May 3, joining Colonel Scott, and became the manager of the telegraph office of the War Department. President Lincoln was a frequent visitor, awaiting war news. Wilson returned to Harrisburg and rejoined the Pennsylvania Railroad in the summer of 1862.

Harrisburg on the tracks of the Pennsylvania Railroad, but Dennison asked that it be halted until firm instructions came from Secretary of War Cameron. At the time, Pennsylvania did not have adequate training camps to handle an excess of fresh troops. Carnegie informed Scott that the train had already departed for Altoona, but it would remain there until further notice. The immediate focus would be on organizing Pennsylvania's new regiments and establishing formal military training camps. Later that day, orders came through to move the Buckeyes eastward with "as great celerity as possible." They would head on to Harrisburg.[18]

Across the Cumberland Valley the third week of April, throngs of enthusiastic young men made plans to travel to Harrisburg to enlist in the new regiments being formed. In downtown Chambersburg, patriotic citizens raised a 120-foot-high flag pole in the center of the town square. The 150 members of a local militia company, the Chambers Artillery, began preparing for war. On the morning of April 19, they assembled and then proudly marched in martial formation past throngs of cheering admirers and well-wishers to the depot on North Second Street. They boarded five yellow CVRR passenger coaches coupled behind the 4-4-0 locomotive *William Penn*, one of the engines Judge Watts had acquired from Wilmarth in 1850. The train steamed away about nine o'clock to the sustained cheers of the populace and headed up to Harrisburg. There, most of the volunteers enrolled in two companies of what became the 2nd Pennsylvania Infantry, with a standard term of enlistment of three months; other local men enrolled in the 3rd Pennsylvania.[19]

On the afternoon of the 19th, five or six horse-drawn wagons appeared on the brow of a hill opposite Chambersburg's Reformed Church. They were filled with inexperienced U. S. Regulars who had hastily evacuated Harpers Ferry upon the approach of hostile Virginia militia troops who were aiming to seize the Federal arsenal and gun manufacturing facilities there. Most of the Federal soldiers were fresh recruits with no previous military experience or training. Lieutenant Roger Jones, realizing he was badly outnumbered, had ordered his 49 men to set fire to the armory and factory buildings and evacuate the town. They missed the train at Hagerstown, so Jones hired several omnibuses to take them to Chambersburg on the turnpike. "The arrival of these troops," businessman Jacob Hoke later wrote,

18 Simon Cameron to A. G. Curtin, April 15, 1861, and Andrew Carnegie to T. A. Scott, April 19, 1861, Records of the Department of Military Affairs, Transportation & Telegraph Department, Record Group 19, Pennsylvania State Archives, Volume 1, page 6.

19 W. A. Culbertson, "Our First Defenders," in *Kittochtinny Historical Society Papers*, vol. X, 317-18.

"increased the excitement in the town, and we were made to feel that the seat of war was coming uncomfortably near." The people of Chambersburg fed the exhausted Regulars, who took the next available train back to their base at the Carlisle Barracks. They received loud cheers along the route of the CVRR during their ride.[20]

Hoke's foreboding sentiment also prevailed across the Mason-Dixon Line in northern Maryland. On April 20, organized groups of secessionists, including a detachment of Baltimore city policemen and state militiamen under the command of former railroad civil engineer Isaac R. Trimble, destroyed several wooden bridges on the Northern Central Railway and the rival Philadelphia, Wilmington and Baltimore Railroad. Their twin actions severed the rail connections from Baltimore to Harrisburg and Philadelphia, respectively. The lengthy repairs left potential passengers scrambling for alternative transportation, including the Franklin Railroad and the CVRR, which both saw a marked short-term increase in ridership.[21]

Chambersburg merchant Henry E. Hoke, Jacob Hoke's brother and business partner, took a crowded train down to Greencastle to deliver a sewing machine to a customer. With seats at a premium, he was forced to ride in the baggage car along with several other passengers. They included two men "whose features were distinctively Southern," in Hoke's opinion. The strangers, each sporting Sharps rifles, were carefully guarding several large wooden chests. Hoke later speculated the mysterious boxes may have contained money or smuggled percussion caps, a commodity the South needed more than cash at the time.[22]

The Initial Military Buildup

With Harpers Ferry in Rebel hands, the War Department began preparations for a campaign against the Confederates. Within days, southbound trains would steam through the valley carrying hundreds of soldiers, usually packed 40 to 50 men per car, to Chambersburg to be staged for future transport into the Shenandoah Valley and the likely commencement of hostilities. If the Union army

20 Jacob Hoke, *Historical Reminiscences of the War; or, Incidents Which Transpired in and about Chambersburg, during the War of the Rebellion* (M. A. Foltz, 1884), 7-8; *Emporia (KS) News*, April 27, 1861; *Polynesian* (Honolulu, Hawaii), June 1, 1861.

21 Scott Mingus, *"This Trying Hour": The Philadelphia, Wilmington and Baltimore Railroad in the Civil War* (Amazon CreateSpace, 2017).

22 Hoke, *Reminiscences of the War*, 9.

planned an aggressive movement south of the Potomac River, "Chambersburg," Jacob Hoke believed, "because of its location in the valley, and because of its excellent railroad facilities and the loyalty of its people, was naturally chosen as the place for this gathering." The 7th and 8th Pennsylvania infantry regiments, under Colonels William H. Irwin and Anthony H. Emley respectively, moved on April 23 from Harrisburg to Chambersburg. They reached town about 10 o'clock at night and marched from the depot up Second Street to Market Street. From there, the new soldiers tramped through the Diamond (the town's center square) and headed out to the old fairgrounds on a hilltop west of town. "This was the first time many of our citizens had seen so large a body of soldiers," Hoke commented, "and their arrival created a great excitement and great interest."[23]

On April 25, several Federal officers soon destined for higher command traveled on the Cumberland Valley Railroad en route to Washington, D. C. Major Fitz-John Porter, Col. Andrew Porter, and Col. Thomas A. Scott left Harrisburg on the early morning train bound for Hagerstown. After the officers arrived at the depot in the Maryland terminus, a carriage transported them down to the capital city. Colonel Scott was a senior executive of the Pennsylvania Railroad and special advisor to Pennsylvania Governor Andrew G. Curtin. One of the most influential and well-connected businessmen in the Keystone State, Scott also sat on the board of managers/directors of the CVRR. That August, the Franklin County native would happily accept President Lincoln's appointment as assistant secretary of war to Simon Cameron. The two Porters, unrelated by blood, would later become Union generals.[24]

Under the direction of state militia Brig. Gen. Edward C. Williams, authorities soon established a new training camp named for the Honorable Eli Slifer, the secretary of the Commonwealth of Pennsylvania. Work crews quickly constructed several spacious wooden barracks on a well-watered field on the Eberly farm southeast of Chambersburg along the turnpike. The site was a short, easy march from the CVRR depot. The quarters were supplied with large piles of straw to be used for bedding. Similar military camps were set up in York and Harrisburg. In addition to the 7th and 8th Pennsylvania (the first occupants of the camp), the

23 Baer, *PRR Chronology 1861*, citing the *Baltimore American*; Hoke, *Reminiscences*, 15. Years later, in his memoirs, Hoke placed the arrival of the two regiments as happening "some time near the end of April—probably the 25th or 26th." Baer and a few other sources state it occurred on April 23.

24 Baer, *PRR Chronology 1861*, citing the *OR*. Andrew Porter was the second cousin of Mary Todd Lincoln.

10th Pennsylvania Infantry and an independent Keystone artillery battalion soon joined them.[25]

President Lincoln issued another proclamation on May 3 calling for an additional 42,034 volunteers to serve for three years in the infantry or cavalry. He thought it "indispensably necessary" to augment the original 75,000 three-months men. In addition, he requested another 22,714 officers and enlisted men for the Regular Army, to serve in eight new infantry regiments, one regiment of cavalry, and a new artillery battery. The Department of War would handle the operational details for both summonses. "In the meantime," the embattled new president urged, "I earnestly invoke the cooperation of all good citizens in the measures hereby adopted for the effectual suppression of unlawful violence, for the impartial enforcement of constitutional laws, and for the speediest possible restoration of peace and order, and with these of happiness and prosperity, throughout our country." Soon, more newly recruited troops began arriving on the CVRR and marching out to the countryside camps around Chambersburg.[26]

"Three Regiments were in yesterday afternoon," Franklin County resident Alex "Ellic" Cressler recorded in a letter to a friend on May 17, "and make a long line of people, who with their glittering bayonets under the rays of the shining sun, accompanied by their Bands, or marshal [sic] music, and the heavy and steady tramp of three thousand men, make all who stand and look on, feel, that they are not soldiers, all this can but give a very faint idea of the appearance of one hundred and fifty thousand human beings marched into the field of battle by the warming and thrilling sound of almost countless drums[.]" Governor Curtin was expected to arrive in town shortly to inspect the troops.[27]

The buildup of military forces and materiel in Chambersburg, coupled with the town's vulnerable location, concerned at least one reporter. "Although there is probably no immediate danger of an attack, the contiguity of Chambersburg to the scene of action— the distance to the Maryland State Line being only fifteen miles, and to Hagerstown twenty-two miles, with a railroad connecting the two points—it is advisable that every precaution should be taken against surprise." He

25 Bates, *History of Franklin County*, 338-39. The 10th Pennsylvania arrived in Chambersburg on May 1 and stayed until June 8, when the regiment departed for Virginia.

26 Abraham Lincoln, "Proclamation 83: Increasing the Size of the Army and Navy," May 3, 1861. Online by Gerhard Peters and John T. Woolley, The American Presidency Project. http://www.presidency.ucsb.edu/ws/?pid=70123. Accessed January 29, 2018.

27 Alex Cressler to Henry A. Bitner, May 17, 1861, Chambersburg, PA, Valley of the Shadow website, UVA. http://valley.lib.virginia.edu/papers/F0700. Accessed February 3, 2018.

noted that pickets were stationed some distance from the various encampments, with the roads leading southward being particularly well guarded. Young Cressler, however, did not think there was any danger. If the Rebels came, he said, "I expect to be prepared for the worst that can happen [to] me. The citizens of Chambrg. are calm, and do not apprehend an attack from the rebels from the South."[28]

The Rebels indeed had no short-term intention of marching on Chambersburg, but they were making a command change at Harpers Ferry. On May 23, Confederate Brig. Gen. Joseph E. Johnston arrived by train to take command of the nine infantry regiments, some 5,200 men, and various unorganized companies that by then had assembled there. Johnston, who graduated from West Point in the same class as Robert E. Lee, was a Mexican War veteran who had been promoted to brigadier general in the U. S. Army in 1860. He resigned to join the Confederate forces after his native Virginia seceded. Shortly after arriving, Johnston met with the senior colonel on duty, Thomas J. Jackson, a mathematics and physics professor at the Virginia Military Institute before the war. After an early misunderstanding as to the overall authority of Johnston, a Confederate Provisional Army general officer, and Jackson, whose commission came from the commonwealth of Virginia, was resolved, they went to work. Johnston began surveying the surrounding terrain that towered over Harpers Ferry. He soon became concerned that in the event of a determined Federal push to retake the town, it was indefensible.[29]

News from Pennsylvania gave Johnston reason to fret about a possible enemy attack. Throughout May, the Federals concentrated several more newly-raised regiments at Camp Slifer. They were formed into brigades and the men given additional training. The press expected that "at least ten thousand infantry and cavalry" would soon arrive. The CVRR, handicapped with a limited number of heavy-duty locomotives and insufficient rolling stock, could only transport a few regiments each day from Harrisburg. With the added military traffic, the transportation manager scaled back the use of the light-weight, underpowered, single-axle locomotives such as the *Pioneer* and *Jenny Lind* in favor of the newer, heavier 4-4-0 engines in the fleet. The older, smaller engines were relegated to light

---

28 "Our Camp Correspondence. Camp Slifer, at Chambersburg," *Philadelphia Inquirer*, May 11, 1861; Alex Cressler to Henry A. Bitner, May 21, 1861, Chambersburg, PA, Valley of the Shadow website, University of Virginia. http://valley.lib.virginia.edu/papers/F0700. Accessed February 3, 2018.

29 For a detailed account of Johnston and his occupancy of Harpers Ferry, see Craig L. Symonds, *Joseph E. Johnston: A Civil War Biography* (W. W. Norton & Co., 1992), 101-108.

duty on work trains and special uses. The company also ordered a powerful new freight engine, the *Col. Gehr*, from Danforth, Cooke & Company of Paterson, New Jersey.[30]

At 7 a.m. on Tuesday, May 28, "our town was thrown into a state of excitement," Jacob Hoke related, "by the announcement that the 2nd and 3d Regiments from Camp Scott, near York, were at the depot." Companies A and B had been recruited largely in Chambersburg, and Company C was from Greencastle, St. Thomas, and other parts of Franklin County. They were coming home, at least temporarily. As word spread, large crowds began gathering to receive them. Their arrival had been kept a secret, other than to a handful of railroad employees and the military authorities. They had left Camp Scott at nine o'clock the previous evening and had marched through the streets of York to the Northern Central Railway's station. The two regiments rode overnight through York, Cumberland, and Franklin counties, and arrived to a hearty reception from friends and relatives. The cheering throngs also gave "a generous welcome to all who composed that splendid body of men," according to Hoke. They disembarked, marched behind Col. Frederick Stumbaugh to sustained applause through the town, and camped at the fairgrounds. Most of the men received furloughs there and hastened to their respective homes to be reunited with loved ones. A long train of supply wagons, loaded with fresh provisions, soon left the Harrisburg commissary warehouses and headed across the Susquehanna River bridge bound for Camp Slifer.[31]

Two days later, shrill steam whistles on the locomotives announced the impending arrival of more troops on the Cumberland Valley Railroad. Colonel James Nagle's 6th Pennsylvania Infantry and Col. Charles P. Dare's 23rd Pennsylvania emerged from the railcars after a lengthy journey from Camp Dare near Perryville, Maryland, at the mouth of the Susquehanna River. They had taken Philadelphia, Wilmington & Baltimore Railroad trains to the City of Brotherly Love and then headed west through Harrisburg to the tracks of the CVRR. That afternoon, still more Federal troops arrived, specifically the 21st and 24th Pennsylvania, which had traveled from Philadelphia. Camp Slifer and the Franklin County Fairgrounds bulged with blue-clad soldiers. On the evening of May 31, nearly a thousand men from the Scott Legion arrived from Philadelphia, bringing

---

30 Comparison of miles served by locomotives from the CVRR annual reports of 1852 to 1865. See also White, "The Pioneer," 251. The *Pioneer* only ran 4,346 miles in 1861 versus and average of 22,000 miles per year in the 1850s.

31 Hoke, *Reminiscences*, 15; "Movement of Troops," *Harrisburg Telegraph*, May 28.

New Oxford, Pennsylvania, amateur photographer Charles F. Himes' image of the Harrisburg Station taken during the Civil War. *"Pennsylvania Railroad Depot, Harrisburg, circa 1860," House Divided Project at Dickinson College*

the total number of troops now in Chambersburg to more than eight thousand. Public buildings such as churches and the county courthouse served as temporary quarters for some of the men. Some regiments camped on the sprawling country estate of Alexander K. McClure north of Chambersburg, while others, including the 2nd and 3rd Pennsylvania, marched to the farm of Christian Bitner three miles south of town and pitched their tents in his fields.[32]

By the beginning of June, the Federal forces assembled at Chambersburg consisted of ten full regiments of infantry and five companies of cavalry. However, four of the infantry regiments had yet to receive their weapons and accoutrements. They were under the local command of William H. Keim, a former U. S. congressman who had received a commission as a major general of Pennsylvania volunteers on April 20. In Washington, General-in-chief Winfield Scott, the old Mexican War hero, was planning to send troops "to threaten

---

32 Hoke, *Reminiscences*, 15; *Shippensburg News*, June 1, 1861. Editor Edward Curriden of the *News* was pleased that "all of the officers" and "a good share of the men" of the Scott Legion had served in the Mexican War.

Harpers Ferry and support the Union sentiments in Western Virginia." He dispatched Maj. Gen. Robert Patterson, the commander of the military's Department of Pennsylvania, to take command of the forces at Chambersburg and environs.[33]

Sunday evening, June 2, saw a rarity in the streets of Chambersburg—a public parade on the Sabbath. That afternoon, the aged General Patterson arrived on a special CVRR train as signal guns boomed. Patterson was born in Ireland in January 1792. The veteran of the War of 1812 had commanded the Pennsylvania state militia for many years before serving as a major general in the Mexican War. Patterson subsequently left the army and returned to Philadelphia, where he ran a business empire of more than 30 cotton mills. He was the older brother of former Pennsylvania Railroad President William C. Patterson. At the outbreak of the Civil War, Robert Patterson became a major general of Pennsylvania state troops. He received orders to proceed to Chambersburg, where he was to take command of the regiments and batteries then assembling there. When his force was sufficient, he was to move his men to Harpers Ferry to capture or disperse the enemy there per General Scott's orders.[34]

A magnificent body of soldiers soon formed along North Main Street in Chambersburg to greet the new commanding officer and his entourage. Patterson and some of his staff entered a waiting carriage and rode through the town with a military escort, including bands playing lively music, in tow. The infantrymen lining Main Street comprised what one observer described as "a sea of glistening bayonets from the Presbyterian church to the German Reformed." The martial spectacle thrilled many of the civilian onlookers; other residents expressed anger and regret at the blatant violation of the sanctity of the Sabbath quiet. Patterson afterward took quarters in the Rosedale Female Seminary while he and his 8,000 anxious men—including his son Francis E. (Frank) Patterson, who commanded the 17th Pennsylvania Infantry—awaited the expected orders to march on Harpers Ferry. Many were confident they would easily whip the Rebels congregated there. A few had misgivings about initiating an aggressive movement against what they perceived to be their fellow countrymen.

33 Thomas L. Livermore and Theodore F. Dwight, ed., "Patterson's Shenandoah Valley Campaign," in *Papers of the Military Historical Society of Massachusetts. Volume 1, Campaigns in Virginia 1861-1862* (Houghton, Mifflin and Co., 1895) 8-9.

34 John H. Eicher and David J. Eicher, *Civil War High Commands* (Stanford University Press, 2001), 418-19; Robert Patterson, *A Narrative of the Campaign in the Valley of the Shenandoah, 1861* (John Campbell, 1865), 31.

General Patterson soon issued a proclamation reassuring his new men, "You are not the aggressor." He blamed the conflict on "a turbulent faction, misled by ambitious rulers… You are going on American soil to sustain the civil power, to relieve the oppressed, and to retake that which is unlawfully held." The following day, the Department of War forbade him to advance toward Hagerstown until certain "indispensable" reinforcements, including elements of the 3rd U. S. Infantry of the Regular Army, arrived in Chambersburg to augment his volunteers. Patterson, doubtful that he could recapture Harpers Ferry with the force at hand, began asking Secretary of War Simon Cameron for more troops.[35]

A man in Shippensburg, in his nightly diary entries, recorded the amount of rail traffic passing through town. On June 1, "[a] long train with soldiers passed through." The next day, 1,000 soldiers rode through Shippensburg, with another 2,000 on June 4.[36] With the massive volume of military traffic passing through the Keystone State, Governor Curtin summoned the leaders of Pennsylvania's leading railroads to a special meeting in Harrisburg to set the standard rates for moving troops and supplies through the commonwealth. They convened on Tuesday, June 4, in the hall of the state House of Representatives. Officials of three railroads—the Pennsylvania, Northern Central, and Sunbury & Erie—believed they would bear the brunt of the long-distance troop movements. They wanted to charge the government the same rates as regular passenger and freight service. The CVRR, Reading, Lehigh Valley, and Pittsburgh, Fort Wayne & Chicago were among those companies that favored a 33% reduction for troops, but regular rates for freight and supplies.

The convention chair, Lt. Col. John A. Wright, the military adjutant to the governor, read General Orders Number 2 from Maj. Gen. George McCall, the commander of the Pennsylvania Reserve Volunteer Corps. The orders announced the formation of a Department of Ordnance and a Department of Transportation and Telegraph, both centered at McCall's headquarters in Harrisburg. Wright would head the latter organization, with the authority to arrange all contracts with the railroads and telegraph companies, and "return a regular and correct settlement of their accounts." The chief of ordnance, quartermaster general, and commissary general had authorization to issue requisitions for the transportation of freight over the railroads, using specific forms that Wright would prescribe.

35 "Proclamation from Gen. Patterson," *Pomeroy (OH) Weekly Telegraph*, June 14, 1861; Hoke, *Reminiscences*, 15-16.

36 "Effects of War News," *Shippensburg Chronicle*, June 19, 1913.

McCall further ordered that all bills would be forwarded monthly to the chief of Pennsylvania's Transportation and Telegraph Department, and that they must have his written approval before they are paid.

Judge Frederick Watts, representing the Cumberland Valley Railroad, offered a formal resolution "[t]hat in the settlement of all accounts from transportation and freight upon the railroads of Pennsylvania—to be settled with the State—the charges should be at a reduction of 33½ per cent for transporting passengers, and that for freight the charges shall be according to their respective tariff rates: provided that no company be required to reduce their charges for passengers below two cents per mile." Most of the railroad executives could live with Watts' proposal, but the Northern Central Railway continued to hold out for full fares. Watts' measure passed by a 15-5 vote, with two executives abstaining. After the delegates debated and voted on additional minor amendments, they sent the final resolution to Governor Curtin for approval. Edward M. Clymer, a New Yorker who served as president of the East Pennsylvania Railroad, presented an additional resolution that the railroads should give free passage to wives visiting their soldier-husbands in camp; the other delegates declared his proposal out of order. Judge Watts returned home and turned his full attention to helping his railroad speed the army's transportation across the Cumberland Valley.[37]

The first priority was moving the first of General Patterson's forces into position near Hagerstown from their staging area at Chambersburg. He would soon need to get his entire army into Maryland. He decided to stay at the Female Seminary in Chambersburg and direct affairs from there until nearly all of his men were on their way to Hagerstown. By June 7, his First Brigade under Brig. Gen. George H. Thomas was near Greencastle, and plans were in place to move his other three brigades as soon as a few last regiments arrived in Chambersburg. General Patterson would have about 18,000 men at his disposal to march toward Harpers Ferry if necessary.[38]

Soon Patterson and his main body departed for Hagerstown, and other regiments arrived at the staging area in Chambersburg to take their place. They included the 900 gray-clad men of the 11th Pennsylvania Infantry, which had been in Maryland guarding the vulnerable route of the Philadelphia, Wilmington &

37 "Important Meeting of Railroad Officers," *Philadelphia Inquirer*, June 7, 1861; Baer, *PRR Chronology, 1861*; "Orders No. 2," *Shippensburg News*, June 29, 1861.

38 "Letter from Chambersburg," *Philadelphia Inquirer*, June 8, 1861. Thomas later gained fame as the "Rock of Chickamauga" for his stubborn defense of Snodgrass Hill during the battle of Chickamauga (Sept. 18-20, 1863) on September 20.

Baltimore Railroad against Rebel mischief. Several railcars of munitions and camp equipage accompanied the regiment. On June 12, the soldiers of 4th Connecticut Infantry, one of the first three-year regiments to take the field, arrived via rail after departing Hartford two days earlier. They were soon brigaded with the 11th Pennsylvania and the 1st Wisconsin, under the overall command of 63-year-old Col. John J. Abercrombie, General Patterson's son-in-law. In July, the 2nd Massachusetts Infantry and a cavalry company and two-gun artillery section would join them.[39]

In mid-June, General Johnston's Confederates evacuated Harpers Ferry out of fear that it was indefensible against Patterson's larger force and that a simultaneous movement by McClellan in western Virginia might cut off the line of retreat to Winchester in the Shenandoah Valley. Very early on the morning of June 14, the Rebels detonated explosives that collapsed the sturdy iron Baltimore and Ohio Railroad bridge over the Potomac River. Any machinery at the U. S. Arsenal that could be moved was put into wagons for future Confederate use. The remainder was destroyed and the arsenal buildings set ablaze. Soldiers also destroyed (or dumped into the river) the railroad engines, fully-loaded coal cars, and other rolling stock. With whatever the supplies he could carry away, Johnston began pulling back toward Winchester.[40]

The unexpected Rebel withdrawal necessitated changes in General Patterson's plans. He consolidated his division by recalling the regiments that had already crossed the Potomac River. By Sunday, June 16, Patterson and his soldiers, by then including the recently arrived 11th Pennsylvania and 4th Connecticut, were encamped at various points over a three-mile distance between Hagerstown and Funkstown. Maryland Governor Thomas H. Hicks visited Patterson that day and toured the camps amid the cheers of the assembled brigades. Rumors spread that the division was to be moved to Washington, D. C. Three other divisions—those of Generals Irvin McDowell, Benjamin Butler, and George McClellan—were also situated at various points in Maryland and Virginia to be in position to counter any Rebel moves. On the Confederate side, Johnston had J. E.

39 "Passage of the Eleventh Regiment of Pennsylvania Troops," *Baltimore Sun*, June 13, 1861; Henry L. Abbot, "History of the First Regiment C. V. Heavy Artillery," in *Record of Service of Connecticut Men in the Army and Navy of the United States During the War of the Rebellion* (Case, Lockwood & Brainard, 1889), 116.

40 Symonds, *Joseph E. Johnston*, 107-108.

B. Stuart's cavalry patrols keep a wary eye on the Potomac fords in case Patterson attempted another crossing.[41]

Well to the southeast, McDowell's Union soldiers readied themselves for a possible move on Manassas Junction, Virginia, where P. G. T. Beauregard's Rebels were ensconced. "It was doubtful whether the Harpers Ferry rebels would have time to join their forces at Manassas junction," a journalist reported. "If not they would be surrounded. If they did so, there would probably be a brief and decisive battle preliminary to the United States occupation of the place." The U. S. War Department suspected that a rendezvous of Generals Johnston and Beauregard was exactly what the Confederates were planning. Patterson's force was to feign an offensive to distract Johnston and keep him pinned in the Shenandoah Valley.[42]

Additional troops continued to pour into the Cumberland Valley to support Patterson and protect the Mason-Dixon Line. The considerable increase in business from the military required the CVRR to run far more trains between Harrisburg and Hagerstown than the normal schedule in pre-war times. Not everyone was happy about the situation. "Night and day, the shrill scream of the Iron Horse," wrote a Chambersburg newsman, "and the deep rumbling of the rolling train is almost constantly sounding in the ear."[43]

A reporter for the *Harrisburg Patriot* opined, "The Cumberland Valley Railroad, which for years has done nothing but a small local trade (enough, however, to pay a handsome dividend), and has always been looked upon as a 'one-horse road,' has suddenly become one of the most important routes for the time being, in Pennsylvania, if not in the Union." These were heady times for Judge Watts' little railroad, which was trying mightily to keep up with the burgeoning demand for its services. "It is not alone the transportation of troops, horses, and munitions of war that has thrown an immense amount of business upon the Cumberland Valley railroad," he added, "but the number of people who travel to Chambersburg to see their friends, as well as those who are attracted there to see the operations and movements of the army, is immense. If the war in the direction of Harpers Ferry continues, and the Cumberland Valley route

41 "Latest News," *Lewistown* (PA) *Gazette*, June 20, 1861; *Baltimore Daily Exchange*, June 19, 1861.

42 "Virginia," *The Deseret News* (Salt Lake City, Utah Territory), June 19, 1861.

43 "Railroad Trains," *Semi-Weekly Dispatch*, June 21, 1861.

continues the great thoroughfare, the Cumberland Valley Railroad will make five times more money than it cost originally."[44]

Over the next two weeks, Patterson's and Johnston's armies stayed largely in position. On July 2, Patterson crossed the Potomac near Williamsport, Maryland, and took the road toward Martinsburg, Virginia. Col. Thomas J. Jackson's Rebel brigade successfully delayed the Yankee advance in a minor engagement on the Porterfield farm near Falling Waters, Virginia, before withdrawing. The relatively few casualties in what was termed the battle of Hoke's Run included 18-year-old Sgt. Warren M. Graham of the 1st Wisconsin Infantry of Abercrombie's brigade. Shot three times, he was taken back to Hagerstown, where he died on August 26.[45]

Patterson, having subsequently received reinforcements, planned to move farther southward to Winchester. However, Rebel cavalry under J.E.B. Stuart now blocked his path. After consulting with his subordinates, Patterson, concerned that a number of regiments were nearing the end of their term of enlistment, decided to cancel the general advance and instead force-march his men to Charlestown, Virginia, southwest of Harpers Ferry, where they camped for the next few days. Meanwhile, on July 18 at Winchester, General Johnston received orders to transfer his 8,800-man newly-christened Army of the Shenandoah to Manassas Junction to reinforce Beauregard. Now unimpeded by Patterson, Johnston marched his soldiers to the Manassas Gap Railroad terminus at Piedmont, where one of his infantry brigades boarded the only available train. His cavalry and artillery marched overland.

In the meantime, the CVRR and its operating subsidiary, the Franklin Railroad, continued to transport additional Union soldiers to reinforce Patterson. On Wednesday, July 10, Pvt. Dilworth Dewers of the 3rd Pennsylvania Infantry stumbled on the FRR tracks near Hagerstown and was run over by an oncoming train. He was rushed to the temporary army hospital at the local academy, where he died on Saturday. That evening, his remains were interred in the local Lutheran graveyard. Trips and falls were not the only dangers the soldiers faced along the line of the railroad. "The few secessionists of this place are becoming desperate," a reporter mentioned, "and the sentinels of the [4th] Connecticut regiment, who are

---

44 "An Ill Wind Blows Nobody Good," *New Albany* (IN) *Daily Ledger*, June 22, 1861, citing the *Harrisburg Patriot*.

45 "Memoirs of Mary Louise Foster Graham 1819-1908," Allen County Public Library, Milwaukee, WI.

acting as a home guard for this town, are most frequently fired on, and even stoned, by concealed foes."[46]

Not all the troops sent through the Cumberland Valley from Harrisburg were destined for short-term service in the South with Patterson. Some were earmarked, by Pennsylvania state law, for the defense of the commonwealth against potential enemy threats. On Friday morning, July 19, the soldiers of Col. William W. Ricketts' 6th Pennsylvania Reserves left Camp Curtin, a sprawling military camp on the north side of the state capital, and headed south to Greencastle, where they disembarked. "Not having been accepted into the United State's [sic] service, they cannot go beyond the Pennsylvania State line," a Harrisburg reporter commented, "They will remain in the camp at Greencastle until another requisition is made upon our State for troops."[47]

Union army quartermasters, many of them new to the role, continued to work with railroad transportation masters to arrange the transport of massive amounts of war materiel and supplies on the lines than ran across the Mason-Dixon Line into the South. "The shipments of army stores over the Pennsylvania Central and Cumberland Valley Railroads are daily of great value," a Pittsburgh correspondent wrote. "Ordnance and food are thus forwarded to the seat of war in Western Virginia, and to the troops at Martinsburg and Winchester. Bread forms no inconsiderable item, while pork, biscuit[s] and crackers are sent in great quantities. Cars of live horned cattle pass over daily. Arms and military equipment are sent, as also clothing, the demand being continual, and no fabric being sufficiently strong to endure, for any length of time, the trials to which it is subjected by exposure to the weather in active military duty."[48]

Many observers, including leading CVRR officials, thought the war and the temporary spike in government-initiated railroad traffic would be short-lived. That thought was proven to be in error in late July when Johnston's and Beauregard's united Confederate forces routed McDowell's Federal army along the banks of Bull Run near Manassas. The news stunned much of the North, bringing into painful focus the fact that the war would continue indefinitely, and now no one was certain of the outcome or duration. Only two regiments from

---

46 "Western Maryland Affairs," *Philadelphia Inquirer,* July 19, 1861.

47 *Harrisburg Patriot & Union,* July 19, 1861; Roger D. Hunt, *Colonels in Blue: Union Army Colonels of the Civil War: The Mid-Atlantic States…* (Stackpole Books, 2007), 137. Ricketts' younger brother Bruce commanded a Union artillery battery on East Cemetery Hill during the battle of Gettysburg.

48 "Shipments to the Army," *Pittsburgh Daily Post,* July 20, 1861.

Pennsylvania, the 4th and 27th, had been involved in the battle, but there were some connections to the Cumberland Valley. In Chambersburg, the *Valley Spirit* mentioned that Union Brig. Gen. Daniel Tyler, who led a division in the battle, was well-known to its readers as the "go-a-head gentleman" who had managed the reconstruction of the CVRR line "so well and so speedily" a few years ago. He had served on the board of directors for several years.[49]

Another officer with more recent connections to the Cumberland Valley, General Robert Patterson, played a critical, but ultimately ill-fated, role in the outcome of the battle at Bull Run, despite not being anywhere close to it. His lack of aggressiveness had allowed Gen. Joseph E. Johnston's much smaller Confederate army to slip away from the Shenandoah Valley on the railroad and join Gen. P. G. T. Beauregard's men at Manassas. Johnston's timely arrival turned the tide of the battle to the Southerners' favor. The dejected Patterson, having failed in his assignment, learned that he had been relieved of command by reading an article in a newspaper. Dejected, he boarded a train at Hagerstown and headed home. Merchant Jacob Hoke noted the general's passage through Chambersburg, where his men had trained only a few short weeks ago. "The contrast between the arrival of Gen. Patterson in our town," Hoke wrote, "and his passing through it on his return, some few weeks afterwards, was decided and humiliating." This time, there was no Sabbath parade through the streets with bands playing and banners flying. "When he returned," Hoke added, "he rode in a regular train, in an ordinary car with others, and with but a few persons to look at him. He may not have deserved the reproach our people heaped upon him, but his case is another illustration of the propriety of the Scriptural injunction, 'Let him not that girdeth on his harness boast himself as he that putteth it off.'" Pride, in General Patterson's case, had indeed come before a fall. Widely criticized in the press and by his peers, he resigned his commission in late July and returned to his cotton milling business. He never again served in the military.[50]

Following the fighting at Bull Run, the three-month term of enlistment for many of the Union volunteer army's new regiments expired and the soldiers began returning home. Many of Patterson's men had not fired a single shot in the nearly bloodless campaign against Joe Johnston. The train station in Harrisburg was busy with new arrivals, both those men heading home and fresh, longer-term troops heading for Camp Curtin. At 3:00 p.m. on Wednesday, July 24, the 3rd

49 "General Tyler," *Valley Spirit*, July 24, 1861.

50 Hoke, *Reminiscences*, 16.

Pennsylvania Infantry stepped off the northbound (or "down") train from Hagerstown. Under the command of Col. Francis P. Minier, six of the companies were returning to Blair County, three to Cambria County, and one to Allegheny County. The men of Col. James Nagle's 6th Pennsylvania soon arrived in Harrisburg by the same route and took temporary quarters in a local Baptist church until they could return to Schuylkill County. A local reporter interviewed many of the returning soldiers. "[W]e are satisfied that a majority of these soldiers will re-enter the service as soon as they can make the necessary arrangements," he wrote, "although it is to be regretted that they did not continue for a month longer under their present organizations."[51]

The sight of so many trains full of soldiers passing through the Cumberland Valley especially thrilled the young boys who lived within earshot of the train whistles. In Newville, if they could not get to the depot in time to see the trains close up, the lads on the southern part of town would head to a nearby hill, where the open fields presented a fine view of the tracks. In between watching the trains, the youths enjoyed "playing around over these fields little caring whether school kept or not." It was an idyllic life, and the CVRR played an important role in the kids' daily routine.[52]

Railroad Affairs in the Second Half of 1861

Frederick Watts and the senior officials of the Cumberland Valley Railroad were always seeking ways to reduce costs and improve efficiency. In August, workers in Chambersburg completed a new turntable in front of the existing engine house. The turntable required only one worker, rather than two or three, to operate it.[53]

Residents throughout the Valley learned in the newspapers in mid-August of a troubling development. A dispatch had reached Governor Curtin, informing him that three alleged Rebel spies had slipped through Federal lines, crossed the Potomac River near Williamsport, and went in the direction of Hagerstown. The information was passed on to the mayor of Harrisburg, William H. Kepner. He

<hr/>

51 *Harrisburg Patriot and Union,* July 25, 1861.

52 "More Reminiscences," *Newville Star and Enterprise,* November 20, 1901; *Newville Valley Times-Star,* April 26, 1950. This area would later be known as "Coal Castle," for five identical company houses that were constructed near South High Street.

53 "New Turn-table," *Semi-Weekly Dispatch,* August 30, 1861.

had Constable Henry Radabaugh and several policemen meet the incoming CVRR train on the morning of August 22. A Union military officer on board identified the men, saying he had followed them from Hagerstown. The policemen swiftly arrested the well-dressed trio and escorted them to a private meeting room in the state capitol building. There, the mayor interrogated them. The men gave their names as Thomas J. Carson, an Irish-born former resident of New York City now living in Baltimore; William M. Pegram of Baltimore; and Walter J. Kelly, who claimed no particular residence but said he was a British subject. Kelly produced a signed pass from the British Consul in Baltimore, countersigned by Secretary of State William H. Seward back in June. Carson carried a pass dated August 9 and signed by Col. Samuel Heintzelman of the Union army, with the counter-signature of Union Brig. Gen. James Cooper, a former U. S. senator and congressman from Pennsylvania. They seemed innocent enough, on the surface, at least.

Still suspicious, the policemen searched the trio, finding on Carson several other passes signed by Confederate officers. He claimed he had obtained them in order to see after his property in several Southern states, including his summer residence, Montpelier, the former home of President James Madison, in Orange County, Virginia. Carson and his brother/business partner, Joseph, were well known to the merchant community in Harrisburg as "high living and decidedly fast men" who were "always ultra in their Pro-Slavery proclivities." They frequently transported large quantities of provisions to and from the capital city. The policemen then opened Pegram's carpet bag and discovered several letters addressed to residents of Baltimore from a Confederate artillery sergeant; however, none were of significant military value. The writer, a participant in the battle of Manassas, merely described his impressions of the fighting to friends and his father, a judge in Annapolis.

Walter Kelly, on the other hand, was much more problematic. His carpet bag proved to be innocuous, but Chief Radabaugh believed that Kelly's shirt looked unusual, so he ordered him to take it off. Kelley turned pale and then faintly asked for a glass of water. The inside of the shirt, when examined, contained several hidden pockets, which were sewn shut. When opened, the pockets contained "an immense number of letters from the South—some from men in the rebel army to their friends in Baltimore—others to men in New York, and a number to Europe. In addition to this, there were various bills of sale, dated at Richmond, for pork and other articles, and large packages of money, principally in notes on banks in the Confederate States." The $3,000 in currency and more than $100,000 in bank drafts were deposited in the State Capital Bank for safekeeping, and the "treasonable letters" and other incriminating papers were handed over to the mayor to deliver to the state attorney general. The suspected secessionists were placed in the county prison until Federal authorities arrived to take charge of them.

Carson, Pegram, and Kelly were "evidently in the North to get specie and arms," the reporter postulated. Later in the day, private detectives Taggart and Franklin, in the company of Deputy U. S. Marshal Henry Sharkey, traveled from Philadelphia to Harrisburg to pick up the three Southerners and take them back to Philadelphia to meet with government investigators. Their train arrived in Philadelphia at 7:00 p.m., and the prisoners were whisked away. They were taken to Washington's Old Capitol Prison, eventually released, and allowed to return home. The trio would not be the last alleged Rebel spies to travel on the CVRR from Hagerstown to Harrisburg.[54]

With the spy scare behind them, the CVRR's board of managers met on September 18 in Philadelphia in the office of secretary and treasurer Edward M. Biddle, a prominent financier who was married to Judge Watts' sister Juliana. On the docket was a discussion of delinquent payments from the Federal government for the transportation of troops. The board instructed Biddle to settle the account at an interest rate of 7.3 percent. If that could not be negotiated, the fallback position was an interest rate of 6 percent.[55]

The CVRR placed advertisements in several newspapers proclaiming that passengers could board the morning mail train in Philadelphia at 8:10 a.m., arrive in Harrisburg at 1:30 p.m., and be in Chambersburg at 4:35 p.m. If they wanted to continue on the Franklin Railroad, the train would arrive in Hagerstown at 6:15 p.m., well in time for dinner. If the passengers preferred overnight service, a train left Philadelphia at 11:00 p.m. and arrived in Chambersburg twelve hours later. At 12:35 p.m., it chugged into Hagerstown. Connections were also available in Harrisburg to take valley residents west to Pittsburgh, should they so desire.[56]

---

54 "Spies Nabbed," *Carlisle Weekly Herald*, August 23, 1861; *Philadelphia Press*, August 23, 1861. Carson, described as "a fine-looking, elderly gentleman," was about 50 years old; his accomplices were in their 30s. Joshua Taggart was one of Philadelphia's leading private detectives in the 1860s and 70s. William Meade Pegram became a Confederate officer and served on Jeb Stuart's staff. He was one of a group of prominent Baltimore men who identified the body of Lincoln assassin John Wilkes Booth. Pegram later became a well-known poet.

55 *Minutes of the Board of Managers of the Cumberland Valley Railroad, January 1840-March 1873*, page 375. Manuscript Group 286, Records of the Penn Central Railroad, Pennsylvania State Archives, Harrisburg.

56 "Passengers," *Shippensburg News*, September 21, 1861.

Before the CVRR's fiscal year ended on September 30, a key order of business was to elect officers and managers for the upcoming year. Notices in local papers appeared announcing that the election would be held at the railroad office in Chambersburg on Monday, October 7, between the hours of 10 a.m. and 4 p.m. At the appointed time, shareholders cast their ballots and reelected Judge Watts as president, Edward M. Biddle as secretary/treasurer, and O. N. Lull as superintendent.[57]

At the same time, Watts was embroiled in a bitter political battle, hoping to be elected to the position of presiding judge. The ardent Republican faced tough opposition in incumbent Judge James H. Graham, a frequent opponent in the past for other local judicial positions. Watts received a strong endorsement from the *Carlisle Weekly Herald*, a paper that had long supported him and his railroad. Watts "is widely and favorably known in connection with almost every important enterprise in our State," read an editorial on September 13. Despite being almost 60 years old, Judge Watts "retains all the vigor of his mental and physical faculties unimpaired," and he had earned "a reputation for legal acumen." Through his work as president of the Pennsylvania Agricultural Society, he had forged strong relationships with the farmers of the Cumberland Valley. The paper confidently predicted victory. In Newville, Watts picked up another ringing endorsement in a letter published in J. M. Miller's *Valley Star* that also cited his favorable impression among farmers in the county.[58]

Watts, however, suffered a stinging defeat in the balloting in early October, ensuring that Graham, who had held the office for ten years, would continue. "The election is over," the editor of the *Herald* rued, "and has resulted in the choice of the entire Democratic ticket in this county." He knew why. "The apathy of our friends," he complained, "and the 'side door' arrangements of the some of the candidates, as well as the withdrawal of our most active young politicians, who are now with the army, has contributed no little to our defeat." While voters in Carlisle strongly supported Watts, in the countryside, it was a much different matter. The newsman blamed "a few groveling politicians in the townships, who call themselves Republicans, but are unworthy of the name. . . . Judge Watts has

57 "Cumberland Valley Railroad Company," *American Railroad Journal*, January 11, 1862, 17-18; *Newville Valley Star*, September 19, 1861.

58 "The Judgeship," *Carlisle Weekly Herald*, September 13, 1861; "The Judgeship," *Newville Valley Star*, September 26, 1861.

great reason to be proud of his vote in the borough." He soon turned his focus back to his beloved railroad.[59]

Railroading in the mid-19th century was a dangerous business at times, and severe accidents were not uncommon. "Fifty-seven persons were killed," the *Shippensburg News* informed its readers, "and two hundred and twenty-four wounded by railroad accidents in this country during the month of September." Fortunately, none of the tragic incidents resulting in casualties had involved the Cumberland Valley Railroad. That good fortune was soon to change.[60]

Tragedy struck the CVRR early on the morning of October 8. About two miles from Carlisle, the engineer of a speeding freight train spotted what appeared to be a man lying across the track up ahead. He quickly reversed his engine but, with the train's momentum, he could not stop in time. The heavy cow-catcher of the locomotive struck the prostrated man and carried him a considerable distance until the train finally came to a halt. The crew scrambled out to render any assistance, but the body was badly mangled. He proved to be a soldier named Myers from Colonel Frederick S. Stumbaugh's newly raised 77th Pennsylvania Infantry, which had taken CVRR cars the previous evening. "He must have fallen from the train," a Carlisle reporter speculated, "and lain on the track all night, and was probably dead before the train struck him. In his pocket was found an instrument of writing, which was so discolored by blood that a name, 'James,' and another name, 'James Hassler, witness,' was all that could be deciphered. The deceased was a young man, with light hair and eyes." The coroner, in accordance with the law, held an inquest that verified the victim's identity. The recruit was from Luzerne County, and had only been a soldier a short time.[61]

Despite the occasional mishaps, the Cumberland Valley Railroad and Franklin Railroad had proven to be reliable partners for the Union army in transporting troops between Harrisburg and Hagerstown. At the end of the fiscal year, the railroad issued its 27th annual report to the stockholders. "Notwithstanding the unusual and extraordinary draughts which, in consequence of the large number of U. S. troops, and the immense amount of stores and munitions necessary for their support and equipment, were made upon this thoroughfare," officials stated, "it is a source of gratification to the Government and gratulation to the management to know that these demands were in every case met with promptness and alacrity."

59 "The Election," *Carlisle Weekly Herald*, October 11, 1861.

60 "General News," *Shippensburg News*, October 19, 1861.

61 "Railroad Accident," *Carlisle Weekly Herald*, October 11, 18, 1861.

He went on to say, "The perfect order in which everything is kept, the almost clock work precision and regularity of its trains, and the entire freedom from accident, are the very best evidence of the efficiency and ability of both officers and employees."[62]

Passenger revenues grew from $70,000 in fiscal 1860 to more than $115,000 in 1861, with freight rising from $107,000 to $129,000. Fees collected from the mail service remained steady at $5,200. Gross receipts, driven by the traffic of General Patterson's forces and by a favorable growing season for crops and other freight, were up 37% over the previous fiscal year. Net earnings rose by almost $43,000. Watts also reported that the company over the past year had purchased "one new locomotive of the largest class, 300 tons of new iron [rails], and 6,000 new white oak sills; new turntables have been put in at Bridgeport and Chambersburg; and two new passenger cars have been built…" The new engine upped the number of operational locomotives to twelve, with a total of 181,087 miles being run over the course of the year (of which 32,757 were on the Franklin Railroad). With the war still raging, Watts expected military traffic to continue to be a steady source of income. The existing motive power and the road itself were "in the best condition in anticipation of the approaching winter, which is expected will be heavy, as the crops of the past season have been above an average." Things were going so well that O. N. Lull, the superintendent of the CVRR, granted free transportation home for the delegates traveling home from the Cumberland County Teachers' Institute, which convened in Newville on December 24. The goodwill gesture received acclamation and widespread press coverage.[63]

It had indeed been a very good year for the Cumberland Valley Railroad. Optimism abounded for the future after the record-setting financial performance. However, Judge Watts and his hard-working employees little guessed how stressful 1862 would prove to be. They would come to know the fury of war firsthand.[64]

62 "Cumberland Valley Railroad," *Carlisle Weekly Herald*, December 20, 1861; *Twenty-Seventh Annual Report of the Cumberland Valley Railroad Company, to the Stockholders, Made October 1, 1861* (The Herald Office, 1861), 6-7.

63 *1861 Annual Report*, 6; *Newville Star and Enterprise*, December 12, 1861.

64 *1861 CVRR Annual Report*, 6-7.

Chapter 3

The Escalating War

January-September 1862

To some observers, Chambersburg was nothing more than a "one-horse town," nondescript and of little importance. In late January 1862, a local reporter rebutted the condescending charge by pointing to the vast amount of freight transported in and out of town on the Cumberland Valley Railroad over the past year. The cargo included large quantities of lumber, coal, iron castings, pig iron, nails, plaster, bricks, paper, marble, cement, furniture, and leather. Foodstuffs included oysters, fish, bacon, pork, potatoes, flour, tobacco, salt, and whiskey. Reflecting the rich agrarian harvest of the region, the railroad also transported seeds, hay, grain, and live cattle, hogs, and sheep. Exports leaving town for Harrisburg and points beyond far exceeded the tonnage of incoming goods. The relative prosperity of the community, as reflected in the rail shipment figures, gave clear evidence of its regional importance.[1]

Later that year, a reporter from the lion of the Democratic press, the *New York Herald*, offered a similar bullish opinion. The correspondent described Chambersburg as "a flourishing borough . . . pleasantly situated on the Conococheague creek, at the junction of the Cumberland Valley Railroad with the Franklin Railroad." He added, "The dwellings in this place are mostly built of brick or stone, and the town exhibits a general appearance of neatness, comfort

---

1   "What We Buy and What We Sell," *Valley Spirit*, January 29, 1862.

and prosperity. It has a fine court house, a bank, a large academy, a female seminary, eight churches and five newspaper offices." The town, he wrote, sat amidst "a cultivated and populous country."[2]

Chambersburg residents often displayed a generous spirit, particularly in providing for sick and injured soldiers at the nearby camps. They also freely put their spare change into collection boxes at the railroad ticket office and post office. Officials used the money to purchase delicacies and other goods for shipment to local soldiers who were at the front. The editors of the *Valley Spirit* newspaper urged "anybody who can spare the money to continue to contribute." The ladies of the town, as well as those in Carlisle and other towns along the route of the Cumberland Valley Railroad, frequently held parties to roll bandages, sew blankets and quilts, cook or bake food, and other activities designed to help the soldiers.

Judge Frederick Watts, a native and lifelong resident of the Cumberland Valley, was justifiably proud of the region and the railroad that served it. In February, he penned a note to Commonwealth Secretary Eli Slifer, enclosing a railroad pass for Governor Curtin, "to ride where he pleases upon our roads," in the event Curtin found "time to ride through our Valley[.]" There is no record that Andrew Curtin took any social excursions that winter or spring, but Federal soldiers continued to pass through Chambersburg and the upper Cumberland Valley with some regularity. At times, they proved controversial. At 11:00 a.m. on May 26, 1862, forty to fifty weary men of the 1st Maryland Infantry arrived in Harrisburg. They told of fighting in Stonewall Jackson's recent Shenandoah Valley Campaign, and said they had participated in the disastrous battle of Front Royal the previous Friday and then the subsequent fighting at Winchester. They had taken a series of trains, including the Cumberland Valley Railroad, to reach the Pennsylvania capital. "Some of the party were slightly wounded," a Telegraph newsman noted, "and all bore evidence of having endured much fatigue and hard usage." The soldiers confirmed previous telegraphic reports that the two engagements had been brutal and savage. They claimed that at Front Royal "the rebels granted no quarter, killing the wounded without mercy, and even disfiguring the bodies of those already dead." Other newspapers across the region soon repeated the sensational story.[3]

---

2 "Sketch of Chambersburg," *New York Herald*, October 11, 1862.

3 "Contributions for the Soldiers," *Valley Spirit*, May 28, 1862; Frederick Watts to Eli Slifer, February 22, 1862, Eli Slifer Papers, Box 11, Folder 1, Dickinson College Archives & Special Collections; "Col. Kenly's Command," *Pittsburgh Gazette*, May 28, 1862; *Pennsylvania Daily Telegraph*, May 27, 1862.

Another reporter, however, had a much different slant on the new arrivals. They were, apparently, not war heroes returning home. "Quite a number of deserters from General Banks' army passed through this place on Monday," he charged. "The first lot, numbering about fifty, took possession of the cars and passed over the Franklin and Cumberland Valley Railroad. They claimed to belong to the First Maryland Regiment, and said they were going to Baltimore. Later in the day, several passed through on horseback having 'contrabands' along, and towards evening a number arrived on foot. We understand orders to arrest those coming this way have been received here, and all who will attempt hereafter to pass this point will be taken up and lodged in jail."[4]

A few weeks later, on June 24, there was no doubt as to the identity of the soldiers riding on the CVRR. Captain Edwin L. Hubbard and Company G of the 3rd Wisconsin Infantry guarded 57 Rebel prisoners, captured in the Shenandoah Valley by Maj. Gen. John C. Frémont's division in a battle against Stonewall Jackson's forces. The Southerners and their guards arrived in Harrisburg at 11:00 a.m. on a train from Hagerstown. In dress and general appearance," a local reporter observed, "[they] differed very little, if any, from the rebels who arrived here two weeks ago, whose imprisonment at Camp Curtin they, for the present, will share." They were the second group of Rebel prisoners to ride the CVRR that month, with 504 captives being sent to Harrisburg on June 15.[5]

On June 16, alarms in Harrisburg sent fire crews scurrying to extinguish several burning shanties along the railroad tracks east of Third Street. Several poor black people living in the shanties were now homeless, despite the fact that the pumping apparatus and firemen had arrived quickly and "prevented the flames from spreading to any great extent," a newsman reported. "The buildings destroyed belonged to the Cumberland Valley railroad company, and were of little value. We did not learn how the fire originated."[6]

Throughout the summer, the CVRR enjoyed strong ridership, both military and civilian, and excellent profits. The war was far away, having shifted east toward Richmond during McClellan's Peninsula Campaign and Pope's subsequent Second Bull Run Campaign, and many Cumberland and Dauphin county residents took advantage of special excursion trains for day trips. One of

4 "Deserters," *Valley Spirit*, May 28, 1862.

5 "Arrival of More Rebel Prisoners," *Pennsylvania Daily Telegraph*, June 24, 1862; "Effects of War News," *Shippensburg* (PA) *Chronicle*, June 26, 1913.

6 "Fire Yesterday," *Pennsylvania Daily Telegraph*, June 17, 1862.

the most popular events took place on Tuesday, August 12, at Mumma's Woods near Mechanicsburg. Advertised as "The Picnic of the Season," the gala, sponsored by the Friendship Fire Company of Harrisburg, featured Weber's String Band. The cars left the Harrisburg depot at 8:05 a.m. and stayed in Mechanicsburg until 6:45 p.m., giving plenty of time to eat, listen to the lively music, and socialize. The firemen warned, however, that "no spiritous of malt liquors will be allowed on the grounds and all persons are positively forbidden to come on the grounds intoxicated." They hoped to raise enough money to make a payment on the company's new steam engine, which would be on display. The railroad charged all passengers twenty-five cents for the train ride, and the firemen collected an addition quarter from the men to gain entry to the picnic grounds. "All respectable ladies," the ad read, "are invited without further charge than their fare."[7]

Less than a week later, a train passed through Mechanicsburg with a much less celebratory group on board—political prisoners being removed from western Maryland to Harrisburg and then on to Baltimore via the Northern Central Railway. Lieutenant Philip A. Vorhees of Company K, 29th Pennsylvania Infantry, escorted six prominent men from Funkstown, Hagerstown, and Smithburg. Five of them had refused to take the oath of allegiance when asked by the deputy provost marshal at Hagerstown and were now on their way to jail. The sixth, John Thomson Mason, Jr., was "imprisoned for causes unknown." A former judge and Democratic U. S. congressman, Mason came from a distinguished family with deep roots in colonial Virginia. His great-uncle, George Mason, had drafted the Virginia Declaration of Rights, a forerunner to the U. S. Bill of Rights. Fortunately, "there was no excitement at the Depot," a reporter noted, "and the prisoners speak in the highest terms of Lieutenant Vorhes [sic] and the guard under his command for their gentlemanly demeanor towards them."[8]

The CVRR continued to transport Union troops, including the newly raised 15th Pennsylvania Cavalry, into the Cumberland Valley. In early August, the War Department authorized Capt. William J. Palmer to raise a battalion of cavalry, and that commission was soon extended to a full regiment. Men from across the state

---

7 "The Picnic of the Season," *Pennsylvania Daily Telegraph*, August 7, 1862.

8 "Secesh Sympathizers on Their Travels," *Pennsylvania Telegraph*, August 18, 1862. Mason had been the collector of customs in Baltimore before the war, where he was an outspoken secession advocate. He had retired to his estate near Clear Spring in 1861. He became Maryland's secretary of state in 1872 but died a year later at the age of 57.

visited recruiting stations, and before the end of the month, more than a thousand men had congregated at the camp of rendezvous near Carlisle. The majority came by rail. Before the war, Palmer, a native of Delaware, spent six months in England studying the railroads and coal mining. As personal secretary to the Pennsylvania Railroad's president, J. Edgar Thomson, he was well acquainted with Thomas A. Scott and other railroad executives. He had been instrumental in the PRR's conversion of several wood-burning locomotives to coal-fired. Despite his Quaker upbringing, Palmer had accepted a commission and raised the Anderson Troop in 1861 to serve as a bodyguard for Brig. Gen. Robert Anderson, of Fort Sumter fame. Now, assisted by Regular Army officers stationed at the Carlisle Barracks, the 15th's officers began training cavalry recruits. They would soon be needed to help defend the commonwealth. The problem was, they had not yet been issued horses.[9]

In late August, as Union casualty lists swelled following the Second Battle of Bull Run, the government asked local doctors "to repair to Washington to attend the wounded from the great battles that had just taken place." A special train arrived in Mechanicsburg around the beginning of September, filled with "a number of physicians from the various other points on the road." Doctors from Dillsburg, Churchtown, and Mechanicsburg joined them, but returned when they learned that their services were not needed.[10]

The Rebels are coming! The Rebels are coming!

The bucolic days of mid-summer gave way to war talk in early September 1862—rumors that the Confederates intended to invade southern Pennsylvania. Anxious newspaper editors throughout the commonwealth speculated as to Robert E. Lee's exact intentions. A strong force would be necessary to oppose Lee if he advanced toward the Mason-Dixon Line. Governor Andrew G. Curtin had previously established the Pennsylvania Reserve Corps, regiments which were intended to stay behind and guard the state's borders. However, the much-needed troops had since been absorbed into the Army of the Potomac in Virginia. Now, as Lee moved north toward the Potomac River, their attachment to McClellan's army, now in Washington, D. C., recovering from the disaster at Second Bull Run,

9   Samuel P. Bates, *History of Pennsylvania Volunteers, 1861-5* (B. Singerly, 1869-1871), vol. 4, 902.

10 "A Day of Excitement," *Cumberland Valley Journal*, September 4, 1862.

left no significant military force to defend the Keystone State. On Thursday, September 4, Curtin issued a proclamation urging the formation of military companies across the state. He also directed all businesses to close at 3:00 p.m. to allow drilling. Curtin was attempting to create a temporary army that he could summon at a moment's notice if Lee came too close to the border. When Curtin made this call, however, Lee had not yet crossed the Potomac into Maryland, and many observers in Pennsylvania did not believe the Rebels would strike north, despite the persistent rumors.[11]

The threat was real; Lee was indeed moving inexorably toward Pennsylvania. The Cumberland Valley, with its lush farmlands and plentiful fresh water, offered an excellent route for a full-scale invasion that potentially could target Harrisburg and its hub of important railroads and industry. From September 4-6, the bulk of the Confederate Army of Northern Virginia, in stages, forded the Potomac ten miles downstream from Harpers Ferry and entered Maryland in the vicinity of Point of Rocks. The officers of the Bank of Chambersburg moved their specie and other valuables to the safekeeping of the Harrisburg Bank. The Hagerstown Bank soon followed suit, sending its money to safety. In the following days, the Hagerstown Savings Bank and the Washington County Bank did likewise.

The Cumberland Valley Railroad took steps to protect its rolling stock and locomotives on September 7. Believing it would be unsafe to leave them at Hagerstown overnight, at 2:00 a.m. crews moved them to Chambersburg. A considerable number of anxious pro-Union refugees from Frederick and Washington counties went with them. Later that Sunday, a train ventured south to Hagerstown. Its crew intended to remain overnight, but at 1:00 a.m. Monday morning, they hastily retreated to Chambersburg upon reports that Jeb Stuart, with 5,000 Rebel cavalrymen, was approaching Hagerstown, the southern terminus of the Franklin Railroad.[12]

The Army of the Potomac had begun to move out of Washington on September 5 in pursuit of the Rebels. General McClellan followed by moving his headquarters 15 miles west from Washington to Rockville, Maryland, on September 7. He moved his army slowly at first, assuming that Lee had far more men under his command than he did in reality. That same day, Lee's lead elements

11 Bates, *History of Pennsylvania Volunteers*, vol. 5, 1147.

12 "From Southern Pennsylvania," *Baltimore Sun*, September 11, 1862, citing the *Philadelphia Press*.

marched triumphantly into Frederick, where they found a cooler-than-expected reception from the populace.[13]

On September 8, a short train with only three cars arrived in Harrisburg on the CVRR line. It had come from Hagerstown, and was "mostly filled with women and children," according to a reporter. "They report that the rebel pickets had been near that city." Concerns over a possible invasion extended eastward beyond the South Mountain range all the way to the Susquehanna River in York County, 70 miles northeast of Lee's advance guard in Frederick. A special Northern Central Railway train arrived in Harrisburg from the borough of York, with the intention of returning with arms and ammunition. "Everybody in York is arming," the reporter added. "Two pieces of cannon and two hundred muskets have already been taken down, and a number more will be taken down this morning, together with ammunition." In Shippensburg, an unidentified diarist recorded, "Great excitement. Report says Rebels have possession of Frederick, Md. Our town full of refugees, farmers, horses, wagons—all going east for safety."[14]

"It is generally conceded that if our State be invaded by the rebels," a *Philadelphia Press* reporter suggested on September 9, "the Cumberland Valley will most likely be one of their points of entry. Its abundant crops, great quantity of horses and cattle, and undoubted wealth will make it a most desirable place for our half-starved foes to visit." The people were well aware of their danger, he believed.17 The War Department ordered the horseless 15th Pennsylvania Cavalry, still encamped near Carlisle, to remain in the Cumberland Valley. Captain William J. Palmer sent 250 hand-picked soldiers, carrying three days rations and 36 rounds of ammunition apiece, on rail cars to Greencastle. There, foragers scattered in all directions to procure good horses for the men. They were only able to obtain 150 animals, so 150 troopers saddled up and headed out to picket the roads leading south.[15]

On September 10, with Lee now in Maryland, Governor Curtin issued a general order for all able-bodied Pennsylvanians to take up arms and form into regiments. All men should bring "such arms that they could obtain," requested

13 For a comprehensive account of the Maryland Campaign, see Ezra A. Carman and Thomas G. Clemens, ed., The Maryland Campaign of 1862, in three volumes (Savas Beatie, 2010, 2012, and 2017).

14 "Pennsylvania Alarmed," Evening Star (Washington, D. C.), September 9, 1862; "Effects of War News," Shippensburg (PA) Chronicle, June 26, 1913.

15 "From Southern Pennsylvania," Baltimore Sun, September 11, 1862, citing the Philadelphia Press; Bates, History of Pennsylvania Volunteers, vol. 4, 902.

Curtin, but if necessary, the state would arm those who could not bring their own. The men were to "hold themselves in readiness to march upon an hour's notice," and would be in service only for the extent of the "pressing exigency." They would go down in history as Pennsylvania's "emergency men," soldiers who would stay in service only until the Rebel threat to the Keystone State abated. The next day, September 11, Lee's advance guard occupied Hagerstown, with Brig. Gen. Robert Toombs' veteran Georgia brigade camping alongside the railroad tracks. In Harrisburg, Curtin, with President Lincoln's permission, made a more direct call—for 50,000 men—when he issued General Order No. 36. The governor noted that additional calls would be made, "as the exigencies should require." He asked the state's railroads to give priority to troop movements above all other traffic and placed Col. Thomas A. Scott, the former assistant secretary of war and Pennsylvania Railroad executive, in charge of the expected mobilization.[16]

Pennsylvanians rushed to the flag in large numbers. In one night, 18 companies were raised. Lincoln and his cabinet assured Governor Curtin that Harrisburg and Philadelphia were in no danger. The president further argued "that the true defense of Harrisburg was to strengthen the column" of McClellan's army. Therefore, the newly raised Pennsylvania state militia would be concentrated around Chambersburg near the commonwealth's southern border. By existing commonwealth law, these temporary troops could not advance beyond the border into another state. They were to be used for defensive purposes.[17]

Perhaps the most alarmed Pennsylvanians were those in Philadelphia. A petition from many of the city's prominent citizens demanded a commanding officer "of known energy and capacity, 'one who combines the sagacity of the statesman with the acuteness and skill of the soldier.'" Secretary of War Edwin M. Stanton replied in his usual, sharp demeanor: "If you know or have heard of any officer coming up anywhere near the description of the one you need, please make me happy by naming him, and I will make you happy by assigning him to your city."[18]

---

16 *Baltimore Sun*, September 11, 1862, *Herald of Freedom and Torch Light* (Hagerstown, MD), September 24, 1862.

17 Ezra A. Carman, Thomas G. Clemens (ed.), *The Maryland Campaign of September 1862: Vol. 1: South Mountain* (Savas Beatie, LLC, 2010), 111, 203.

18 Ibid., 203.

Attention soon turned to Brig. Gen. John Fulton Reynolds. A native of Lancaster, Reynolds had originally commanded the Pennsylvania Reserve Corps, which was originally charged with defending the state's southern border. Reynolds, however, greatly disliked that position, and much to his delight was incorporated into McClellan's army fighting in Virginia. However, with invasion imminent, Washington officials thought Reynolds an ideal choice to handle the militia, and asked McClellan if he could be spared. While McClellan was chagrined to lose one of his best divisional commanders, Curtin and other state officials were relieved to have a competent favorite son at the helm of the assembling militia force.

In the meantime, Curtin requested that Lincoln provide heavy protection for all railways linking Washington and Harrisburg, as well as requesting "not less than 80,000 disciplined men" to be sent via these railways to Harrisburg, an outrageous and unrealistic request. Curtin added that an order should be drafted for all states on the East Coast to send "every available man to hasten to [Harrisburg]… where he would concentrate in a few days as many of the Pennsylvania militia as he could muster." Lincoln's response—that "the best possible security for Pennsylvania is putting the strongest force into the enemy's rear"—made it clear that any defense of Harrisburg would have to be undertaken by Pennsylvania militia. Deepening Curtin's dismay, civil engineers inspected the west bank of the Susquehanna River, opposite Harrisburg at Bridgeport, but found the location unsuitable for a defense against Lee's whole army.[19]

At 11:30 a.m. on September 10, the regularly scheduled CVRR train arrived in Harrisburg carrying several hundred ladies and gentlemen from Hagerstown and Chambersburg. A reporter conversed with "a highly intelligent citizen from Hagerstown." The man had left that place late last night, but no Rebels had yet made an appearance and the people there "were unduly excited." He told the newsman that "the very extravagant stories circulated in reference to secesh movements there were utterly false; that the nearest approach of the enemy's scouts was thirteen miles east of Hagerstown." The reporter also chatted with "one the most respectable and substantial citizens of Chambersburg," who confirmed that the recent report of the capture of a Rebel spy in that town, with several maps and plans of the Cumberland Valley in his possession, "was a complete fabrication of excited imagination."[20]

19 Ibid., 203-205.

20 "Preparations for Meeting the Rebels," *Baltimore Sun*, September 10, 1862.

Things changed almost overnight as additional rumors spread of an impending Confederate advance north through the Valley. Panic began to set in, and the trains, including several specials added to the schedule, were packed full. On September 11, several CVRR trains arrived at the sprawling depot in Harrisburg, bringing "several hundred Union citizens and a number of contrabands from beyond Chambersburg," a reporter wired to his editor at the *Philadelphia Inquirer*. "The panic in that direction is represented as fearfully intense. The people at Chambersburg now regard an advance on that place by the Rebels as near at hand, perhaps tonight."[21]

The Reverend Benjamin S. Schneck, the pastor of St. John's Reformed Church of Chambersburg since 1855, had taken a trip west to Cincinnati and Dayton, Ohio, in early September. He cut his journey short when he received word that the Rebels would likely march from Hagerstown toward Chambersburg. He took an overnight train and returned to the Franklin County seat on September 11 about noon. "We are in the midst of a frightful panic...," he wrote to his sister the next day. "I found our folks packed, ready to start with Mr. [CVRR director Thomas B.] Kennedy in [his] carriage and baggage wagon." When the Rebels failed to make an appearance, he wrote that "things look rather more favorable. Indeed, I doubt whether the Rebels will come here at all. I think it's a feint to draw troops from Washington." However, he cautioned, "Should they come, we must just submit—we are defenseless—I myself will stay, but the females will go first to Carlisle, and if things prove worse, across the mountain into Perry County."[22]

No one, least of all Judge Frederick Watts and the nervous officials of the vulnerable Cumberland Valley Railroad, was quite sure when or if the Rebel raiders might arrive. A correspondent for the *Philadelphia Inquirer* traveled south from Greencastle to collect information on reported Rebel movements. He set out for Williamsport, Maryland, where a shallow ford in the Potomac River near Hagerstown was a likely crossing spot for the enemy forces. He reached a wooded hill about three-quarters of a mile from the town when he spotted Rebel cavalry "riding rapidly and frantically about." The reporter surmised, "It was evident from their semi-crazed action that they had found an abundance of bad whisky somewhere, and had imbibed freely... They seemed to relish the whisky, poisonous as it is, with more than usual gusto. With my glass I could see them

---

21 "Important from Harrisburg," *Philadelphia Inquirer*, September 12, 1862.

22 Benjamin S. Schneck to My Dear Sister, Chambersburg, PA, September 12, 1862, FCHS.

flourishing bottles about, and occasionally they turned them, drinking deeply and long." Drunken or not, it was clear that advance elements of the Army of Northern Virginia had already crossed the Potomac into Maryland. Where the Rebel army was headed next was anyone's guess. The newsman rode to Hagerstown, where he planned to take the evening train up to Chambersburg. He found the town filled with refugees as the Confederate vanguard approached the region. "I suspect Jackson will attempt a flank movement to catch the rolling stock of the Cumberland Valley Railroad below Chambersburg if he intends seriously to advance towards Harrisburg," he penned on September 11. "There is no rolling stock save a single locomotive and two cars which only come this far below Chambersburg."[23]

It was evident that a major clash between the armies was imminent, most likely near Hagerstown or Frederick, but also possible in southern Pennsylvania should the Rebels venture that far. Confederate advance cavalry patrols had reached the Mason-Dixon Line that marked Pennsylvania's southern border. Several residents in the most threatened areas began making travel plans. On September 14, the head of McClellan's Army of the Potomac met portions of Lee's Army of Northern Virginia in battle along the slopes of South Mountain in western Maryland. At the time, Stonewall Jackson's Confederate forces were besieging the outnumbered Union garrison in Harpers Ferry just south of the Potomac, while the rest of Lee's army was in Maryland. Lee dispatched a portion of his army to defend the mountain gaps, which they were to hold at all costs so Lee could reunite his dispersed army a few miles to the west, near Sharpsburg, Maryland, to face McClellan. After a bloody series of assaults, Federals under Maj. Gen. William B. Franklin finally forced their way through Confederates at Crampton's Gap by sundown, but too late to save the distressed Harpers Ferry garrison, which was forced to surrender to Jackson on September 15.

John Reynolds, meanwhile, had assumed command of the hastily assembled volunteer Pennsylvania state militia force in Harrisburg. He informed his sisters on September 14, "The real designs of the enemy it is very hard to conceive, they are evidently avoiding some important movement before they unmask their real intention." He believed the threat of an invasion through the Cumberland Valley was "very serious, there is nothing to prevent their doing great injury... There is nothing in the valley to stop them and our army is too far behind them to retard and overtake theirs if they push on boldly. You are not alarmed, I see, in Lancaster,

---

23 "Our Greencastle Letter," *Philadelphia Inquirer*, September 13, 1862.

that is alright, do not allow yourselves to become so. Burn this up and do not let anyone see it."[24]

So far, the majority of the militiamen who passed through Harrisburg's Camp Curtin had enjoyed a relatively pleasant time. "My first day in the Regt. Like it well," recorded one newcomer, Pvt. Henry Bilighous, in his diary. Charles F. Henry and 20 fellow volunteers were grouped with several men from Selinsgrove to form Company D of the 18th Pennsylvania Volunteer Militia. After electing officers, they took a train to Harrisburg and then marched to Camp Curtin. Later that day, they formed into ranks and marched to the Pennsylvania Railroad's impressive station. There, they received their first meal as soldiers, "which consisted of a piece of dry bread and cold ham and a tin of good coffee." They spent the night quartered on the second floor of the Capitol. "We did not sleep much as the boys were singing and dancing just as if they were at some great frolic," Private Henry recalled. "But it was the boys' time and they preferred dancing to sleep before they returned home. . . . We surely were a motley crowd, dressed in style, all in their nearly best. I had a braided cloth coat, satin vest, big black silk neck tie, graded calf boots and the rest were dressed equally as good and some much better. Our army equipment," he continued, 'consisted of a Harpers Ferry musket with bayonet, haversack made of cloth and a canteen. We had to carry our ammunition in our haversack." The ladies of Selinsgrove presented every man in Company D with an oil-cloth haversack. In addition, most of the young soldiers carried wreaths with them made by their mothers, sisters, or sweethearts.[25]

Through September 14-16, General Reynolds moved the untrained force of militia towards Chambersburg via the Cumberland Valley Railroad. Colonel Thomas Scott faced the logistical nightmare of transporting thousands of soldiers 53 miles over the line, which typically ran two passenger trains and one freight train per day. To solve the dilemma, Scott commandeered engines, cars of all sorts, and manpower from the Pennsylvania Railroad. Not everyone was overjoyed at the military buildup. Carlisle resident Jacob Bretz informed his son George, "You would of thought all Hell had broke loos[e], to see the trains pass hear [sic] and the men Hallowing." Governor Curtin and some of his staff and aides were among the first to travel to Chambersburg, taking a special two-car private train. He

---

24 John F. Reynolds to dear Sisters, September 14, 1862, Eleanor Reynolds Scrapbook, FM.

25 Henry A. Bilighous Diary, September 15 and 17, 1862, Ronald D. Boyer Collection, Box 1, USAHEC; Henry F. Charles Memoir, Ronald D. Boyer Collection, Box 1, USAHEC.

wanted to be near the militia encampments to make decisions on the spot, as needed. According to a rumor that circulated through the camps, Curtin had a attached a car to a CVRR engine and "beat the record on a flying trip." The governor stayed a few days before returning to Harrisburg.[26]

Curtin's special transportation advisor, Colonel Scott, knew the CVRR did not have the necessary capacity to transport so many men in so a short time. He arranged for the Pennsylvania Railroad to supply locomotives, cars, and crewmen to augment the CVRR's available rolling stock and limited manpower. Scott, in his role supervising the railroad during the emergency, asked CVRR Superintendent O. N. Lull to relocate temporarily, from the company offices in Chambersburg to Bridgeport. There, Lull had the responsibility of making up the troop and supply trains, clearing the right of way, and sending them on their way in an orderly fashion. Scott, at the insistance of Brig. Gen. Herman Haupt of the U. S. Military Railroad, brought in another veteran railroad man, Joseph D. Potts, to oversee operations on the Franklin Railroad from Chambersburg down to Hagerstown. The 33-year-old Potts, formerly the assistant superintendent of the Western (or Mountain) Division of the Pennsylvania Railroad, had recently been selected as the new general manager of the Philadelphia and Erie Railroad. Earlier in the war, he had served on Governor Curtin's advisory staff with the rank of lieutenant colonel. Potts had supervised the commonwealth's transportation and telegraph operations from the war's onset until December 1861 when the Federal government assumed the duties.[27]

Still, there were frustrations for the militiamen, many of whom were in their first military campaign. The bureaucratic delays that plagued rail service greatly annoyed many, including Pvt. John S. Witmer of Company H, 2nd Pennsylvania Volunteer Militia. The men were equipped and "told that we were to march to the railroad to get transportation, for Hagerstown," he wrote. But he was disappointed when, after waiting a long time for the cars, they arrived already full with another regiment, "owing to some mistake." Witmer and his comrades

26 Westhaeffer, *History of the Cumberland Valley Railroad*, 69-70; Jacob Bretz to George Bretz, October 8, 1862, Dickinson College Archives and Special Collections, Carlisle, PA; Manuscript memoir, attributed to William B. Bigler, Brooks-Bigler Family Papers, 125-11, CCHS. See also RG 19 Subgroup B Records of Transportation and Telegraph Department, 1861-1869, Military Dispatches Received and Sent, Pennsylvania Military Telegraph Department (PMTD), A. G. Curtin to T. A. Scott, September 10, 1862.

27 J. H. Kennedy, ed., "The Railroad Men of America: Joseph D. Potts," in *Magazine of Western History Illustrated*, vol. IX, 1889, 746-49.

waited through the night, lying on the ground in their blankets without the comfort of any fires.[28]

Throughout the northern part of the Cumberland Valley, grateful citizens lined the railroad as Reynolds' "emergency men" proceeded southward via train from Harrisburg. On Sunday, September 14, the men of the 2nd Pennsylvania Volunteer Militia embarked for their jaunt down to Chambersburg. "The regiment proceeded out to near Camp Curtin and got aboard a train of freight cars, which had been provided with seats for the transportation of troops," Louis Richards, a youthful private from Reading, related. "A long delay, with the explanation of which we were not furnished, ensued; but about 3 the train started. A halt of an hour or more was made in town. A tremendous and enthusiastic crowd was out to see us off. Moved over the Long Bridge and stopped another half hour west of the Susquehanna. Chambersburg, our destination, was fifty-two miles distant. Passed successively through Mechanicsburg, Carlisle, and Shippensburg, at each of which places short stops were made."

At Mechanicsburg, the tracks passed just yards from the Irving Female College, where the entire student body came out to cheer their fellow Pennsylvanians. "Were struck with the great natural beauty of the Cumberland Valley region," Richards noted. "Crowds of people came out to the stations to meet us, and black and white, old and young, all joined in the heartiest demonstrations of welcome." He added, "[We] were also greeted from the houses and roadsides all along the line by people waving their handkerchiefs and swinging their hats. At Mechanicsburg a whole girls' school was out to see us. This was a specially engaging sight to some of our number, who thought that that village would be a good place to camp."

The train continued steaming southward. On board, the new soldiers were enjoying the festivity. "At Carlisle I met Mr. R. S., whom I knew," Private Richards added. "The elite of the town were at the station, and S. pointed out to me the leading beauties of the place—I mean the ladies. Soldiers of a day, we already began, in the midst of these inspiring scenes, to feel like real veterans. Between stops the men beguiled the time singing, jesting, smoking, etc., and every one was in the best possible humor. Private T. H., among the rest, favored the company with a curious song in Pennsylvania Dutch called 'Babbel Maul,' which performance his delighted auditors compelled him frequently to repeat. It was generally agreed that the most desirable way of marching was by railroad." About

28 John S. Witmer to Dear Grandfather, September 29, 1862, MG 7, PSA, PHMC.

9 o'clock that evening, they passed through Chambersburg. About a mile or two southwest of town, the train halted in a wood brightly illuminated with campfires and "resonant with the cheers of soldiers." The weary men piled out of the converted freight cars and began establishing their campsite.[29]

Thousands of state emergency militiamen soon poured into Chambersburg and the surrounding countryside. General Reynolds left Harrisburg on the morning of September 15 to meet his men. "Camp McClure," named in honor of prominent Chambersburg newsman/farmer/businessman Col. Alexander K. McClure, was established just north of town. "Camp Misery," the home of the 8th Militia, was about five miles south of Chambersburg off of the turnpike to Hagerstown. It appears neither of the sites were held in high esteem by their inhabitants, as Camp Misery's name implies, but the same goes for the former. Private Richards simply described it as "a large stubble field west of the railroad, in a position which had been dignified by the title of 'Camp McClure.'" Regardless of their location, the Pennsylvanians established shanties in the surrounding woods. They would do so by placing a center pole surrounded by rails taken from surrounding fences leaning against it. After snatching some straw from a nearby barn and corn-fodder from various neighboring farm fields, the rough shelters were thought complete. "[B]ut as the shed was built up the side of a hill," reminisced Private Witmer, "the men slid down in the night and we were rolled out into the woods which was not very pleasant especially as it was raining."[30]

The trains running up and down the valley included motive power, rolling stock, and crews on loan from the Pennsylvania Railroad. Veteran PRR engineer Ephraim Jones had brought his train to Harrisburg on September 13 following an all-night trip from Altoona. There, he met the PRR Middle Division superintendent, Samuel D. Young, who ordered Jones to head out on the CVRR. He took the throttle of the Wilmarth 4-4-0 locomotive *Robert Morris* and pulled a load of ammunition to Chambersburg. The following morning, he, his crew, and the train narrowly averted capture when they unexpectedly rolled into a

29 Louis Richards, *Eleven Days in the Militia During the War of the Rebellion; Being a Journal of the "Emergency" Campaign of 1862* (Collins, 1883), 22-24. Irving Female College was named in honor of popular author Washington Irving, whose works include *Rip Van Winkle* and *The Legend of Sleepy Hollow*.

30 Reynolds to Eleanor Reynolds, September 14, 17, 1862, Reynolds Scrapbook, FM; Richards, Eleven Days in the Militia, 21-26; Bilighous Diary, September 15 and 17, 1862, Boyer Collection, Box 1, USAHEC; John S. Witmer to dear Grandfather, September 29, 1862, Manuscript Group 7, PSA, PHMC; James Fuller Queen, "Sketches with the Co. B 8th Reg., Pa. Ma," painting at Library of Congress.

Confederate camp just north of Hagerstown. He quickly reversed the engine and steamed away. Based out of the CVRR telegraph office in Chambersburg, Jones stayed alert for emergency runs. On the afternoon of September 15, General Reynolds and his staff appeared. They climbed aboard the engine as it sat on a siding and ordered Jones to take them to Hagerstown. The engineer stubbornly refused, telling the general that he only took orders from the military superintendent of the railroad. Jones found himself under arrest, but soon received vindication when a northbound train barreled through town. If Jones had listened to Reynolds and pulled onto the main line, a head-on collision would have been the result. When the conductor returned from the telegraph office with the authorization, Jones complied and took Reynolds to Maryland as requested.[31]

The infantry regiments heading west across the river from Harrisburg and then south through the Cumberland Valley included Col. James Armstrong's 6th Pennsylvania Militia. On the morning of September 15, they were marched to the arsenal to receive their muskets and twenty rounds of ammunition. The regiment halted on Fourth Street for more than an hour "like Roman sentinels," according to Capt. James Elder of Company K, as the men's wives, sweethearts, and relatives came out to wish them a fond farewell. Tears flowed down the faces of many family members, anxious about the possible fate of their beloved soldier boy. "About eleven o'clock we boarded the cars, and soon were on our way to the front," Elder wrote. "The train was composed of freight-cars of various descriptions, but principally of the box pattern, air-tight everywhere excepting at the two side-doors." Toward evening, the train arrived at Chambersburg. The soldiers were quartered for the night in various parts of town; two companies slept in the county courthouse.[32]

At 1:00 a.m. on September 16, a special train chugged north from Chambersburg to Harrisburg. Colonel Grimes Davis's Federal cavalrymen, who had escaped the surrender of the Harpers Ferry garrison, captured Confederate Maj. Gen. James Longstreet's wagon train and 300 horses and mules near Williamsport, Maryland. The troopers drove the 75-80 wagons north to Chambersburg and then headed back to Maryland to report to the Army of the Potomac. Carlisle preacher J. A. Murray recorded the ammunition train's passage through town, as well as several other trains as the day wore on: "A company of

---

31 Westhaeffer, *History of the CVRR*, 71.

32 William Henry Egle, ed., *Notes and Queries Historical and Genealogical Chiefly Related to Interior Pennsylvania* (Harrisburg Publishing Co., 1895), vol. 2, 322.

troop[s] from Dauphin County arrived. Soldiers in the A.M. passenger cars. A large train passed up [southward] with the Grey Reserves from Philadelphia, over a thousand noble lot of men." Murray, the pastor of a local Presbyterian church, also noted three other trains that passed through Carlisle that day, including a CVRR train that carried the 20th Pennsylvania Volunteer Militia from Philadelphia and late at night a Pennsylvania Railroad train "filled with soldiers."[33]

By sundown on September 16, as multiple troop trains rolled through the Cumberland Valley, General Lee had established a defensive position in front of the small town of Sharpsburg, a short distance north of the Potomac River. Parts of McClellan's army crossed Antietam Creek and engaged the Rebels in a series of inconclusive skirmishes. The next day—September 17—would be the bloodiest single day in American military history. The battle of Antietam started at dawn and lasted well into the afternoon. Lee held the blood-soaked field at the end of the day despite suffering about 23,000 casualties. He and his exhausted army soon retired south of the Potomac, being too damaged to campaign further. The day was busy for the CVRR. In the morning, a train passed through the valley heading for Harrisburg carrying Rebel prisoners, while five more troop trains went south at various intervals hauling more militia to the front. "Reported victory at Sharpsburg, Md.," the Reverend Murray noted in his diary. "A troop of 120 horsemen arrived in town from Chester county. I saw a rebel gun captured from a S. C. rebel."[34]

In camp that same morning near Chambersburg, John Reynolds' Pennsylvania emergency militiamen had been awakened "just before daylight with orders to pack our knapsacks and prepare to march," Private Witmer recalled. "We hastily got our blankets rolled up, and all our goods packed into our knapsacks with the exception of our plate and tin-cups and awaited breakfast— fully expecting to be hurried off immediately." After a meal of beef and hardtack "as usual," they continued to wait as the battle of Antietam was already raging. "We heard very heavy cannonading which continued all day," remarked Witmer. "The report was that little Mac was driving the rebels on [north] towards our camp." As the sun began to set, "we thought certainly we would be allowed to sleep once more in our shanties," yet they then received orders to fall in and

---

33 D. W. Thompson, ed., *Two Hundred Years in Cumberland County* (Hamilton Library & Historical Association of Cumberland County, 1951), 205-206. The Corn Exchange Association of Philadelphia was a commercial business trade organization whose members were merchants of flour, grain, and similar produce.

34 Ibid.

prepare to march with 50 cartridges. They were informed that they would be embarking via train for Hagerstown. "Every one seemed in good spirits," Witmer recalled. "They apparently did not know that in order to reach that place, the state line had to be crossed." The rumor proved to be unfounded; indeed, state law prohibited such a movement. After marching about one-and-a-half miles, the militiamen waited before finally heading south toward the Mason-Dixon Line.[35]

Preparations were being made in Harrisburg to circumvent or change the existing regulations. On the evening of September 17, General Reynolds rode down to the battlefield from his temporary camp near Keedysville, Maryland, and saw firsthand the destruction and killing which had gone on earlier in the day. Colonel Scott, in the governor's office in the Capitol building in Harrisburg, sent a telegram to Reynolds. He advised, "There are engines and cars in Chambersburg sufficient to move 1,000 men to Hagerstown, and there is on the way to Chambersburg a train with a regiment and another train with Crossman's Battery, all of which you can use in sending troops through to Hagerstown. By moving them briskly tonight you can throw 4,000 to 5,000 men into Hagerstown by daylight tomorrow. We will endeavor to start three or four regiments early in the morning."[36]

One of the emergency regiments headed for Hagerstown that day was the newly raised 13th Pennsylvania Volunteer Militia, under the command of Col. James Johnson. On the morning of September 17, the men marched to the state arsenal and received their muskets, knapsacks, haversacks, canteens, and blankets. Each company received a single box of ammunition to split among the men. The regiment formed in the rear of the Capitol grounds and marched a mile to the waiting cars. At 5:00 p.m., the train moved slowly across the Susquehanna River and followed the CVRR track through the Valley. "The reception which awaited us," a soldier in Company F from Bradford County related, "was that of the wildest enthusiasm on the part of the inhabitants… Wild huzzas rent the air, as the train swept by; the ladies smiled their sweetest welcome, and displayed their whitest pocket handkerchiefs to testify their gratitude to those who were ready to face death for their protection." However, according to the soldier, the train made slow progress. He complained that there was only a single track, "and the detentions consequently frequent." It was the middle of the night when the train

---

35 Witmer to dear Grandfather, September 29, 1862, Manuscript Group 7, PSA, PHMC.

36 Department of Military Affairs, Transportation & Telegraph Department, Scott to Reynolds, September 17, 1862.

arrived in Chambersburg, which the men thought was their destination. However, after a lengthy delay, the cars headed south to Hagerstown, arriving after daylight on Thursday, September 18. The men wearily piled out of the cars and camped on the outskirts of town in a spot where the Rebels had camped the previous Sunday.[37]

That same morning, September 18, Thomas Scott sent additional fresh troops through the Cumberland Valley to Hagerstown, while withdrawing other soldiers to Harrisburg. "About 9 a.m. a train came down [south through Carlisle]," the Reverend J. A. Murray wrote, "having on board a few militia that had declined crossing the [state] line—also 6 deserters from the rebel army, & the dead body of one of the Anderson Troop. Soon a large train of soldiers passed up, & the Telegraph operator said that 10 or 12 more trains would pass up and down during the night."[38]

On September 18, from his headquarters at Keedysville, General Reynolds wrote to his sister in Lancaster. He informed her that he had left Chambersburg yesterday and arrived on the battlefield last night. "I had to get my troops at the field at Genl. McClellan's request but they do not seem to relish the idea and I don't know what will be the up shot of the affair," he noted. "I think if the Penna. Militia did not turn out to fight they had better have remained at home—the Battle here was limited yesterday. It has not been resumed today. We had the advantage of the Rebels, I think, tho' not much to boast of."[39]

Reynolds and his emergency militiamen indeed saw no combat action, as he predicted. However, their presence along the border was a testimony to Governor Andrew Curtin and Col. Thomas Scott. From September 12-19, the energetic duo coordinated the movement of some 25,000 militiamen, including Reynolds' untested command, and their supplies and equipage south on the CVRR and Franklin Railroad lines toward or across the Mason-Dixon Line. It was a significant accomplishment, given the unparalleled need to move that many armed men through the Cumberland Valley. An even more impressive feat happened at same time.[40]

---

37 "Notes from My Knapsack," *The Bradford Reporter* (Tonawanda, PA), October 2, 1862.

38 Thompson, *Two Hundred Years*, 205-206.

39 John F. Reynolds to My dear sister, September 18, 1862, Eleanor Reynolds Scrapbook, Reynolds Family Papers, Franklin & Marshall College Archives, Lancaster, PA.

40 Scott oversaw sending and receiving of hundreds of messages over a three-week period and rarely left the capitol building. Transcripts are in the Pennsylvania State Archives.

The Amazing Antietam Ammunition Run

Major General George B. McClellan's Federal forces expended a significant amount of ammunition battling General Lee's Army of Northern Virginia to a tactical stalemate at Antietam, and reserves were now dangerously low. During the early afternoon of September 17, "Little Mac" drafted an urgent telegram to Maj. Gen. Henry Halleck, the general-in-chief of the Union army, in Washington. He asked Halleck to "please take military possession of the Chambersburg and Hagerstown railroad that our ammunition and supplies may be hurried up without delay. We are in the midst of the greatest battle of the war, perhaps of history. Thus far it looks well, but I have great odds against me. Hurry up all the troops possible; our loss has been terrific, but we have gained much ground." After giving some updates on the particulars of the fighting, McClellan closed with, "I hope that God will give us a glorious victory." He entrusted the message to an orderly, who galloped north along the turnpike toward the nearest telegraph station, in Hagerstown.[41]

Just past Boonsboro, the messenger encountered William Bender Wilson of the Pennsylvania Railroad. Since Maj. Gen. John Pope's defeat in late August at the Second Battle of Bull Run, PRR officials had worried that the Confederates might turn north and threaten their railroad and communication lines. Wilson had left his role as the company's lost car agent in Harrisburg and resumed his early war status as a telegrapher. This time, however, he did not base his operations in Governor Curtin's office in the state capitol building. Instead, he packed a pocket relay and "a coil of fine helix wire for opening up telegraphic communication whenever convenient and practical." Armed with this portable telegraph, he and Capt. William J. Palmer (also a former Pennsylvania Railroad employee) had headed down the Cumberland Valley as the Maryland Campaign began, scouting the enemy's movement and strength. "My offices as opened, were improvised from fence rails, tree stumps or crevices in decayed trees," Wilson recalled his primitive work conditions, adding, "from these, however, I was able to give the Government officials the first information of the fall of Harpers Ferry, the fight at Boonsboro Pass of the South Mountain and the evacuation of Hagerstown by Longstreet." Now, with McClellan's note in hand, Wilson rode to the nearest

---

41 William Bender Wilson, *A Few Acts and Actors in the Tragedy of the Civil War in the United States* (s. n., 1892), 75.

telegraph line and sent the message to Washington about 4:30 p.m. via the relay station in Harrisburg.[42]

Meanwhile, as the fighting at Antietam thundered around him, General McClellan became increasingly concerned about replenishing the long-range rounds for his heavy guns, which had been particularly active. By 5:30 p.m., the situation was becoming desperate. Lieutenant Samuel N. Watson of Battery E, 2nd U. S. Light Artillery, had fired his final round. Several other batteries were also out of ammunition or dangerously low. McClellan, a pre-war railroad executive, sent another courier to Wilson near Hagerstown with instructions for the army's chief of ordnance, Brig. Gen. James W. Ripley: "If you can possibly do it, force some 20-pound Parrott ammunition through to-night, via Hagerstown and Chambersburg, to use near Sharpsburg, Maryland." About dusk, Wilson received the note and dutifully tapped out the message to Washington. However, for some reason, Ripley did not receive the message, despite its urgency, until almost ten o'clock that evening.[43]

Wilson's task was not yet finished. At 9:30 p.m., he received instructions to wire General Ripley and request that he send duplicate loads of ammunition, split equally between Hagerstown and Frederick. Signed by Lt. Col. N. B. Sweitzer, McClellan's aide-de-camp, it specifically mentioned "twenty-pounder Parrott, ten-pounder Parrott, twelve-pounder Napoleon and thirty-two pounder Howitzer ammunition, and small arms ammunition except .54, .58, .69 and .57; Sharp's ammunition and pistol ammunition." This time, Ripley received the message rather quickly; Washington acknowledged receiving the telegram at 10:00 p.m.[44]

Ripley and other supply officers quickly sprang into action. Lieutenant Colonel George D. Ramsay, the capable commander of the Washington Arsenal, issued the needed artillery ammunition and had it ready to ship by 1:00 a.m. Colonel Daniel H. Rucker of the quartermaster department arranged with President John W. Garrett of the Baltimore and Ohio Railroad to provide the needed engines and cars. Assistant Secretary of War Peter H. Watson further told Garrett, "This train must have the right of way on the entire route, and must be

42 Wilson, *From the Hudson to the Ohio*, 47-48. After the war, Palmer moved to Colorado, where he co-founded the Denver & Rio Grande Railroad and served as its president. In 1894, he received a Medal of Honor for his conduct at the battle of Red Hill, Alabama, while serving as the colonel of the 15th Pennsylvania Cavalry.

43 *Report of the Joint Committee on the Conduct of the War, in Three Parts* (Government Printing Office, 1863), part 1, 490.

44 Wilson, *A Few Acts and Actors*, 76-77.

run as fast as any express passenger train could be run. It must be ready to start in two or three hours from this time. Can you make the necessary arrangements to push it through via Harrisburg?" Meanwhile, at the arsenal, Ramsay soon acknowledged the orders, sending McClellan a message at 11:00 p.m. that "a special train will soon leave with the 20-pounder ammunition asked for. It will go in charge of an ordnance officer, and will be in Hagerstown to-morrow morning. Other ammunition will follow to Frederick and Hagerstown as soon as possible."[45]

At midnight, Secretary of War Stanton added his personal stamp to the urgency of the matter, addressing a telegram "to the officers or any of them of the Northern Central Railroad, Pennsylvania Central Railroad and Cumberland Valley Railroad at Harrisburg, Pa." He ordered the ammunition train "to be run through at the fastest possible speed so as to reach its destination to-morrow morning early. It must have the right of way throughout, as General McClellan needs the ammunition to be used in the battle to be fought to-morrow. It is expected you will use every possible effort to expedite the passing of this train." For further emphasis, Secretary Stanton closed with, "By order of the President of the United States."[46]

In Harrisburg, the orders reached Col. Thomas A. Scott, who had charge of railroad logistics for the mobilization. He sent a courier racing to the home of Joseph N. DuBarry, the youthful, energetic president of the Northern Central Railway. Called out of bed shortly after midnight, DuBarry rushed to the telegraph desk at the sprawling station the Northern Central, CVRR, and Pennsylvania Railroad shared in the capital city. He quickly worked with military and railroad officials to move the special B&O four-car ammunition train across the Northern Central road north to Bridgeport, where he was to turn it over to *Judge Watts* and the CVRR. During the night, workers in Washington feverishly loaded the quartet of freight cars with crates of much needed ammunition. When they had finished the arduous task, a locomotive pulled the train, under the command of Lieutenant Bradford of the Ordnance Department, the 40 miles north to Baltimore. Despite the original plans to leave at 1:00 a.m., it was hours later before the train finally departed Washington. It finally arrived at Camden Station at 7:27 a.m. on the 18th. There, horses pulled the railcars almost two miles along the Basin (today's Inner

45 Ibid., 77; Report of the JCCW, 842.

46 Wilson, *A Few Acts and Actors*, 78.

Harbor) to the Northern Central's Bolton Street Station, where a powerful freight engine awaited.[47]

Time was short because of the late start. DuBarry and his employees quickly cleared the right of way on the single track for the ammunition train, which raced through rural Baltimore County across the Mason-Dixon line and into southern York County. It steamed through the Howard Tunnel and rolled at a perilously high speed through the countryside, careening on the iron T-rails around the many curves in the hilly region. After passing through downtown York, the special train arrived in Bridgeport at 10:20 a.m., where DuBarry passed control to the CVRR. It had been the fastest that any train had ever run on the Northern Central's tracks. The engineer, at DuBarry's urging, had completed the 84-mile run from Baltimore to Bridgeport in a record 2 hours and 53 minutes. It had averaged some 30 miles an hour, an unheard-of speed for a fully loaded freight train.[48]

There remained the necessity of getting the special train down to Hagerstown, where McClellan's empty supply wagons waited. Just before the train arrived at Bridgeport, Assistant Secretary of War Watson reassured McClellan that "2,500 rounds of this ammunition was ordered with the least practical delay from the arsenal, and arrangements made to run it through in all the roads at express passenger speed. It is now at or near Harrisburg, Pennsylvania, and will reach Hagerstown by noon to-day."[49]

At Bridgeport, the Northern Central locomotive was decoupled and the CVRR's appropriately named *Judge Watts* took its place to provide the motive power for the final leg. It only took 24 minutes to swap the locomotives, allow the journal boxes of the hard-worked ammunition cars to cool somewhat, and add an additional freight car filled with ammunition from the Pennsylvania State Arsenal. The journal boxes covered the ends of the axles, which spun on friction bearers in a bed of oil-soaked rags or cotton packing. As the oil dried out, the bearings overheated and could catch fire, a situation that railroaders of the day called a "hot box." That was the situation facing the CVRR. The Northern Central had run the

47 Ibid., 73. The Federal arsenal in Washington later became part of Fort McNair. On July 7, 1865, four of the Lincoln assassination conspirators including Mrs. Mary Surratt, the first woman to be executed by the Federal government, would be hung on gallows erected in the courtyard.

48 For more on the NCR and its interactions with the Cumberland Valley Railroad, see Scott Mingus, *Soldiers, Spies, and Steam: A History of the Northern Central Railway in the Civil War* (CreateSpace, 2016).

49 Report of the JCCW, part 1, 490. Watson had replaced Thomas A. Scott as assistant secretary of war in January 1862.

cars so fast that the journals were almost to the point of igniting, which could be catastrophic considering the cargo. There was no time to replace the packing and bearings, so the train would have to proceed after the short break. CVRR Superintendent O. N. Lull had assigned Joseph Miller as the engineer, Henry Ward as fireman, and Andrew Stepler as the brakeman. They formed a capable, experienced crew.[50]

At 10:44 a.m., the Judge Watts rolled out of Bridgeport with the tender and the five heavily laden cars in tow. It soon picked up speed and headed south toward Hagerstown. With few bridges or curves, the CVRR could make up the lost time, although the journal boxes remained a major concern. At Newville, the train had to stop for ten minutes as maintenance workers swarmed around the trucks of the freight cars. "As will be remembered by our older citizens," the local newspaper would recall almost four decades later, "that when this train passed this place the flames were flying from the boxes of one of the cars and it stopped, oil and packing put in and away it went over the grade."[51]

Resuming the journey at speeds that at times reached 45 miles an hour, Miller and his highballing train roared through Shippensburg, startling the residents. Eighteen-year-old Mary Emma Hollar lived in a house on Railroad Street (now Earl Street). She later recalled "the thunder of the ammunition train rushing to supply the troops." All along the route, the hard-charging train turned heads. It stopped again in Chambersburg at noon for another ten-minute break to cool the journal boxes and then sped to Hagerstown, arriving at 12:42 p.m. Crews began unloading the ammunition.

Years later, military telegrapher William Bender Wilson marveled, "Such running was never before experienced on the Cumberland Valley Railroad before, and has not been equaled since. When the train entered Hagerstown all the journal boxes on the four Baltimore and Ohio cars were ablaze; of this fact I was an eye witness." Amazingly, the ammunition cars had not caught on fire, a disaster that could have leveled a portion of the town. Wilson later wrote, "When it is considered that the train was composed of four Baltimore and Ohio freight cars, controlled by hand-brakes, with none of the more modern appliances, their journal boxes smoking most of the distance, and running over a road imperfectly ballasted, ironed and aligned, it will readily be seen how remarkable was the run, a

---

50 "More Reminiscences," *Newville Star and Enterprise*, November 20, 1901, citing the diary of O. N. Lull.

51 Ibid.

run never tried before nor equaled since, and the unusual nerve of the man who directed it."[52]

The trip was a triumph for all involved in the desperate endeavor. The special ammunition train had made the 158-mile trip from Baltimore to Hagerstown over the B&O, Northern Central, and Cumberland Valley railroads in only 4 hours and 31 minutes, averaging an astounding 37 mph (including the unplanned 10-minute stops at Newville and Chambersburg). Normally, trains running on the same routes averaged 20 to 25 mph. However, there would be no immediate need for the new ammunition. Neither McClellan nor Lee attacked on September 18; the two armies sat idle, watching each other all day.

Credit should also be given to telegrapher W. B. Wilson for his unique role in the Maryland Campaign, one that involved the railroad. "The enemy threatened Greencastle, and the few troops we had there departed," he wrote, "leaving me with two scouts as the sole garrison. Taking position on a hand-car, I put my instrument in circuit and flying the American flag over the town, I bid defiance to the enemy, and from my unique office kept the authorities advised of his movements…The combination of Palmer and myself was the medium of information which enabled Governor Curtin to guide McClellan's army in the Antietam campaign."[53]

Curtin, with traffic resumed on the CVRR, left Harrisburg at 3:00 p.m. on September 18 in a special gubernatorial train for Hagerstown. He brought welcome relief to the wounded of Antietam. His aide, Col. John A. Wright, Pennsylvania's Surgeon General Henry H. Smith, and surgeons from all parts of the commonwealth had assembled in Harrisburg in anticipation of their services being required. They brought loads of medical supplies to take to the field hospitals in and around Sharpsburg. Trainloads of wounded soldiers would begin to head north into Pennsylvania for treatment and recuperation.[54]

Frustrations Mount with the Railroad

For the next two weeks, scores of other troop, munitions, and hospital trains, including those pulled by the locomotive *Robert Morris* and its engineer Ephraim Jones of the PRR, steamed up and down the Cumberland Valley. None matched

---

52 Wilson, *A Few Acts and Actors*, 78.

53 Wilson, *From the Hudson to the Ohio*, 48.

54 "Harrisburg: Sept. 17," *Daily Intelligencer* (Wheeling, VA), September 19, 1862.

the speed or urgency of the special September 18 ammunition run. While newspapers lauded the unique achievement, not everyone was happy that it was only a one-time event. "If the same energy had been shown in sending forward relief for the wounded how many noble and precious lives would have been saved at Antietam!" Charles J. Stillé, a Philadelphia-based agent for the United States Sanitary Commission, later complained.[55]

Illustrative of Stillé's frustrations was the case of one of the commission's volunteer field inspectors, Dr. William M. Chamberlain, who was based in New York City. On September 18, Chamberlain, a Dartmouth-educated physician and a former army surgeon, received a request from Frederick L. Olmsted, the general secretary of the Sanitary Commission, to travel to Philadelphia. Chamberlain was to do whatever he could to expedite the transportation of much-needed medical supplies from Harrisburg to the Antietam battlefield. He would have the authority to travel to Antietam if that seemed advantageous to him. Chamberlain met with Stillé after arriving in Philadelphia. The agent urged him to hop a train at once to Chambersburg and assist the local USSC agents working there. During their conversation, Stillé received a telegraph advising him that "no further supplies should be sent via Chambersburg, on account of obstructions to transportation in the railroad." Hearing this, Chamberlain immediately determined to make his way there. He left Philadelphia at 11:00 a.m. on Friday morning, September 19, on a train bound for Harrisburg. He arrived there at four o'clock in the afternoon. He was more than distressed to confirm that there was no train being sent to Chambersburg that day.

That evening, however, he heard that a special train was leaving to carry two regiments of Pennsylvania state militia to Hagerstown. Chamberlain climbed on board expecting to climb back off at Chambersburg. What he did not know, however, was that it was an overnight express without a single stop along the way. The train sped through the town too fast for him to hop off, so he proceeded to Hagerstown, getting there at 9:00 a.m. on Saturday morning. Once there, he conversed with another Sanitary Commission doctor who agreed to head back up to Chambersburg to pick up the stores there—assuming they had been forwarded from Harrisburg—and forward them to Maryland. Dr. Chamberlain proceeded to the Antietam battlefield to lend what aid and comfort he could.

---

55 Charles J. Stillé, *History of the United States Sanitary Commission* (J. B. Lippincott & Co., 1866), 265.

On Sunday morning, he was back in Hagerstown, where he received a telegram that his associate Charles Stillé still had not reached Chambersburg, and the promised supplies would not arrive that day. Noticing boxes of blankets and bandages near the Franklin Railroad station, he went to General Reynolds, whose headquarters was then in town, and received his permission to seize the supplies for the wounded soldiers. He filled two captured Confederate supply wagons with the blankets and bandages and other goods he scrounged and, with a cavalry escort provided by Reynolds, Chamberlain returned to the field hospitals to deliver the badly needed relief supplies. Later, he learned that the medical supplies, plus thirteen casks of whiskey and wine, and a large cask of brandy, had finally arrived. He had them taken to the railroad's storehouse and left them in the hands of railroad officials with the full expectation they would send them on to the hospitals on Monday.

The next day, September 23, Dr. Chamberlain received a request to take charge of a train containing 347 wounded men and conduct them to Harrisburg. It proved to be a most frustrating experience. After many delays, the train finally left Hagerstown at 3:00 p.m., but made poor time chugging northward with all the traffic jammed on the single track. Hours were lost sitting on sidings waiting for the all-clear signal. Finally arriving at Chambersburg, he met the local USSC agent, Dr. Edward A. Crane, and gave him a complete report, including the delays. The two discussed how best to counter the railroad's inability to move supplies and wounded quickly.

At Shippensburg and Carlisle, during delays there, local women came out to the train and supplied the wounded men with abundant quantities of tea, coffee, fruit, bread, and butter. "The enthusiasm of the ladies was wonderful," Dr. Chamberlain later wrote. "They were clamorous that the wounded should be left among them to be nursed and feasted, and when they could no longer find anyone to eat and drink their good things, they gathered in groups and sang the 'Star-Spangled Banner,' and the 'Red, White, and Blue,' which was answered by the men with cheers for the flag and cheers for Gen. McClellan." The train of wounded finally reached Harrisburg at 1:00 a.m. on Wednesday, a full ten hours after leaving Hagerstown. Dr. Chamberlain returned to Philadelphia, where he reported to Stillé, who informed him of the reasons for the delay in the shipment arriving in Hagerstown. The liquors had last been seen in Harrisburg "or at some station on the Cumberland Valley Railroad," Stillé added, "with an assurance from the superintendent that he would see them forwarded immediately." That promise had, unfortunately, taken two full days to fulfill while the wounded lay suffering at Antietam. His finally mission over, Chamberlain took a train to New York City to

Union Brig. Gen. Herman Haupt, a prewar civil engineer, commanded the United States Military Railroads for much of the Civil War. *Library of Congress*

report to the Sanitary Commission's executive committee, which for a full report.[56]

The Military Temporarily Takes Over the CVRR

Hermann Haupt, a pre-war civil engineer and noted bridge builder in south-central Pennsylvania, now was a brigadier general serving as the Chief of Construction and Transportation for the United States Military Railroads. He was frustrated, as were many in the War Department in Washington, that after Lee's Confederate army had re-crossed the Potomac River on September 19 and marched back into Virginia, General McClellan had not moved aggressively after the enemy forces. Haupt was also concerned that the movement of supplies and troops on the Cumberland Valley Railroad did not meet with the standards of efficiency he had set for military railroads.

56 "Sanitary Commission No. 48," in Documents of the United States Sanitary Commission, vol. 1 (United States Sanitary Commission, 1866), 1-8; "Dr. W. M. Chamberlain's Death," *New York Times*, November 1, 1887.

The same day Lee was leaving Maryland, Col. Thomas Scott took action to help alleviate supply problems. In a demonstration to Haupt and the War Department that he was taking steps to improve the Cumberland Railroad's military volume, he sent a telegram to his colleague Enoch Lewis, the general superintendent of the Pennsylvania Railroad, requesting the services of Robert Pitcairn, the PRR's superintendent of transportation, along with his top three dispatchers. Pitcairn arrived in Chambersburg late the next day, September 20, with the authority to oversee all of the line from Hagerstown to Harrisburg. Scott planned to move O. N. Lull from Chambersburg back to Bridgeport to help there, but Watts wanted him to stay at the company offices in Chambersburg. Judge Watts tersely wired Scott, "Mr. Lull's direction here is essential to the management work to be done. He will remain here." Scott acquiesced and allowed Lull to remain in place, to Watts' satisfaction.[57]

The next day, September 21, with Governor Curtin still in Hagerstown, Scott sent a telegram to Pitcairn, asking, "Are you getting hold of things?" Pitcairn soon responded, telling his chief that he proposed to run regular passenger trains on September 22, along with one freight train each way. He would establish a schedule "and some rules to govern trainmen." He planned to flag freight trains intended for the military, keep the track clear for them, and run by telegraph if the trains were much behind schedule. Scott replied, "All right, make your schedule to move trains with regularity. When this army of Pennsylvania begins to move [homeward] you will have a busy time of it for 3 or 4 days." However, the same problems that had plagued Lull and Watts returned that same day. Pitcairn, clearly frustrated, wired Scott that he was "prepared to take all the trains they could give us," but he had just been informed that "nothing can be done at Hagerstown tonight as there is not a soldier there to unload cars." He would have to hold all trains at Harrisburg that night. "That will set us back," he mentioned, "but [I] can still catch up if you will assure a force for that duty in the future."[58]

In Hagerstown, J. D. Potts soon began making some progress in clearing the massive backlog of railcars. He telegraphed to Colonel Scott on September 22 that

57 Westhaeffer, *History of the CVRR*, 77, citing the Pennsylvania Military Telegraph Department files for September 19-20 at the Pennsylvania State Archives. The dispatchers who accompanied Pitcairn were his kinsman John Pitcairn of West Philadelphia, Daniel McCann of Altoona, and Samuel Kennedy of Pittsburgh. All were veterans of the PRR.

58 PMTD files, September 20-22, 1862. Using the telegraph to track movements of trains was not common at the time. The CVRR typically used flaggers if trains were running behind schedule. With the added volume, Pitcairn would not allow trains to leave until telegraphic confirmation the single track was clear, if necessary.

he was working with a new system. "Slowly all will be cleared out today," he declared. "Gen. Reynolds at my request has sent to Gen. McClellan for a regiment to guard stores and trains, and 200 contrabands for a day and night labor." The contrabands, black men who had escaped from slavery, provided welcome labor to unload the heavily laden cars. Potts arranged with an army quartermaster "to erect a storehouse and provide wagons and canvas for stores unloaded on the ground." Adding to the confusion, Federally-provided supplies for McClellan's Army of the Potomac were intermixed with Pennsylvania's stores intended for John Reynolds's emergency militiamen. Cars had been forwarded from Harrisburg without the proper manifests, "and no one knows their destination," Potts complained. His system was working; "The goods are now being selected, loaded, and manifested." He informed Scott that he was resuming regular passenger service on the entire line later that day, and would resume regular freight service from Hagerstown to Chambersburg on the morrow.[59]

Things were still not going as smoothly as the army needed, despite Colonel Scott's reinforcements from the Pennsylvania Railroad. On September 25, in accordance with Special Orders No. 248 issued by Quartermaster General Montgomery C. Meigs, General Haupt dispatched one of his trusted assistants, William Wierman Wright, to Harrisburg "to take charge of the transportation on the Cumberland Valley Railroad." He gave Wright a copy of Meigs' new Special Order as well as previous instructions sent to the CVRR. He also included a message from E. C. Wilson, Meigs' assistant quartermaster in Harrisburg, complaining about poor management of the railroad. The general instructed Wright to proceed to the state capital, see Wilson, and "ascertain fully the character and magnitude of the evils complainted of and, if necessary, assume the direction of train movements on the Cumberland Valley Railroad."[60]

Wright, a native of York Springs in northern Adams County, was quite familiar with the geography, people, and railroads of south-central Pennsylvania. A Quaker by lineage, his father and mother were among the most active conductors on the Underground Railroad in the region, having helped hundreds of freedom seekers move toward the Susquehanna River. Haupt had been young Wright's instructor at a private academy in Gettysburg. Later, Wright began his distinguished career as a civil engineer under the tutelage of Samuel W. Mifflin,

---

59 Ibid.

60 Herman Haupt and Frank A. Flower, *Reminiscences of General Herman Haupt* (Wright & Joys, 1901), 138.

William Wierman Wright, a Quaker with strong family connections to the Underground Railroad in south-central Pennsylvania, was the capable assistant of Brig. Gen. Herman Haupt of the U. S. Military Railroad. *Library of Congress*

another Quaker who had charge of the Mountain Division of the Pennsylvania Railroad. Mifflin himself had been a long-time conductor on the Underground Railroad, as had his parents, at Wrightsville along the Susquehanna River in eastern York County. Under Mifflin's capable mentorship, Wright flourished and went on a successful career in the U. S., South America, and England.[61]

General Haupt told Wright that generally it was desirable that railroads used wholly or partially for military purposes be operated by those railroads' regular officers, "but when the management is characterized by incompetency, or inefficiency, it [may become] necessary to assume military possession and place in charge agents and officers who will promptly forward troops and government supplies." He added another far-reaching proviso: "When the amount of rolling stock is insufficient, requisitions must be made upon connecting roads." He reminded his assistant that he had found it necessary the previous week to take possession of the Franklin Railroad and had placed J. D. Potts, "a very efficient officer," in charge at Chambersburg and Hagerstown. Wright was to consult with Potts in regard to train arrangements. Haupt had the impression that very little government business would be required between Harrisburg and Hagerstown, as alternatives existed through Sandy Hook and Harpers Ferry.

Haupt insisted that three points required "special attention" in properly managing military railroads. Supplies were not to be moved to the advance terminus until actually required, and even then, only that amount that could be

61 *American Society of Civil Engineers, Proceedings*, vol. VIII, December 1882, 118-19.

promptly moved. Cars should be promptly unloaded and returned to their point of origin. And, finally, trains should never be permitted to leave late. If extra freight was required, the train should leave at the appointed time and the railroad should form an extra train to send the additional materials, "if the proper accommodation of business requires them."[62]

These three items requiring special attention pointed to Generals Meigs' and Haupt's main frustration with the joint Cumberland Valley Railroad/Franklin Valley Railroad management group. Despite pressing PRR crews and equipment in place, the sheer amount of government traffic had overwhelmed the CVRR's scheduling and supporting logistics, despite having Superintendent O. N. Lull strictly focus on the Harrisburg-to-Chambersburg segment while Potts ran the Franklin Railroad operations south from Chambersburg to Hagerstown. Trains arrived with either too much or too little of the freight needed at the moment. With inadequate sidings or warehouses, several trains had stacked up at Hagerstown needlessly for days, blocking the tracks to more important oncoming ones. No competent person was in charge before Potts arrived. Troops and supplies from the north were taken to Chambersburg and dropped off with little planning as to how to stage them for transportation to Hagerstown, or troops and supplies arrived in Maryland at government expense, but were not needed. Haupt had seen first-hand some of the issues back in September 19 when he took the Northern Central and CVRR from Baltimore to Chambersburg. Plagued by "many delays caused by passing trains," he had not arrived in Chambersburg until well after his scheduled arrival, certainly not the efficiency he needed to win a war.[63]

The CVRR and FRR were not only railroads in the region to frustrate General Haupt. He also censured Northern Central Railway and the Baltimore and Ohio. He believed that management was too reliant on the telegraph to dispatch trains exclusively, covering up for a lack of strict adherence to established schedules and protocols. "I believe that it is always possible with good management to run the trains by schedule," he informed General-in-chief Henry Halleck, "the telegraph, although valuable as an auxiliary, should not be used as a principal. It is desirable that uniformity should be introduced in the management of all railroads used for military purposes."[64]

62 Ibid., 138-139.

63 Ibid., 139-40.

64 Ibid., 142-43.

The *Utility* was a small and relatively lightweight 0-4-0 tank engine and used exclusively to shuttle trains across the wide Susquehanna River bridge between Harrisburg and Bridgeport until it was involved in a frightful accident. After repairs, it served as a yard engine in Chambersburg. *Mike Marotte*

With the principles, theories, and expectations of Meigs and Haupt as guideposts, William W. Wright took over active management of the Cumberland Valley Railroad, with the title of military superintendent. It did not take long for him to face a major crisis.

Tragedy Strikes the CVRR

For several years, Judge Frederick Watts had routinely touted the sterling safety record of the Cumberland Valley Railroad in his annual reports to the stockholders. That all changed in an instant on the morning of Friday, September 26, under the watch of the newly arrived W. W. Wright. A fully loaded, 20-car troop train pulled out of Greencastle and headed north through the Valley to Harrisburg. On board were members of Col. William B. Thomas's 20th Pennsylvania Volunteer Militia who were heading home to be discharged after the immediate threat from Lee's army had receded. They had left their campsite and piled into uncomfortable freight cars pressed into service to haul soldiers. The train had fallen well behind schedule as it sat on the siding at Greencastle awaiting the passage of a train from Carlisle. Time ticked away, but the southbound train did not arrive. Finally, officials cleared the troop train to proceed to Harrisburg. The weather was so foggy that the engineer and fireman could barely discern objects along the trackside. The situation demanded extreme caution, particularly on a single-track railroad.

Shortly after 7:30 a.m., the troop train was within a half-mile of the bridge over the Susquehanna River at Bridgeport when disaster struck. The engineer, peering into the fog bank, suddenly noticed a large, dark shape in his front. Too late, he recognized it as a locomotive sitting idle on the main line. It was the *Utility*, the small engine that was only used to pull trains across the bridge, and it was too late to avoid a head-on collision. The sound of it jolted the residents of Harrisburg from all the way across the wide Susquehanna river. The first car of the troop train smashed into fragments, killing or maiming almost all of the occupants as the second car slammed into it. Several soldiers were maimed when the third car left the ground and came down on the wreckage of the second car. Bodies, parts of bodies, and badly injured men littered the scene as shock and numbness gave way to the wails and screams of the dying and injured.

Quickly, the survivors rushed to lend assistance, collecting the wounded and taking them to nearby farm houses. Two men went racing up the tracks to warn any other oncoming trains that a major collision now blocked the route, hoping to ward off an even greater disaster. Someone headed for Harrisburg to fetch as many surgeons as possible. Several men were in critical condition. They included Hampton Harris, "a colored man," according to a newspaperman, who had deserted "from Jackson's army, had one arm and both legs badly crushed; not expected to recover." The train's engineer had a broken leg, but no other railroad employees had been harmed. Some later accounts placed the number of injured as high as 63, many of whom were now unfit for further service.[65]

A reporter for the *Harrisburg Telegraph* soon arrived on the gruesome scene. His vivid description conveys the horror of what he witnessed and his lingering trauma: "Inside the cars could be seen brave men struggling in the last gasp of death—others writhing and imploring Heaven to end their suffering—others again dead, crushed, mangled, torn, without a single warning of the cause which produced their end." He added, "So sudden was the crash, that the loud and boisterous cheers of soldiers, just then approaching as they had reason to believe,

---

65 "Distressing Railroad Accident," *Pittsburgh Daily Post*, September 27, 1862. In other accounts, Harris is mentioned as a "negro servant, from Hagerstown." More conservative estimates suggest 40 men were injured.

the last change of cars which were to carry them home, were, as it were, instantly changed to the groan, the stifled cry of pain, the yell of agony, and such demonstration as men only make who are suddenly driven to despair and terrible death." As he peered into the interior of the crushed cars, the reporter's heart "fairly sickened at the sight. We never desire to look on such a scene again. The cries of those wounded men still ring in our ears; while the sight of mangled and torn dead will be a spectacle which it will be impossible to dispel from our view for some time to come."[66]

"A sad and terrible accident occurred near here this morning," a *Philadelphia Inquirer* correspondent stationed in the state capital reported, "casting a gloom over a city which yesterday was full of merrymaking and congratulations on the return of our gallant and self-sacrificing State militia." The news spread "with the swiftness of an electric shock, until the whole city was alive with excitement, and the bridges across the river were crowded with men, women and children, on their way to one of the most terrible scenes I ever witnessed. Surgeons, physicians and nurses were wanted, and the medical fraternity of Harrisburg responded nobly."[67]

The first car behind the tender of the troop train contained Company I from Reading and Berks County, under the command of Capt. Frederick S. Boas. Some of these men had perished immediately; others suffered devastating, crippling injuries. In the second car, Company F, from the Corn Exchange (an early type of commodities exchange that now was primarily a financial institution in Philadelphia), also had many casualties. "When your correspondent arrived on the spot," the Philadelphia reporter noted, "men were being taken out from the wreck, and many were still buried in the mass of timber and iron." He soon learned that a warm friend, Albert Werner of Reading, lay lifeless in the wreckage. Werner was "loved by all who knew him for his gentle qualities and manly bearing;" the reporter mourned, "a young man, too, just in the spring-tide of life, of no mean intellectual abilities, promising him honorable promotion in life hereafter." Another family member, Cpl. Alexander Werner, was injured.[68]

Two miles distant from the crash site, William Bigler and his fellow students at the White Hall Academy (in present-day Camp Hill) "heard the collision, and we all ran from there to the scene of the wreck." They were in for a horrific sight,

---

66 *Pennsylvania Telegraph*, September 27, 1862.

67 "Terrible Accident on the Cumberland Valley Railroad," *Philadelphia Inquirer*, September 27, 1862.

68 Ibid.

eyeing "the mangled bodies of twelve dead men" lying beside the track, "side by side, all covered with army blankets[.]" Bigler was particularly taken by a "drummer boy, of scarcely 15 years, whose right arm was crushed to the elbow."[69]

Wagons and other wheeled conveyances began arriving to take the patients to a hospital in an old factory in Harrisburg, opposite the Capitol. The 20th PVM's commander, Col. William B. Thomas, arrived there to succor his men; he was "unceasingly active in his attentions," and was "doing all that he can for their comfort." He had plenty of help in his ministrations. "The ladies of Bridgeport and Harrisburg were very attentive," the Philadelphia correspondent added. "They brought bandages, delicacies, wines and medicines, and more than all, loving, tender hearts, a feeling a self-sacrifice and martyrdom, that prompted the noble action. Kind friends and loving relatives at home could have scarcely taken better care of the sufferers." Thomas and the badly shaken survivors of the regiment soon headed home to Philadelphia on another train, leaving a squad of ten men under Maj. William H. Sickles to attend to the sufferers and take charge of the deceased. One mangled body, that of 19-year-old Cpl. Frederick V. Harmer of Philadelphia, was crushed between the cars and could not be removed until workers began removing the shattered wreckage. The firm of Boyd & Sloan placed the dead soldiers in coffins and supervised their shipment to Reading, Pottsville, and Philadelphia.[70]

Almost immediately, people started looking for the underlying reason for the disaster, a calamity unmatched in CVRR history. The *Valley Spirit* ruled out mechanical problems, considering it likely human error: "The editors do not know who to blame but are certain that the accident was the result of gross carelessness on somebody's part." In Harrisburg, the editor of the Pennsylvania Telegraph was far more certain. "The whole cause of the accident was carelessness on the part of

---

69 Manuscript memoir, attributed to William B. Bigler, Brooks-Bigler Family Papers, 125-11, CCHS. Bigler later served as a corporal in the 1st Pennsylvania Militia, raised during the 1862 Emergency. The injured drummer boy is uncertain, but both drummers in the front two cars were injured. Alexander Brown of Company F was "saved principally by his brother's presence of mind. He is not dangerously hurt," according to the Philadelphia Inquirer, September 27, 1862. Jacob Hamilton of Reading's Company I had his "head bruised and hip dislocated."

70 "Terrible Accident on the Cumberland Valley Railroad," *Philadelphia Inquirer*, September 27, 1862; "The Dead of the Railroad Catastrophe," *Pennsylvania Telegraph*, September 27, 1862. The dead men were identified as Cpl. Frederick V. Harmer of Company B; Cpl. Robert T. Graves, Pvt. John W. McIntosh, Pvt. P. William McFeeters, and Pvt. Richard "Reed" McKay of Company F (all from the Philadelphia area) and Sgt. Henry Fleck, Pvt. Albert B. Werner, Pvt. Daniel Seiders, and Pvt. Augustus Keller of Reading's Company I. In addition, black civilian Henry Hampson of Virginia also perished. Two other men later died of their injuries.

an engineer of the Cumberland Valley railroad. The Pennsylvania railroad, which had the entire charge of the transportation of troops, exercised all due caution. The shifting engine [the *Utility*] of the Cumberland Valley Railroad, instead of stopping at the bridge and inquiring the whereabouts of the troop train, passed on, and the collision was the result."[71]

The national press also was quick to assign blame for the tragedy, finding fault with the CVRR management team. Calling the accident "deplorable," the editor of the *Philadelphia Inquirer*, measuring his words, stated, "It is difficult to write with temperance about such a disaster, which could not have occurred with any proper system of precaution, or fidelity in the observance of it. Here were large bodies of citizen-soldiers, who had gone forth at the call of their State to defend it from outside enemies, having accomplished their gallant mission, and returning to their homes with the honest sense of a dangerous duty well done, when a number of them are suddenly killed, and variously and cruelly maimed through the simple negligence of parties having charge of their transport." The newsman added that if the railroad was tasked with an unusually large amount of travel, it should have put in place extra safeguards against collisions and other misfortune to prevent such "murderous mishaps." Company managers needed to ensure that such safety precautions were in place, and their agents and employees trained and competent to make the safeguards effective. That was the only way to "relieve themselves of the just odium of the guilt of this calamity." The paper called for a legal investigation, with severe punishments "stinted only by the limits of the law." Even then, that "might not satisfy public indignation against the perpetrators of the outrage."[72]

The *Inquirer* correspondent who had rushed to the scene only to find his friend Albert Werner dead singled out one man for blame. "The fog, at the time of the accident, was very dense, and the noise of shifting trains close by prevented a detection of any opposing trains by sound," he wrote. Nevertheless, "some feeling was manifested against Mr. Pitcairn, the new superintendent of the road. That gentleman has been newly appointed to his position and had arrangement of transportation, &c., on the road." He went on to say, "There will shortly be a judicial investigation, when the real facts of the case will be known. I informed you before of the danger of traveling on this road at a time when the business of

---

71 *"Terrible Railroad Accident," Valley Spirit*, October 1, 1862; *Pennsylvania Telegraph*, September 27, 1862.

72 "Railroad Slaughter," *Philadelphia Inquirer*, September 27, 1862.

transportation is unprecedented, and all cars run on but a single track, with sidings at each station, where they wait for opposing trains to pass."[73]

In Chambersburg, the *Valley Spirit* quickly jumped to the defense of the railroad management, deflecting the blame onto the Federal officials who had taken over the line. The editors reminded their readers that the government had absolute control of the railroad since September 21, and no officer of the company had participated in its operation since then.[74]

While the newspapers vied in placing blame, one of the critically injured soldiers, 22-year-old Cpl. Edwin F. Scott of Company K, 20th Pennsylvania Volunteer Militia, expired on Sunday morning, September 28, in Harrisburg. He had suffered a fracture of his right leg and a severe compound fracture of his left. Grieving family members in his hometown of Philadelphia soon placed a notice in the *Inquirer*, informing the public, "His male friends are requested to attend his funeral, from his father's residence, No. 308 South Sixteenth street, this (Tuesday) afternoon, the 30th inst., at 3 o'clock, without further notice." Fueled by the appalling toll of dead and maimed soldiers, public sentiment continued to be against the railroad company.[75]

Soon, CVRR officials found themselves with another stain—although much smaller in scale than the Bridgeport accident—on their once impeccable safety record. "A Franklin County resident by the name of Todd was killed by a train on Friday morning at Rohrerstown," the *Valley Spirit* reported on October 1. "It is believed he fell off the train while it was in motion."[76]

A week later, the newspaper returned to its persistent defense of the Cumberland Valley Railroad officials for the still-raw Bridgeport disaster. This time, it shifted guilt from the Federal government to a new pair of scapegoats—the Union army and the commonwealth's most powerful railroad. "The editors protest the attempt by certain parties in Harrisburg to blame the Cumberland Valley Railroad for the recent accident on its line. As the editors note, the line was under the control of the military and was being operated by the Pennsylvania Railroad at the time. It is they who should take responsibility. The

---

73 "Terrible Accident on the Cumberland Valley Railroad," *Philadelphia Inquirer*, September 27, 1862.

74 "The Cumberland Valley Railroad," *Valley Spirit*, October 1, 1862.

75 "Died," *Philadelphia Inquirer*, September 30, 1862.

76 "And Still Another," *Valley Spirit*, October 1, 1862.

Cumberland Valley Railroad should welcome an investigation, as it would surely absolve them."[77]

The *Philadelphia Inquirer* sharply disagreed, lambasting the CVRR officials for trying to deflect the blame onto the Federal government when the shifting engine, the Utility, was directly under the supervision and management of the railroad. It agreed with the *Harrisburg Telegraph* that the engineer should have stopped at the telegraph office and asked if the road was clear before pulling onto the main line. "He could have easily discerned the fact that a train was due and coming when he left the other side of the bridge." It did not behoove the railroad company "to shift the responsibility to the Government. Upon that Corporation, therefore, appears to rest the responsibility of the consequences of the collision." The newspaper called upon the management of the Pennsylvania Railroad, as controlling owners of the CVRR, to launch an immediate investigation.[78]

The members of the Corn Exchange Association of Philadelphia, grateful for the swift and compassionate response of the people of Harrisburg, passed a resolution on October 2 to thank them for "their extreme kindness, unremitting attention and constant devotion to the sufferers from the late accident." The group singled out Dr. Schultz, who had charge of the local hospital, and William Buehler, "who so freely gave their attention and sympathy to the relief of the wounded." Many of the wounded were still suffering in great pain.[79]

One of the most seriously injured soldiers, John Matchett of Company F, lingered for several weeks before succumbing to his injuries. He was the last victim to expire. His body was shipped home on the railroad to Philadelphia, where numerous friends, including the members of Lodge No. 37 of the American Protestant Association, attended his funeral on October 27. In the ensuing weeks, several of the surviving passengers threatened to initiate legal proceedings against the Cumberland Valley Railroad. Judge Watts, perhaps realizring that the tide of public opinion weighed heavily against his company, responded by telling the press that the railroad would "pay reasonable damages to avoid a lawsuit." He set aside $25,000 to cover the contingency.[80]

77 "Cumberland Valley Railroad," *Valley Spirit*, October 8, 1862.

78 "The Railroad Sacrifice in the Cumberland Valley," *Philadelphia Inquirer*, October 2, 1862.

79 *Pennsylvania Telegraph*, October 15, 1862.

80 "Funeral of Volunteers," *Philadelphia Inquirer*, October 28, 1862; "The Late Accident on the Cumberland Valley Railroad," *Valley Spirit*, December 3, 1862.

His efforts met with praise, at least in Reading, where many of the injured soldiers lived. "We learn that certain parties on behalf of the Cumberland Valley Rail Road Company," the *Reading Times* reported in December, "have been in this city trying to settle with parties injured in the collision which occurred on that road near Harrisburg when some of our State Defence men were returning home. How they have succeeded we cannot precisely tell, but we know that they have paid some of those injured on that occasion; the sums ranging from $60 to $1600." The reporter was pleased. He went on to opine, "This shows a desire, at least, on the part of the Company to do justice, as near as can be, in the premises, and we have no doubt they will have matters all their own way, if they are liberal enough, as people do not like to go to law when it can be avoided, without losing too much by so doing."[81]

The railroad's problems, however, were far from over. "The Pennsylvania Railroad company has been peculiarly unfortunate in running its trains upon the Cumberland Valley road," the *Carlisle Weekly Herald* declared on October 10. "During the short time that the U. S. Government was running the road, no less than three considerable accidents have occurred, resulting in the killing and maiming of no less than thirty persons." He went on to describe the latest incident. "A fourth occurred, on Monday morning last, near Carlisle, at the point where the State road crosses the Railroad. The train coming down encountered a bull upon the track. The engine struck him throwing the body upon the bank at one side. Mr. Bull rolled back upon the train just in time to come in contact with the latter end of it, causing the smashing into fragments of half a dozen of them. No further damage was done."[82]

Ingratitude

The negative publicity the Cumberland Valley Railroad received in the regional press following the Bridgeport accident and the resulting feuding as to culpability soon led to other expressions of dissatisfaction. Chambersburg's residents found themselves defending against claims that they had mistreated the soldiers at Camp Slifer and the other nearby military encampments. Some of the accusations were that the townspeople and merchants overcharged for basic

---

81 "Settling Up," *Reading Times*, December 6, 1862. The *Utility*, after being repaired, was sent to Chambersburg to be used as a switching engine in the rail yard there. The *Tiger* replaced it as the bridge service engine for the rest of the war.

82 "Railroad Accidents," *Carlisle Weekly Herald*, October 10, 1862.

services, or failed to provide expected aid and assistance in a timely manner, or not at all.

The criticisms reached the editors of the *Valley Spirit*, who, not surprisingly, fired back in a lengthy article on October 8. "These complaints are entirely uncalled for and unjust," the editor wrote. "Ever since the breaking out of the rebellion the people of our town, rich and poor, have vied with each other in their efforts to minister to the comfort of the soldiers passing through the town." He insisted that no carload of men in uniform could pass through Chambersburg without being surrounded by men, women, and children with baskets of provisions to relieve their hunger. The townspeople took care of any sick or wounded soldiers, lavishing money and time without reservation and freely opening their doors and bedrooms. The only thanks they needed was a heart-felt "God bless you" from their guests as they departed for the camps. Citizens volunteered at the temporary military hospitals, "smoothing the pillows of the sick and wounded, and lightening to some extent the long hours of sickness and pain."

Despite all the residents were doing, several militiamen still complained about the lack of hospitality. The editor noted that some of the so-called protectors of the Valley were in fact thieves and vandals. "Fences burned for fuel," he wrote, "young timber wantonly destroyed, whole fields of growing corn cut down and carried away, and numberless other vandalisms attest the kind of 'protection' their property received." Many residents feared the state militiamen more than the Confederates. The editor concluded, "We cannot but admire and applaud, the patriotism that prompted these men to leave their homes for the purpose of repelling the Rebel hordes from Pennsylvania soil, yet at the same time, we must be permitted to denounce the conduct of some of them who say they came to save property, but instead wantonly destroyed it."[83]

Soon, the citizens would learn first-hand of the conduct of Rebel soldiers. Jeb Stuart would pay a visit to the Cumberland Valley.

---

83 "Unreasonable Complaints," *Valley Spirit*, October 8, 1862.

Chapter 4

Torches in Chambersburg

October-December 1862

The residents of Cumberland Valley were about to face a more significant problem than trying to sooth their wounded pride and defend their actions while John Reynolds' state militiamen were encamped there. A much more unwelcome visitor was about to come calling—and his name was James Ewell Brown Stuart. So famous was he, and so familiar was his extravagant image, that people often forgot that "Jeb" Stuart was old-school Regular Army.

Born in January 1833 in Patrick County, Virginia, Stuart graduated from West Point in 1854 and served with the Army on the western frontier in Texas and Kansas. As a lieutenant, he drew attention as Robert E. Lee's aide-de-camp during the capture of John Brown and his accomplices at Harpers Ferry in 1859. At the outbreak of the Civil War, Stuart resigned from the Army to "go South," throwing in his lot with the Confederacy. The energetic officer quickly rose to command Lee's cavalry. More than his resume, however, was Stuart's attention to style—the reason for his ear-war celebrity. With his lithe figure, wearing his ostrich-plumed hat cocked at a rakish angle, gray cape with red lining, golden sash, majestic beard and knee-high boots, Stuart embodied the dashing cavalier—the *beau sabreur*. Stuart achieved national renown in mid-June 1862 with an audacious ride around Maj. Gen. George McClellan's Army of the Potomac, which had marched up the Virginia peninsula and was threatening Richmond from the east. His reconnaissance mission helped set the stage for how General Lee would fight the bloody and consequential Seven Days' Battles soon to follow.[1]

Following the battle of Antietam in September, McClellan's bloodied but still powerful army had remained inert in a general area that stretched from Harpers Ferry to Bakersville a few miles northwest of Sharpsburg. Clearly frustrated by the inactivity, President Abraham Lincoln met with his reticent general on Friday, October 3, at the Stephen Grove farm to urge him to push aggressively after Lee. Lincoln had used the opportunity of the Confederate withdrawal to announce on September 22 the preliminary Emancipation Proclamation, which would go into effect on New Year's Day, 1863. However, he realized that to win the war in the East and give teeth to the proclamation, McClellan would have to defeat Lee's army. And, unfortunately for Lincoln, it appeared that McClellan did not share his vision. The president's personal visit and exhortations accomplished little, and the main Union army remained idle, to Lincoln's exasperation. On October 6, General-in-chief Henry Halleck ordered McClellan to pursue Lee, but to no avail; "Little Mac" was going nowhere: he continued to overestimate the number of men in Lee's army and believed his own forces needed to rest and retrofit before resuming the campaign.

Taking advantage of his overly cautious foe's prolonged inertia, Robert E. Lee decided to act. He dispatched Col. John D. Imboden's 62nd Virginia Mounted Infantry to disrupt the Baltimore and Ohio Railroad and the Chesapeake and Ohio Canal, both significant carriers of coal and other consumables for the Union war effort. That was to be a diversion for the main event. Lee planned to send Jeb Stuart's cavalry northward to Pennsylvania to sever the Cumberland Valley Railroad. He also wanted to secure fresh horses, mules, supplies, and food to replenish his depleted reserves. He sent instructions to Stuart on October 8 to cross the Potomac above Williamsport, keeping Hagerstown and Greencastle off to his right, and march to the rear of Chambersburg. There, he was to "endeavor to destroy the railroad bridge over the branch of the Conococheague. Any other damage that you can inflict upon the enemy or his means of transportation you will also execute." Another significant goal was to collect "all information of the position, force and probable intention of the enemy." Secrecy was imperative, so Stuart was to arrest all citizens that he believed might give information to the enemy. If Stuart encountered any state or Federal officials, he was to detain them

---

1   H. B. McClellan, *I Rode with Jeb Stuart: The Life and Campaigns of Major General J.E.B. Stuart* (Indiana University Press, 1958), 146.

Confederate General James Ewell Brown (Jeb) Stuart led a mounted raid on Chambersburg and Scotland in October 1862 that created significant consternation throughout south-central Pennsylvania. *Library of Congress*

to be used as hostages for possible future exchanges for Confederate political prisoners being held by the Union. Lee reminded Stuart that "such persons will, of course, be treated with all the respect and consideration that circumstances will admit." After accomplishing the goals, Stuart was to "rejoin this army as soon as practical." Lee further admonished Stuart, "Reliance is placed upon your skill and judgement in the successful execution of this plan, and it is not intended or desired that you should jeopardize the safety of your command, or go farther than your good judgement and prudence may dictate."[2]

Stuart selected 1,800 cavalrymen—split fairly evenly in three divisions under Brig. Gen. Wade Hampton, William "Grumble" Jones, and W. H. F. "Rooney" Lee (the army commander's second son)—for the daring mission. It would be Stuart's second "ride around McClellan," duplicating his celebrated circuit during the Peninsula Campaign earlier in the year. Taking along a four-gun battery of artillery under his beloved subordinate Maj. John Pelham, Stuart departed camp at Darkesville (just south of Martinsburg, in western Virginia), on the evening of October 9. Before breaking camp, he sent a circular to his men. "You are about to engage in an enterprise which, to insure success, imperatively demands at your hands coolness, decision, and bravery." He ordered them to obey their orders implicitly and to maintain "the strictest order and sobriety on the march and in bivouac." He did not reveal his plans or his destination, but insisted, "The orders which are herewith published for your government are absolutely necessary, and must be rigidly enforced." He also sent instructions to his three brigade commanders on how he wanted them to conduct their troops and their assignments, including the seizure of "public functionaries, such as magistrates, postmasters, sheriffs, &c." This was "a measure of justice to our many good citizens who, without crime, have been taken from their homes and kept by the enemy in prison." Stuart camped for the night near Hedgesville in western Virginia.[3]

Before dawn on Friday, October 10, the vanguard of Wade Hampton's mounted force splashed across the Potomac River at McCoy's Ford west of Williamsport, Maryland, about eight miles south of the Mason-Dixon Line. The Confederate riders did not do so unseen. A patrol of the 12th Illinois Cavalry spotted the Rebel movement and quickly relayed word to their headquarters. About 8:00 a.m., the Confederates captured a Union signal station on Fairview Mountain. Hampton continued north in thick fog toward Clear Spring and the National Road, where his advance detachment captured about ten stragglers from Maj. Gen. Jacob D. Cox's six regiments of Union infantry that had recently passed along the highway on their way back to western Virginia after fighting at Antietam. Stuart's column entered southern Franklin County, Pennsylvania, by early

2 OR 19, pt. 2, 55.

3 Ibid., 55-56. Darkesville is now in West Virginia, a state created on June 20, 1863. Jones and Rooney Lee had both been recently promoted from colonel to the rank of brigadier general.

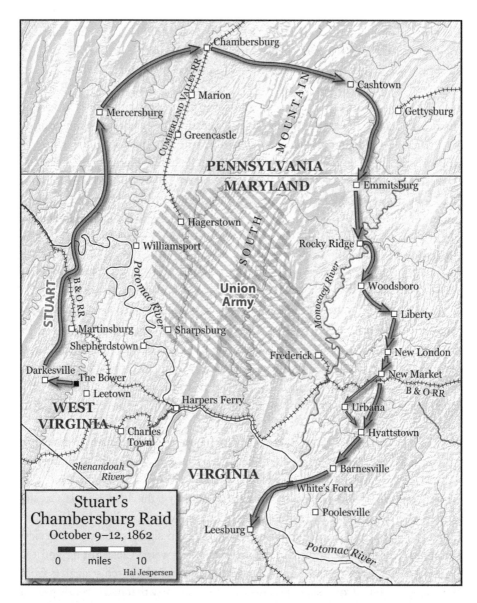

Stuart's
Chambersburg Raid
October 9–12, 1862

0   miles   10
Hal Jespersen

morning, where they began appropriating horses and supplies from startled residents.

Hugh Logan, a trusted scout attached to Stuart's staff, was a native of Waynesboro, Pennsylvania. He knew the geography and key roads of Franklin County from his antebellum adventures with his brothers Daniel and Alexander while hunting fugitive slaves in the region. Logan had headed south when the war began and volunteered his services to the Confederacy. Now, he guided the lengthy Rebel column north toward the Cumberland Valley as storm clouds thickened. About noon, the first Southern soldiers rode into Mercersburg, where they freely entered stores and took clothing and shoes, paying with Confederate scrip, a worthless commodity in the Keystone State. Rebels took nine citizens, including the chief burgess and postmaster, as hostages before leaving about 2:30 p.m. Several soldiers sported roasted turkeys, hams, and beef strapped to their saddles. Others carried bread, cheese, and other foodstuffs taken from the locals.[4]

As light rain began to fall, Stuart's force headed for Chambersburg, where, according to merchant Jacob Hoke, the townspeople had been alerted to a potential raid following "the arrest of several suspicious persons traveling along the railroad from Hagerstown to Harrisburg." That afternoon, five or six soldiers dressed in blue overcoats arrived at the Bratton Hotel, some four miles west of Chambersburg. The old proprietor, assuming them to be Federals, welcomed the strangers, "Well boys, get off and come in, and if you will keep old Jackson away, I will treat." After some light banter and a few drinks, the soldiers admitted, "We are rebels." They unbuttoned their coats, revealing the Confederate gray.[5]

About 6:00 p.m., a refugee from St. Thomas, a village on the turnpike about nine miles west of Chambersburg, rode into the square and reported he had been chased by Rebels "half ways to town." An excited crowd soon gathered around him, peppering him with questions. The Rebels had hauled down St. Thomas's Union flag, took over the town, and then pursued him for several miles. Many Chambersburg residents "shook their heads dubiously, believing the thing impossible." The courthouse bell began ringing, and Chambersburg's 50-man home guard company, the "Phil Kearny Infantry," turned out, receiving muskets from one of the warehouses along the railroad. Captain John S. Eyster of the 12th Pennsylvania Reserves, in town visiting friends and family, took command of them. By now, it was dark and rainy, adding to the gloom and confusion.[6]

Hampton's vanguard arrived in the vicinity of Chambersburg about 7:00 p.m. from the west. Before the Rebels could sever the telegraph wires, the Atlantic and

4 McClure, "An Episode of John Brown's Raid," 282; OR 19, pt. 2, 57. Some accounts suggest that Logan held the rank of captain in the Confederate army. Robert J. Trout, in his book They Followed the Southern Plume: The Story of J.E.B. Stuart and His Staff, calls him a civilian scout attached to Stuart's staff. Logan was a pre-war acquaintance of A. K. McClure, and warned him not to reveal himself as a Union colonel, else Stuart might arrest him. Daniel Logan and a friend had captured John E. Cook, one of John Brown's band, near Chambersburg back in 1859.

5 Hoke, Reminiscences of the War, 30.

6 "The Rebel Raid on Chambersburg," Pittsburgh Daily Gazette and Advertiser, October 15, 1862. Hoke said there were two refugees; the newspaper article mentioned only one man.

Ohio Telegraph Company's youthful operator, W. Blair Gilmore, tapped a message to warn Governor Curtin and Brig. Gen. W. T. H. Brooks, commanding the Federal troops in Hagerstown, that "a large force of rebel cavalry" was within ten miles of Chambersburg. Gilmore also sent the message up to Harrisburg before he packed his instrument and headed to safety in the state capital. In Curtin's office at the Capitol building, the military telegrapher on duty quickly relayed the alarm to the War Department in Washington. The CVRR hastily sent three locomotives and ten cars steaming north to Harrisburg for safekeeping.[7]

Several residents, after becoming aware of the Rebel approach, raced south almost two miles along the Franklin Railroad tracks to intercept the regularly scheduled train from Hagerstown, which was due to arrive about the same time as the enemy soldiers. The citizens managed to stop the train and warn the engineer not to approach Chambersburg. He quickly reversed his course and steamed backwards to Hagerstown. "Had it not been for the timely warning," a reporter later claimed, "another locomotive would have been added to the list of those destroyed, and several officers and soldiers, who were on the train, would have been captured, to say nothing of a pretty considerable fright the remainder of the passengers would have experienced."[8]

General Hampton had hoped to enter Chambersburg before darkness fell, but with the steady rain and muddy roads that action proved impossible. "When we discovered the lights of the town," the burly South Carolinian later reported, "it was so dark that no reconnaissance could be made." Hampton was unable to ascertain if there were Federals in the town. According to General Stuart, "I did not deem it safe to defer the attack till morning, nor was it proper to attack a place full of women and children without summoning it first to surrender. I accordingly sent in a flag of truce," he continued, "and found no military or civil authority in the place, but some prominent citizens who met the officer were notified that the place would be occupied, and if any resistance were made the place would be shelled."[9]

After Pelham's four field guns took position on a knoll commanding the town, Hampton dispatched Lt. Thomas C. Lee of the 2nd South Carolina Cavalry and 25 troopers with a white flag to deliver the demand. Seeing the Rebels

7 Ibid., 65; *Philadelphia Inquirer*, October 11, 1862.

8 "The Daring Rebel Raid into Pennsylvania!", *Philadelphia Inquirer*, October 13, 1862.

9 "General J.E.B. Stuart's Report of His Cavalry Expedition into Pennsylvania, October, 1862," *SHSP*, vol. 3, 72.

Views of Chambersburg, Rebels raiding a merchant, and the burning of warehouses near the Cumberland Valley Railroad during Jeb Stuart's 1862 raid. *Harper's Weekly*

approach, Captain Eyster and the local home guardsmen commanded them to halt. When they told him they had come to demand the town's surrender, Eyster retorted emphatically, "Go to h—l!" The Rebels were escorted into town while the Phil Kearny Infantry scattered to their houses and secreted their arms. Three citizens, including Alexander K. McClure, the abolitionist editor of the *Franklin Repository* and a friend of Lincoln, came forward to ask Lieutenant Lee about the terms. McClure described Lee as a "clever-looking butternut, dripping wet, without any mark of rank, bearing a dirty white cloth on a little stick." Lee refused to give his name or that of his commander, nor did he offer any terms. Given half an hour to surrender before the artillery opened fire, McClure and the others talked things over and finally mounted their horses to ride west to meet with General Hampton. The South Carolinian repeated his demand for the unconditional surrender of the town. He assured the trio, however, that "private persons should be protected and private property unmolested, except such as should be needed for the use of the army." The delegation quickly accepted the terms, and Hampton's men rode into Chambersburg about 8:00 p.m. and established "a rigid provost guard." After designating Hampton as the town's military governor, Stuart and his staff checked into the Franklin Hotel and signed the register.[10]

In a driving rain, Stuart dispatched Capt. Thomas Whitehead and Company E of the 2nd Virginia Cavalry to destroy the railroad bridge over the Conococheague Creek at Scotland, some five miles north of Chambersburg. The Rebels, however, soon heard reports from several locals that the bridge was made of iron and could not possibly be burned or chopped down with axes. Whitehead realized he had neither the time nor the materials to blow it up, so he and his detachment returned to Chambersburg and camped in the streets on a "disagreeably cold" evening, in a drizzle.[11]

"The people have surrendered Chambersburg," Governor Curtin tersely wired Secretary of War Stanton in Washington. At 9:10 p.m. that evening, General Halleck sent an urgent message to McClellan, informing him, "A rebel raid had been made into Pennsylvania to-day, and Chambersburg captured. Not a man should be permitted to return to Virginia. Use any troops in Maryland or Pennsylvania against them." McClellan quickly dispatched infantry to guard the likely river crossings and sent out cavalry patrols to watch the roads in the area. Fifty minutes later, he telegraphed Halleck that "every disposition has been made to cut off the retreat of the enemy's cavalry, that to-day made a raid into Maryland and Pennsylvania." Meanwhile, Hampton's men tightened their grip on Chambersburg. A patrol headed to the local bank, but the soldiers found that the vault had been emptied and its contents carried off to safety. Stuart and his staff officers boarded at a private house on the east side of Chambersburg near the toll gate on the turnpike to Gettysburg.[12]

The town leaders had agreed that the Rebels could search for horses, hats, shoes, and articles of military value, but prohibited the soldiers from entering private houses. "It was a sad spectacle to see rebel soldiers on every street and

---

10 OR 19, pt. 2, 57; "A Highly Interesting Yankee Account…," *Richmond Daily Dispatch*, October 24, 1862; *Pittsburgh Daily Gazette and Advertiser*, October 15, 1862; Hoke, *Reminiscences of the War*, 30. McClure's two companions were Francis M. Kimmel (a retired judge) and Thomas B. Kennedy (who, like A. K. McClure, held the political brevet rank of colonel). Kennedy, an attorney by trade, served on the board of directors of the CVRR and had been its legal counsel since the mid-1850s. In 1873, he became the president of the CVRR and served in that capacity for the next 32 years.

11 Bates, *History of Franklin County*, 359. It is often misstated that the CVRR bridge at Scotland during the Civil War years was made entirely of iron. The metal one came after the war. The one during the war was mostly timber, which may have been reinforced with iron in places.

12 Ibid., 59, 65.

street-corner," a reporter later recounted, "or galloping through every alley, breaking open and entering the stables of our citizens, and taking out their best horses." He went on to say, "Out citizens generally retired to their houses about 11 o'clock; but good order reigned throughout the night, the rebels priding themselves on their good behavior. General Stuart asked one of our citizens if they were as bad as they had been represented, and was told that the devil was never as black as he was painted."[13]

Stuart remained concerned that the steady rain, which at times came in torrents, might swell the mountain streams and eventually cause the vital Potomac fords to become impassable, trapping him north of the river. He decided to pull out of Chambersburg as early as possible. Knowing the Yankees would be heavily guarding the fords closest to Chambersburg, the general determined to head well east across the South Mountain range and then push south toward Emmitsburg, Maryland. From there, guided by Capt. B. S. White, a native of Poolesville, Maryland, he expected to cross the Potomac at White's Ford. Hopefully, it would be unguarded. Stuart's quartermasters worked well into the night to prepare the column to move out. "Numbers of horses had been taken from Pennsylvania farmers and were corralled that night ready for distribution," one of Major Pelham's artillerymen wrote. "The four teams for guns and caissons were now supplied with fresh horses and the colors being selected to match. Seldom had a more attractive artillery outfit been seen."[14]

Hundreds of soggy Rebel troopers camped on the grounds of "Norland," A. K. McClure's sprawling country estate a mile north of Chambersburg. Many fed their horses in his 60-acre cornfield. McClure's wife Matilda and her domestic servants served coffee, tea, and bread to more than 100 officers and men before the bugles called and they departed at 4:00 a.m. That gave McClure the opportunity to report on the Rebel presence in Chambersburg. Very early on Saturday, October 11, he sent a message via the Shippensburg railroad office to Governor Curtin that "Stuart's and Hampton's cavalry, about 3,000 in number, occupied the town last night." He relayed the terms of the surrender and mentioned that the Rebels had taken about 500 horses, including ten of his own, "but did not interfere with citizens or destroy anything. One regiment encamped before my door, and the officers spent most of the night with me. They behaved

13 "The Rebel Raid on Chambersburg," Pittsburgh Daily Gazette and Advertiser, October 15, 1862.

14 Robert J. Trout, ed. *Memoirs of the Stuart Horse Artillery Battalion: Moorman's and Hart's Batteries* (University of Tennessee Press, 2008), 195.

very well, and talked freely about everything but their movements." He suggested they might try to return to Virginia by crossing the Potomac near Leesburg.[15]

Amid fears that Stuart might continue northward instead of trying to return to the Old Dominion, the CVRR suspended all passenger service from Harrisburg as a precaution. "Much excitement prevails here," a correspondent in Carlisle wrote. "All the rolling stock of the road except four engines have been brought here." For some time, the Anderson Cavalry had camped near Carlisle in case of any Rebel mischief there. To watch for any threatening Rebel movements coming north from Chambersburg, Irish-born Capt. David H. Hastings, a Mexican War veteran, led Company D of the 1st United States Cavalry from the Carlisle Barracks on the 30-mile ride to the town. In an effort to locate the Confederates, early in the morning General McClellan dispatched a locomotive north on the Franklin Railroad from Hagerstown toward Chambersburg. He had deployed his infantry and cavalry to intercept the Rebels' anticipated return, but complained about "the want of cavalry, as many of our horses are over-worked and unserviceable."[16]

Fresh horses were also on Stuart's mind, as was evading the expected heavy Union presence along the river between Hagerstown and Williamsport. He began to withdraw his troops eastward, toward Gettysburg, before heading south toward Emmitsburg. A. K. McClure recalled Stuart's presence in the town's "Diamond," the center square: "About seven o'clock I went into town, and found that the First brigade, under Gen. Hampton, had gone towards Gettysburg. General Stuart sat on his horse, in the centre of the town, surrounded by his staff, and his command was coming in from the country in large squads, leading their old horses and riding the new ones they had found in the stables hereabouts. General Stuart is of medium size, has a keen eye, and wears immense sandy whiskers and mustache. His demeanor to our people was that of a humane soldier. In several instances his men commenced to take private property from stores; but they were arrested by General Stuart's provost guard. In a single instance only that I have heard of did they enter a store by intimidating the proprietor. All our shops and stores were closed, and, with very few exceptions, were not disturbed." The public stores, however, were another matter. Stuart's quartermasters collected as much as they load into wagons. Stuart paroled 275 to 280 wounded or ill Federals found

15 *OR* 19, pt. 2, 71.

16 "The War in the East," *Wyandot Pioneer* (Upper Sandusky, OH), October 17, 1862.

recuperating in Chambersburg hospitals and in private homes and then left town.[17]

When, about 9:00 a.m., the last of the main body of Confederates departed for Cashtown, about twenty miles to the east, two-thirds of the way to Gettysburg Stuart's rear guard remained behind. The cavalrymen destroyed whatever public stores could not be carried off. The remaining Rebels scurried about Chambersburg to fulfill their commander's instructions. Captain W. H. Cowles of the 1st North Carolina Cavalry received orders to burn the railroad depot and the nearby storehouses of Wunderlich & Nead, a government contractor and freight forwarder. They contained a large supply of arms (including an estimated 5,000 rifle-muskets), hats, military uniforms, and ammunition of all sorts. The cavalrymen kept several new revolvers and plenty of new clothes (often discarding their own tattered garments), and then torched everything else. They also exploded boxes of ammunition found in some railcars on the siding.[18]

"The first act of the rebels…," Judge Watts later recalled, "was to take possession of our depot buildings, hence nothing escaped the torch of the incendiaries, which was applied the next morning… and immediately before they left the town. The Wood-shop, Machine-shop, Blacksmith-shop, Engine-house, Wood-sheds, and Passenger Depot were totally consumed, and with the Engine-house, three second-class engines were injured by fire but not so destroyed that they may be restored to usefulness. All machinery in the Wood-shop was totally destroyed and most of that in the Wood-shop was so injured as to render it useless. Our entire loss has been estimated at $50,000." All of the company's maps, road profiles, repair and maintenance records, blueprints, and many other important technical papers were also now gone. The three locomotives would be repaired and put back into service, but three freight cars were a total loss.[19]

A. K. McClure penned his own account of the destruction of the trackside structures: "The railroad station house, machine shop, round house, and the warehouses filled with ammunition, were then fired and the last of the rebels fled

17 *Richmond Daily Dispatch*, October 24, 1862.

18 *OR* 19, pt. 2, 58-59; "The Situation," *Pennsylvania Telegraph*, October 11, 1862. The Rebels reportedly took an estimated 700 rifle-muskets, 400 pistols, and 468 boxes of ammunition when they left. For more details on Stuart's raid, see Conrad and Alexander, *When War Passed This Way*, 89-92.

19 *1862 CVRR Annual Report*; "The Daring Rebel Raid into Pennsylvania!", *Philadelphia Inquirer*, October 13, 1862; Westhaeffer, *History of the Cumberland Valley Railroad*, 78.

The CVRR's venerable 2-2-2 tank engine *Pioneer* and the attached combination car both predated the Civil War, on display here in Mount Alto, Pennsylvania, in 1910. Today, the *Pioneer* is housed at the Smithsonian Institution and the combo car at the Pennsylvania State Railroad Museum. *Mike Marotte*

the town. In a little while a terrific explosion told that the flames had reached the powder, and for hours shells were exploding with great rapidity. The fire companies came out as soon as the rebels left, but could not save any of the buildings fired because of the shells. They saved all the others, however." Even the new brick warehouse that Wunderlich & Nead had erected had collapsed from the explosions. The noise from the largest explosion could be heard in Shippensburg, more than ten miles away.[20]

Some of the Rebels sported as many as three new hats and were carrying as much clothing, boots, extra pistols, and ammunition as they could possibly carry on horseback. Others stuffed their haversacks with goods and supplies taken from Chambersburg as Hampton's rear guard left to rejoin the main column on the way toward Gettysburg. The Confederates also took a large U. S. government supply wagon and two or three army ambulances, all fully loaded with uniforms, hats, and other military clothing and related goods. "After the guard departed," merchant Jacob Hoke wrote, "some of our citizens endeavored to save the burning buildings, and adjoining property, but they were much annoyed by the exploding

20 *Richmond Daily Dispatch*, October 24, 1862; *Pittsburgh Daily Gazette and Advertiser*, October 15, 1862.

shells. These did not go off at once as some feared, but gradually as the fire reached them. Fearing for the safety of the sick and wounded in the lower end of town, in case the whole of the ammunition in the burning warehouse would explode at once, many of the ladies who had been ministering to their necessities went to their assistance, and at the usual hour at noon these good Samaritans had dinner prepared for the men."[21]

Several daring residents pursued Stuart's rear guard to watch their movements. They brought in a prisoner taken at Stoufferstown, where he had stopped to have a shoe put on his horse. He was brought back to Chambersburg and placed in the jail, where he soon had company. Three residents—Michael Geiselman, Joseph Deckelmayer, and William Glenn—reportedly had expressed active sympathy for the Rebels during their visit. Geiselman had given the cavalrymen alcohol and regaled them in his house, and the other two had openly congratulated them on their visit; one of them had supposedly declared his allegiance to the Confederacy and said he would fight for them, before being compelled to be quiet. All three men were incarcerated as they awaited bail. "It is in times of invasion that suspected persons should be watched," a reporter opined, "for then they will [be] likely to expose their treasonable feelings." He lamented the fact that "the rebels had sympathizers from our midst giving them information."[22]

Jeb Stuart's jubilant men proceeded eastward on the macadamized turnpike toward the gaps in the South Mountain range, taking horses from the stables and fields along the way. At Thaddeus Stevens' Caledonia Ironworks near the Franklin-Adams county line, a worker named Cramp sent a message to the authorities "that the Rebel cavalry are in Cashtown, at the foot of South Mountain, in Adams county in considerable force. They have been driven back from the Potomac, and are trying to escape. Every effort is being made to cut them off here and at Mercersburg. They have Logan, a man from Franklin county, with them, a superior guide, and they may escape. Our citizens all have arms, and will join the troops in cutting them off."[23]

---

21 "The War News," *Civilian & Telegraph* (Cumberland, MD), October 23, 1862; Hoke, *Historical Reminiscences of the War*, 32; "Effects of War News," *Shippensburg Chronicle*, June 26, 1913.

22 "The Rebel Raid on Chambersburg," *Pittsburgh Daily Gazette and Advertiser*, October 15, 1862. Stoufferstown is located on the turnpike just east of Chambersburg; just east of today's US 30 – I-81 interchange.

23 "The Latest News! The Late Rebel Raid," *Philadelphia Inquirer*, October 14, 1862.

Stuart lost another man shortly after riding through Cashtown. In the late afternoon, "the farmers attacked their advance 5 miles west of Gettysburg, and captured 1 prisoner," Governor Curtin informed General McClellan. "He says the whole force will be in Gettysburg to-night; prisoner is on his way to Harrisburg, by railroad." Curtin urged McClellan to put a force in Stuart's rear, to cut off any retreat to Fulton or Bedford counties to the west. Three infantry regiments under Col. James Beaver and a battery were moving on the Northern Central Railway toward Hanover Junction and Gettysburg to confront Stuart. They would be far too late, as would another detachment that was sent north from Hagerstown.[24]

The latter force consisted of the men of the 2nd and 5th Vermont Infantry. Encamped outside of Hagerstown, on October 11 they were marched into town to the Franklin Railroad station and hastily loaded, with their supplies and equipment, into cars for the 22-mile journey north to Chambersburg. By the time they arrived, however, Stuart's cavaliers were well on the road east. An officer in the 4th Vermont, which had stayed behind in Hagerstown, likened the fruitless expedition of the 2nd and 5th to Chambersburg as locking the barn door after the horse was gone. The two regiments would remain in town for five days before taking the cars back to Hagerstown midday on the 16th.[25]

Another unit hastily pressed into duty was the 153rd Pennsylvania Infantry, a new regiment organized in September in Northampton County. The men were being trained and drilled at Camp Curtin north of Harrisburg. Officers awakened the men very late on the night of October 10 with news of Stuart's raid. Anxious to meet the Rebels, the fledgling soldiers began cheering lustily. They stood in line in a drenching rainstorm to receive three days' rations of hardtack, sugar, and coffee. In the morning, they learned their assignment was to guard the bridges over the Susquehanna River in case Stuart threatened the state capital. They marched to the State Arsenal, where each man drew a musket and forty cartridges. The process took all afternoon, and they did not return to Camp Curtin until almost sundown. The men gathered the rest of their equipment and accoutrements and marched to the train station, where they boarded several "old cattle cars." By now, it was almost midnight, and they still were not on their way across the river. After waiting for some time, the Sons of Northampton learned that the officials of the Cumberland Valley Railroad had not been able to produce a locomotive to pull the

---

24 OR 19, pt. 2, 72; "A Rebel Raid into Pennsylvania," *Harper's Weekly*, October 25, 1862.

25 Paul G. Zeller, *The Second Vermont Volunteer Infantry Regiment, 1861-1865* (McFarland & Co., 2002), 102-103, quoting Maj. Stephen M. Pingree of the 4th Vermont.

train. The grumbling men disembarked and marched back to camp, having accomplished nothing. On Sunday, the 153rd Pennsylvania again headed to the depot, this time with orders to go to the defense of Carlisle. Again, they were disappointed and wearily headed back to Camp Curtin "with sour faces and many imprecations."[26]

"The rebel raid against Chambersburg is not deemed important here," a reporter in Harrisburg sniffed. "The disposition of the Federal troops at Cumberland, Chambersburg, and other points, will force the rebels to a speedy return to Virginia by way of Hancock, or to make a detour above Cumberland. In either case the movements of the rebels must be rapid to escape capture." He did not realize that Stuart was not headed west toward Hancock or Cumberland, into the teeth of the assembled Federal troops, but east and south toward Leesburg, Virginia.[27]

Stuart easily managed to elude the various Federal detachments and slip back into Virginia on October 12 at a Potomac River ford near Leesburg, ending his second ride around a frustrated McClellan. The Virginia cavalier soon reunited with Lee's army, bringing more than 1,200 fresh horses (many of them large, ponderous draft horses more used to the plow than to cavalry service), large quantities of supplies, and several civilian hostages. His road-weary troopers had traveled more than 125 miles since leaving Darkesville, with only minimal losses. Their unfortunate comrade captured by the home guard near Gettysburg had been taken eastward to York on the Hanover Branch Railroad and the Northern Central.[28]

Many Pennsylvanians did not realize the Rebels were actually gone from their state. "The town is alarmed," a Shippensburg man scribbled into his diary on the night of October 13. "Our church bells rang out an alarm and news given out that the Rebels are at the mountain." A six-man detachment of home guard cavalry left town and rode over the mountain to Beam's saw mill, but encountered no enemy. They returned home before dawn.[29]

26 Lochard H. Lovenstein, *In Lieu of a Draft: A History of the 153rd Pennsylvania Volunteer Regiment* (AuthorHouse, 2012), 40-42.

27 "Latest: Harrisburg, October 11," *Muscatine (IA) Weekly Journal*, October 17, 1862.

28 "Important War News," *Raftsman's Journal* (Clearfield, PA), October 22, 1862. Mercersburg attorney and postmaster Perry Rice, one of the hostages taken to Richmond's Libby Prison, became desperately ill and died in prison in January 1863. The other men were eventually released.

29 "Effects of War News," *Shippensburg (PA) Chronicle*, June 26, 1913.

Chambersburg residents, stunned by the unexpected Rebel incursion and resultant destruction to their vital railroad, soon began describing their experiences. "Such a surprise and such a humiliation!" the Reverend Benjamin Schneck informed his sister on October 13. "We were helpless…" The local home guard had proven entirely unready to meet the Rebels, or there might have been significant bloodshed, he reckoned. He was thankful that the Rebels had not exacted vengeance upon the populace. "One must give credit for two things:" he added, "gentlemanly conduct in their intercourse with our people, and intrepidity and boldness. They had several men with them formerly from this county; hence they knew every nook and corner."[30]

William Heyser, who owned a store in the South Ward, quickly assigned blame. "It was all the fault of A. H. Lule, Supt. of the railroad shops," Heyser complained in his diary that evening. "He should have sent the war supplies back to Carlisle, instead of keeping them here, being warned as early as three o'clock the past afternoon. However, this saved our stores from being pillaged as they got enough at the depot. Everybody out on the streets seeking news." Fortunately, the CVRR's tracks and ties had escaped significant damage.[31]

Several Confederates described their recent exploits in letters sent home. Private Edward D. Cottrell of the 10th Virginia Cavalry wrote to his grandmother from Stuart's camp at Martinsburg, mentioning that they had destroyed $300,000 worth of Federal government property, including coffee, sugar, molasses, bacon, flour, boots, shoes, hats, and "clothing of every description." He hauled off a large amount of booty: "I equiped myself fully. I got 8 pair of boots 4 over coats 5 pair of pantaloons 2 hats 6 pair of socks 6 pr. draws 6 over & under shirts some coffe & sugar." Cottrell regretted that he had not been able to get items from the depot before it was torched, "There were things of all Description there. I wish I could have gotten some of them home." He bragged, "We went all round the enemy's lines and landed in Old Virginia safely, having only one small fight those we routed directly I believe its is the greatest thing that has ever been done." Like many of the cavalrymen, he had been forced to swap his played-out horse, Fanny, for one appropriated from the Pennsylvanians. "Fanny I traded for a horse smaller," he

30 Benjamin S. Schneck to My Dear Sister, October 13, 1862, Chambersburg, PA, CVRR files, FCHS.

31 Jane Dice Stone, ed., "Dairy of William Heyser," *Papers Read Before the Kittochtinny Historical Society* (Mercersburg Printing, 1978), vol. 1:54-58. Heyser likely meant O. N. Lull, not A. H. Lule.

noted. "I found she could not stand it so I thought I better trade her as I would never get home safe & sound again."[32]

With the Rebels gone from Pennsylvania and the excitement finally subsiding, the Cumberland Valley Railroad resumed full service on October 13. Early accounts placed the gross damages from Stuart's raid into the Keystone State at more than $200,000. Of this amount, officials estimated the loss to the CVRR as $80,000. Southern soldiers had torched the car house, engine house, wood and water facilities, and other railroad structures. The large, multi-story frame building used as a combination ticket office, telegraph office, and company headquarters was a total loss. Superintendent Ormond N. Lull had his furniture in storage in his residence on the upper floor of the depot; he lost it all. A few nearby houses suffered damage. "We must confess," a newsman from Harrisburg opined, "that if the citizens had used a little more energy their houses might have been saved."[33]

"For a space of 300 square yards," another reporter noted in a Philadelphia paper, "there is now nothing left but the blackened and smouldering ruins." The well-stocked warehouses of Wunderlich & Nead were a total loss. They had contained a significant amount of ammunition and military supplies, including 700,000 cartridges, 700 new muskets, and a quantity of explosive shells, loose gunpowder, and other munitions. Stuart's men, of course, likely did not realize that these same trackside warehouses had played a role in John Brown's controversial 1859 raid on Harpers Ferry. During the summer, the abolitionist and his followers had stored pikes and weapons in wooden crates marked "farm implements" as they prepared and planned for the October incursion.[34]

Rebels also had discovered a railcar loaded with revolvers; they carried off all of them. Fortunately, Stuart respected private property and ordered his men to not disturb two long trains, loaded with goods consigned to private individuals. His

32 E. D. Cottrell to My Dear Grandma, October 16, 1862, Cottrell Family Papers, Mss2 C8297, Box 1, Virginia Historical Society, Richmond.

33 "The Escape of Stuart's Cavalry," *Waynesboro Village Record*, October 17, 1862; "From Chambersburg," *Pennsylvania Telegraph*, October 13, 1862. The postwar Pennsylvania Border Claims Commission estimated the damages from Stuart's raid at $123,000. That was based on claims filed and adjudicated, and does not include any damages suffered by Pennsylvanians who did not take the time to submit the required paperwork and supporting eyewitness testimony. The border claims from Franklin County are held in the Pennsylvania State Archives in Harrisburg. CVRR Superintendent O. N. Lull, who lived with his wife above the depot in space provided by the CVRR, filed a claim with the commission for $475.

34 "The Confederates in Chambersburg," *Richmond Dispatch*, October 23, 1862, citing the *Philadelphia Inquirer*.

men, however, took more than 800 horses from the stables and farm fields in the area. In some cases, the Confederates left behind "a number of skinny, attenuated equines" in trade for the better steeds. "General Hampton appeared to be in command," the reporter added, "and appeared anxious that the citizens should not suffer. Soon after he entered the place he rode up to a house to shoot down any private that attempted to enter the houses, unless accompanied by an officer, and he would protect them in the course." One of Stuart's officers supposedly carried around a long list with the names of the most prominent Union men in the vicinity, and claimed he was well aware of the political feelings of the people in this section of Pennsylvania.[35]

Reactions to Stuart's raid varied among the people of the Cumberland Valley. Many Unionists were appalled at the Rebel intrusion into their region; others were upset at the Federal and state governments for not properly protecting them. For some residents who were not there to understand the situation, it was inconceivable that the townspeople of Chambersburg did not put up any significant resistance to the Rebels. "I suppose you thought of packing up & leaving when you heard of the Rebels being in Chambersburg," Pvt. James H. Maclay of Battery B, 1st Pennsylvania Light Artillery, chided his older sister Jennie in a letter from McClellan's sprawling camps near Sharpsburg. "You had not more than time be at Home when thay [sic] entered the town. I think the people of Chambersburg did not show verry good pluck or thay never would have let them leave the town alive." His unwarranted braggadocio showed as he continued his letter, "I think if I had of been some of them I would have poisoned Gen. Steward or some of there leaders. It would cause no little excitement in the town when they sent in for its surrender... How did Uncle Charles behave[?] I suppose he left the village."[36]

Maclay was not alone in his sentiment that the residents—especially Chambersburg's home guard company, despite its inexperience and lack of training—had not done enough to fend off Stuart. Others realized that armed resistance might have subjected the town to unwanted Confederate reprisals. One plucky Unionist lady, with more confidence than common sense, reportedly had cried out as Stuart's men rode into town, "The dirty rebels! To come when they

---

35 Ibid.

36 James H. Maclay to Dear Sister (Jane Ellen "Jennie" Maclay), Camp near Sharpsburg, MD, October 17, 1862, in Richard Rogers, *James Hemphill Maclay: His Civil War Letters* (Pussycat Productions, 2011), 57-58. The Maclays were from Lurgan Township, northwest of Shippensburg.

knew we weren't prepared for them!" Stuart's column had substantially outnumbered the few available defenders, prepared or not.[37]

While Stuart's men rode through Pennsylvania after attacking the Cumberland Valley Railroad, down in Hagerstown, hundreds of U. S. army supply wagons were rumbling back and forth from McClellan's vast quartermaster camps to the railroad depot. According to a reporter, "Long trains of burden cars are constantly arriving and discharging immense quantities of freight, which is immediately loaded upon the wagons and conveyed to its destination, presenting a scene of business activity, bustle and noise which has never before been witnessed in this town." He added, "At a low estimate, six or eight hundred wagons are continually on the move, passing and repassing each other in our streets, and lining the turnpike leading to and from the various camps in long and almost interminable rows. An army of the magnitude of Gen. McClellan's requires an immense amount of supplies of every description for its subsistence, and these are chiefly transported on the Franklin Railroad." Stuart's failure to destroy the Scotland Bridge kept the CVRR and FRR lines fully operational.[38]

In late October, a couple weeks after Stuart's raid, the editors of the *Valley Spirit* visited the burned-out railroad depot and warehouse. The newsmen complimented the railroad officials and the warehouse owners for their determined efforts to rebuild.[39] Indeed, the CVRR and nearby businesses were busy reconstructing their physical assets and properties. What could not be readily replaced, as Judge Watts rued in his annual report, were the "books, accounts, vouchers, and papers of the auditing department," the loss of which curtailed the ability to construct a detailed financial statement for the fiscal year that had just finished prior to Jeb Stuart's arrival. Of perhaps greater concern, the vouchers for the past transportation of Federal troops were also lost in the fires and, as a result, many of the most recent ones had not yet been submitted to the government for remuneration. Clerks were busy recreating and issuing duplicate statements for future settlement. Fortunately, the office of the treasurer, Edward M. Biddle, and the company accountants was located off-site and was still intact. That would enable the railroad executives to at least submit a complete list of receipts and expenditures, including the expenses for the new passenger and freight depot

37 "The Rebel Raid on Chambersburg," *Pittsburgh Daily Gazette and Advertiser,* October 15, 1862. The article was first published in the *Chambersburg Weekly Dispatch.*

38 *New York Times,* October 12, 1862, citing the *Hagerstown Mail.*

39 "The Depot," *Valley Spirit,* October 29, 1862.

under construction in Carlisle, to the shareholders as part of the annual report. Of significance, Watts and the board still planned to pay the normal dividend to the stockholders, despite the recent financial setback. The railroad expected to continue to operate in the black.[40]

Stuart's raid—widely acclaimed in the South, decried as a disgrace and embarrassment in the North, and reported in several international newspapers, including *The Times* in London—proved to be among the final straws for Abraham Lincoln in his already strained relationship with George McClellan. In early November, Lincoln summarily dismissed the so-called "Little Napoleon" and replaced him with Maj. Gen. Ambrose Burnside. McClellan had proven to be long on organizational and logistical skills but short on the aggressiveness that Lincoln desperately sought in his generals.

Chambersburg residents had mixed opinions of the change in army commanders, but one thing was certain. No one wanted to endure a repeat visit from the Rebels. A. K. McClure later wrote to a friend that he hoped "I shall never again be called upon to entertain a circle of rebels around my fireside." Little did the newsman know that in less than a year, he would make the unwelcome acquaintance of former U. S. congressman, now Confederate brigadier general Albert Gallatin Jenkins and his "circle of rebels."[41]

Another Rebel Threat Does Not Deter Reconstruction

With Jeb Stuart's raid now a painful memory, the CVRR and its partner telegraph company returned to routine business as best as they could. Through the energetic efforts of Col. John H. Berryhill, the president of the Atlantic and Ohio Telegraph Company, the telegraph wires were soon repaired and the Chambersburg office reopened when telegraph operator Gilmore returned. Communications were re-established with General McClellan's headquarters in Maryland and with Governor Curtin in Harrisburg. Chambersburg was no longer isolated from the outside world.[42]

Soon, Judge Watts and the beleaguered CVRR finally had something to celebrate. The new depot at Carlisle was finished and put into operation. The first

40 *Twenty-Eighth Annual Report of the Cumberland Valley Railroad Company, to the Stockholders, Made October 1, 1862* (The Herald Office, 1862), 5-7.

41 *Richmond Daily Dispatch*, October 24, 1862.

42 "The Latest News! The Rebel Raid," *Philadelphia Inquirer*, October 14, 1862.

floor housed the telegraph and ticket offices, with a large front room for general passengers. At the rear was a smaller waiting room reserved for ladies. The decor showed "taste and elegance," according to a local reporter, and the station had all the modern improvements. The second story contained the offices of the CVRR's secretary and treasurer, E. M. Biddle. The offices of accountants John M. Gregg and Alexander McCullough were in an adjoining room. Two smaller rooms were vacant at the time. A passageway connected the third story to the adjacent Mansion House. The popular hotel used this floor as overflow sleeping rooms. "The outside appearance of the building is that of neatness and beauty," the newsman added, "and reflects great credit upon the projector, Col. O. N. Lull, under whose efficient and careful superidentence the working of the Cumberland Valley Railroad has become a proverb for regularity and despatch. With Judge Watts as President, General Biddle, Secretary and Treasurer, and Col. Lull, Superintendent, this road has been so well managed, and its profits so certain, that the stock, even at the enormous premium it commands, can scarcely be purchased."[43]

The company's leadership still drew the unwanted attention of the War Department, especially the impatient Secretary of War, Edwin M. Stanton. He had sent a terse note on October 17 to Brig. Gen. Herman Haupt of the U. S. Military Railroad, instructing him to "proceed immediately" on a personal inspection tour of the CVRR. Haupt was to "take such measures as may be necessary to enforce promptness and efficiency in the transportation and delivery of military supplies on that road from Harrisburg to Hagerstown." It was certainly not a new topic, given Stanton's and Haupt's temporary takeover of the railroad back in September. "It is represented that the service is inefficiently performed by the agents of the Company," Stanton charged, "that private and express freight is given preference to Government supplies, and that agents are not present to dispatch cars." As had happened previously, Stanton authorized Haupt to "take possession of the road and its stock, and employ the agents needed for running the road as a United States Military Railroad route."[44]

As it turned out, Haupt did not need to seize control of the Cumberland Valley Railroad for a second time in 1862. However, that became a distinct possibility the next month, when fresh rumors of another Confederate invasion

43 "Year During War Cumberland Valley Teachers Institute and CVRR," newspaper clippings, CCHS. The Mansion House sat at the southwest corner of West High Street and Pitt Street, along the railroad tracks.

44 Haupt, *Reminiscences*, 145.

led to more reports that "the rebels are coming." On November 11, Chambersburg residents heard that Rebels were at Mercersburg and again headed their way. Anxious townspeople gathered to hear the latest news. People travelling through the town soon confirmed the startling report, and the excitement ran even higher. The town's merchants quickly closed their stores and took down their signs. "Everyone was looking after his own affairs," commented a reporter on the scene. "Old shot guns were brought out and cleaned, and pistols and bowie knives showed conspicuously on many persons, in belts, coat pockets, &c." Local railroad officials took the precaution to have the engineers fire up their locomotives, ready to start at a moment's notice for safety across the Susquehanna River in Harrisburg. Four or five hundred army draftees who were encamped two-and-a-half miles from Chambersburg received orders to march into town. They arrived about dusk and occupied the public square for two hours before being told to return to camp. By 9:00 p.m., everything had quieted down. No Rebels were imminent; the report had been a false alarm.[45]

Throughout the fall and early winter, CVRR work crews feverishly continued to rebuild many of the railroad buildings—including the depot, engine house, and machine shops—that Stuart's Confederate raiders had destroyed. The new buildings were bigger and better than the ones destroyed and, according to a reporter, should improve "the appearance of things about the depot." Superintendent O. N. Lull and ticket agent W. Blair Gilmore were among a group of merchants and soldiers who endorsed a safe made by the Philadelphia firm of Farrel, Herring & Company. "One of the freaks of the Rebels in their recent raid was to burn our Depot…," they stated in a newspaper advertisement for the safe manufacturer, "in which one of your safes was subjected to a very severe test of four days. In justice to you, we will say that we were present at the opening of the safe, and found the contents in an excellent state of preservation."[46]

Judge Watts reported that the company owned 12 locomotives, 8 passenger cars, 4 baggage, mail, and express cars, and 79 freight cars, an area of recent expansion as the railroad continued to try to supplant the long-established network of freight forwarders. The engines—including the newest addition, the T.

45 "Excitement in Chambersburg—Another Rebel Raid Expected," *Philadelphia Inquirer*, November 13, 1862.

46 "Rebuilding," *Philadelphia Inquirer*, October 27, 1862; "Cumberland Valley Railroad," *Valley Spirit*, December 31, 1862; "More of the Rebel Raid," *Philadelphia Inquirer*, November 1, 1862. The other signatories were Chambersburg merchants A. S. Hull and J. H. Eyster and army Assistant Quartermaster George A. Ceitz.

B. Kennedy, acquired from Danforth, Cooke & Company—had run more than 165,000 combined miles, carried more than a quarter of a million passengers, and shipped 106,000 tons of freight. Net earnings were a little less than $100,000. The CVRR purchased the remaining outstanding shares of the Franklin Railroad for $304,169.82 in cash and stock equivalents. The CVRR board decided to continue to operate the FRR as a stand-alone legal entity through the rest of the war and then fully integrate it.[47]

As the year ended, the Cumberland Valley Railroad Company was still recovering from Stuart's raid, but profits from the military traffic enabled the company to fulfill its financial obligations to suppliers and stockholders. Fortunately for the railroad, the Confederates' main target, the vital bridge over the Conococheague Creek, still stood, and trains routinely steamed safely over the watercourse. That fact, in itself, gave Judge Watts hope for the future, as long as the Rebels did not pay a return visit. That possibility remained worrisome, given the Cumberland Valley's vulnerability.

47 *The Commercial and Financial Chronicle* (William B. Dana & Co.), vol. 3, July 21, 1866, 71; *American Railroad Journal*, vol. XXXIII, no. 14, April 7, 1877, 427.

Chapter 5

1863: Another Year, Another Invasion

1863 began, Judge Frederick Watts and the CVRR board of directors were still reeling from the tragic collision at Bridgeport and the resulting legal ramifications. "The Cumberland Valley Railroad Company are devoting a portion of their profits to the compensation of the sufferers by the collision at Bridgeport last summer," newspapers across the Mid-Atlantic region announced. Watts hoped this public gesture of goodwill would discourage damaging lawsuits and additional bad press. He needed to restore confidence in his company, particularly to maintain what was left of the once lucrative government troop and supply transport contracts.[1]

Advertisements in Philadelphia's major newspapers informed the traveling public that the Pennsylvania Central Railroad's 8:00 a.m. mail train and the 10:40 p.m. through express both connected at Harrisburg with CVRR trains for Carlisle, Chambersburg, and Hagerstown. Over time, passenger traffic recovered, but with the Federal army finally having moved away from the Sharpsburg area to Northern Virginia, military traffic had plummeted since the halcyon days of running trains filled with supplies to George McClellan's Army of the Potomac. "Little Mac" himself was gone, having been replaced by Maj. Gen. Ambrose Burnside. He, too, had failed to inspire much confidence from the War Department, following a disastrous defeat at Fredericksburg, Virginia, in

1 *The Evening Star* (Washington, DC), January 13, 1863.

December 1862 and the subsequent ill-fated "Mud March." By the end of January 1863, the bewhiskered Burnside was out and yet another new commander, Maj. Gen. Joseph Hooker, was in place. As a division commander, he had earned the nickname "Fighting Joe," and many in the North hoped he would finally bring Robert E. Lee's vaunted Army of Northern Virginia to bay.[2]

Over the winter months, CVRR did not haul much military freight, other than to supplement the B&O occasionally in supplying Maj. Gen. Robert H. Milroy's division of the Eighth Corps in Winchester, Virginia, in the northern Shenandoah Valley. The 8,000 or so troops had arrived there to guard the southern approaches to Hagerstown and the Cumberland Valley by way of the Shenandoah Valley, and to augment the Federal forces that had re-occupied Harpers Ferry. The fear of another invasion loomed large, particularly along the route of Jeb Stuart's October 1862 incursion, so Milroy's men began expanding several abandoned Confederate fortifications on the low hills overlooking the Valley Turnpike, a major thoroughfare that continued northward through Maryland and Pennsylvania to Harrisburg.[3]

Meanwhile, efforts continued well into the spring to rebuild the CVRR's burned-out buildings at its Chambersburg hub. "We learn that the Cumberland Valley Railroad Company intend beginning to rebuild their depot at this place, within a month," the *Valley Spirit* commented in early March. "The plan of the new building has not altogether been decided upon, but it is to be larger than the old building, is to be much more conveniently arranged, having the cars run under a shelter, and is to be an entirely new and tasty structure, the Company having an eye to the ornamental as well as the useful." The editor added, "We hope to see the new Depot under roof at an early day, as it will be no small accommodation [for] the traveling public, and likewise the officers of the road themselves." Stuart's raid had given Judge Watts the opportunity to modernize the railroad facilities to meet current passenger and freight demand.[4]

While attention focused on rebuilding the infrastructure of the CVRR, a mechanical defect caused an accident that could have been much worse than it was. On Monday, March 16, a northbound freight train passed over a broken

---

2 "Railroad Lines," *Philadelphia Inquirer*, January 31, 1863.

3 For more on the defense of Winchester, see Eric J. Wittenberg and Scott L. Mingus, Sr., *The Second Battle of Winchester: The Confederate Victory That Opened the Door to Gettysburg* (Savas Beatie, 2016).

4 "A New Depot," *Valley Spirit*, March 4, 1863.

T-rail near Mechanicsburg, sending almost a dozen heavily laden burden cars careening off the track. Six of them belonged to private freight forwarder Oaks & Linn, one or two to C. W. Eyster and Co., and several others were railroad property. They mostly contained flour; about half of the load was lost. Two or three of the crew suffered slight injuries. Fortunately, despite the sudden derailment, no one was seriously injured. Accidents of the sort were relatively rare on the CVRR, compared with some other lines in southern Pennsylvania such as the Northern Central Railway, so the incident made headlines.[5]

War news continued to dominate the papers of the Cumberland Valley as the spring thaws enabled the opposing Union and Confederate armies to resume their maneuvering. In the first week of May, the Army of the Potomac suffered a significant defeat at the hands of Lee at the battle of Chancellorsville. However, Lee's "right arm," Lt. Gen. Thomas J. "Stonewall" Jackson, soon died of complications following the amputation of his left arm. His own men had inadvertently shot him and some of his party in the darkness as they returned to Confederate lines after reconnoitering Federal positions. In Washington, War Department confidence in General Hooker waned after his tentative performance at Chancellorsville, and President Lincoln began considering other options in the seemingly endless string of unsuccessful army commanders.[6]

The Rebels are Coming! The Rebels are Coming (Again)!

Fresh off his stunning victory at Chancellorsville, Robert E. Lee met with Confederate President Jefferson Davis and other senior government officials to discuss another invasion of the North. Lee had several objectives, not the least of which was to win a decisive victory on Northern soil, one that might force the Lincoln administration to the negotiating table. Short on food and supplies, Lee timed the incursion to secure the fruits of the summer harvest and ship them back to Virginia for his army's long-term use. He also hoped to disrupt the Federal railroad network in Maryland and south-central Pennsylvania, including the Cumberland Valley Railroad. Lee reorganized his army following Jackson's death,

---

5 "Railroad Accident," *Valley Spirit*, March 25, 1863; "Railroad Accident," *The Star and Enterprise* (Newville, PA), March 26, 1863. Samuel Linn had replaced the retired Abraham Caufman as David Oaks' partner in the freight-forwarding business.

6 For an overview of the battle of Chancellorsville, see Chris Mackowski and Kristopher D. White, *That Furious Struggle: Chancellorsville and the High Tide of the Confederacy, May 1-4, 1863* (Savas Beatie, 2014).

1863: Another Year, Another Invasion

changing from a two-corps structure to three smaller corps and installing two new lieutenant generals, Richard S. Ewell and A. P. Hill, to join holdover James Longstreet. He added fresh troops and made plans to march to the Keystone State. A network of spies, scouts, and mapmakers provided much needed intelligence on key roads, railroads, towns, industries, and watercourses.[7]

Lee set two of his three corps in motion in early June, heading northwest from his Rappahannock River line near Fredericksburg toward the Shenandoah Valley. He left Hill's Third Corps behind to hold Hooker's Army of the Potomac in place. A sharp clash at Brandy Station, Virginia, between Jeb Stuart's Confederate cavalry, many of them veterans of the raid on Chambersburg the previous fall, and Brig. Gen. Alfred Pleasonton's Union horsemen gave evidence that Lee was on the move. No one was quite sure of his intended target, with Ohio, Pennsylvania, and western Virginia the most likely targets, assuming Lee did not turn and strike at Washington or Baltimore.[8]

With rumors of a Southern incursion again swirling throughout the North, the U. S. War Department took initial steps to defend the Keystone State. In June 1863, officials created two new military departments to organize the Pennsylvania militia recruits that Governor Curtin (at Lincoln's request) called into service in response to Lee's threatened invasion. Both departments were headed by capable and reliable commanders, both with stellar records in the Army of the Potomac. Haste was the order of the hour, so much so that the War Department's original general orders establishing the boundaries of the two units were full of errors and had to be reissued. A new Department of the Monongahela was created, tasked with defending that portion of Pennsylvania west of Johnstown and the Laurel Hill range of mountains (now known as the Laurel Highlands); Columbiana, Jefferson, and Belmont counties in the state of Ohio; and Hancock, Brooke, and Ohio counties in what would be, on June 20, 1863, the newly created state of West Virginia. Under the command of West Point-educated Brig. Gen. William T. H. Brooks, the department had its headquarters in Pittsburgh.[9]

Brooks' counterpart to the east was Maj. Gen. Darius N. Couch and his Department of the Susquehanna, designed to defend "that portion of the State of

---

7 For more on Lee's plans and his march north, see Robert Orrison and Dan Welch, *The Last Road North: A Guide to the Gettysburg Campaign, 1863* (Savas Beatie, 2016).

8 On June 22, Pleasonton was promoted to major general, the rank he would hold at the battle of Gettysburg.

9 OR 27:3, 54-55; Ezra J. Warner, *Generals in Blue: Lives of the Union Commanders* (LSU Press, 1964), 47.

Pennsylvania east of Johnstown and the Laurel Hill range of mountains." A New York native and, like Brooks, a West Pointer, Couch had graduated in the class of 1846 alongside George B. McClellan and Thomas Jonathan Jackson. After serving in the Mexican War, he resigned his commission in 1855 and entered the copper fabricating business in Massachusetts. At the outset of the war, Couch served as colonel of the 7th Massachusetts Infantry, but rapidly rose through the ranks until he received an appointment as a major general in July 1862, due in large part to the influence of his former classmate George McClellan. Couch rose to the command of the Second Corps, but, thoroughly disgusted with Joseph Hooker, requested to be relieved from duty with the Army of the Potomac after the disastrous debacle at Chancellorsville in May.[10]

On June 10, 1863, Secretary of War Stanton telegraphed news of these appointments to the governors of Ohio, Pennsylvania, and West Virginia and to Maj. Gens. Ambrose E. Burnside in Cincinnati and Robert C. Schenck in Baltimore. Among the others Stanton notified that day was his scandal-plagued predecessor at the head of the War Department, Simon Cameron, at his Harrisburg residence. In his note to Cameron, Stanton explained Couch's appointment and requested that Cameron assist Couch as he acquainted himself with the duties at hand: "I wish you would see him, and give him what aid you can. I have given him a letter of introduction to you." Couch took a Northern Central train to Harrisburg to meet with Governor Curtin. The new department leader had less than 250 men under his command at the time. Many more would be needed to defend the capital in the event of a Rebel incursion that far north.[11]

In Shippensburg on June 11, "[a]n extra long train of cars passed down the road. Great anxiety to know what it means," a diarist recorded. The excitement was running high during the week, and citizens were discussing raising a home guard company for local defense in case the Rebels came through the Cumberland Valley. People gathered at the stores and public places debating what to do in that event.[12]

Meanwhile, as Curtin and Couch made preparations to resist them, the Rebels continued their irresistible surge toward the Potomac River. Ewell's Second Corps, in the vanguard of the Army of Northern Virginia, entered the Shenandoah

---

10 OR 27:3, 55; Warner, *Generals in Blue*, 95. Brooks was promoted to major general in June 1863, but this was later revoked.

11 OR 27:3, 54-55.

12 "Effects of War News," *Shippensburg* (PA) *Chronicle*, July 3, 1913.

Valley and, from June 13-15, destroyed General Milroy's division in and around Winchester. Milroy lost more than half his number, including more than 4,000 men taken as prisoners, in one of the worst disasters inflicted on Federal forces during the entire war. Confederate losses were less than 300 men. The one-sided victory buoyed Southern confidence, established (at least temporarily) Ewell as a worthy successor to Jackson, and opened the pathway to the Cumberland Valley and, ultimately, Harrisburg, should the state capital be in the Rebels' plans. The Army of the Potomac, still in Virginia, began pursuing the Confederates, but, with uncertainty as to Lee's true intentions, proceeded cautiously to protect the roads to Washington and Baltimore should the Rebels turn eastward. Martinsburg soon fell, and Harpers Ferry looked to be next.[13]

"Fight at Martinsburg. Rebels coming this way," the Shippensburg diarist recorded on June 14. "On Sunday evening," a Chambersburg newsman recounted, "dark clouds of contrabands commenced rushing upon us, bringing the tidings that Gen. Milroy's forces at Martinsburg had been attacked and scattered, and that the rebels under Gen. Rhodes [Robert E. Rodes] were advancing upon Pennsylvania. With due allowance for the excessive alarm of the slaves, it was manifest that they were about to clear out the Shenandoah Valley, and, that once done, the Cumberland, with all its teeming wealth, would be at rebel mercy."[14]

It had also been a busy Sunday in Chambersburg. Amos Stouffer, a young farmer from Guilford Township who was visiting town, reported, "The excitement is very great." To avoid a repeat of the past October, workers were busily removing the government stores from the town in a frantic effort to ship them off to safety before the Rebels arrived. Steam locomotives prepared to pull railcars laden with supplies northward on the Cumberland Valley Railroad, providing a short-term financial windfall for the company. Wagonloads, carts, and all sorts of conveyances lined the main roads leading from town.[15]

Chambersburg's assistant prothonotary (chief clerk) John F. Glosser, helped pack Franklin County records for shipment to safety. He recalled, "During the day

---

13 For more, see Wittenberg and Mingus, *The Second Battle of Winchester.*

14 "Effects of War News," *Shippensburg (PA) Chronicle,* July 3, 1913; "Invasion of Pennsylvania!" *Franklin Repository,* July 8, 1863.

15 Amos Stouffer diary entry for June 13, 1863, William Garrett Piston, ed., "'The Rebs Are Yet Thick About Us': The Civil War Diary of Amos Stouffer of Chambersburg," *Civil War History,* vol. 38, no. 3, September 1992. Stouffer, son of Jacob and Eliza Stouffer, lived near Falling Spring, a community just southeast of Chambersburg.

Confederate Brig. Gen. Albert Gallatin Jenkins commanded the advance cavalry of Richard Ewell's Second Corps during its march through the Shenandoah Valley toward Harrisburg. *Library of Congress*

our merchants were busy packing and shipping off their goods." Storekeeper Jacob Hoke confirmed, "On Sunday evening… information was received of the disaster to our forces in the Valley, and the approach of the enemy. Immediately, as upon former occasions, when news of rebel approaches were received, great confusion and excitement prevailed. The usual work of sending away and secreting merchandise and other valuables was begun. We opened our store and packed and sent away some of our goods; and during the next day we stored the balance of our stock in a beer vault, under the back building of the residence of Dr. [Henry] Langheim, adjoining our store." Hoke added, "The railroad men here were also prompt to prepare for the emergency, and by noon of Monday had all their portable property ready for shipment at their pleasure."[16]

Brigadier General Albert G. Jenkins, a former U. S. congressman, commanded Ewell's forward brigade of Virginia cavalry and mounted infantry. The Confederates forded the Potomac River early on Monday, June 15, and headed north through the thin strip of western Maryland. Northern telegraph wires buzzed with the news. Several times during the war, workers hauled the heavy iron safe of the Chambersburg National Bank to the railroad's shop yards and placed it on a flatcar. When the Rebels threatened, an engine would be coupled to the car and the safe and its contents taken to Harrisburg, out of the enemy's presumed reach. Now, with Jenkins heading toward Pennsylvania, the bankers repeated the precaution and sent the safe to the state capitol. Judge

16 Hoke, *Historical Reminiscences of the War*, 34, 180.

Frederick Watts suspended all rail traffic toward Hagerstown and ordered the CVRR's rolling stock and locomotives to prepare to steam northward. After moving some of the most valuable equipment out of Hagerstown, youthful CVRR station agent and self-titled "assistant to the superintendent" Thomas R. Bard left at 9:30 a.m. pumping a hand car in the company of the local military telegrapher. They headed the 22 miles north to Chambersburg and presumed safety. It would be a long, grueling trek. Scarcely a half-hour later, the first of Jenkins' Rebels entered Hagerstown.[17]

General Milroy had evacuated part of his wagon train from Winchester before Ewell arrived with his legions. The heavily-laden supply wagons, escorted by a detachment of 1st New York cavalrymen, thundered into downtown Chambersburg that same morning. To most observers, they appeared panic-stricken. "[They] dashed through the town at a furious rate, the teamsters shouting 'The rebels are coming!'" a *Valley Spirit* reporter related. "'They are close after us!' Such a scene of wild excitement and consternation we have never witnessed before. Drivers were swearing and yelling at the top of their lungs; wheels were run off from wagons, and horses fell dead in the streets from sheer exhaustion; and still the grand stampede continued, every man and horse seeming animated with the one desire of saving himself from rebel clutches." The astonishing sight of Federal soldiers fleeing through their streets alarmed the populace, who were still recovering emotionally—and financially, in some cases—from Stuart's October visit. Reports circulated that Rebel horsemen were on the heels of the wagon train.

"This extraordinary spectacle served to alarm our citizens seriously," the newsman continued. "The merchants at once proceeded to close their stores and to remove and secret their most valuable merchandize; and the timid and fearful prepared to 'skedaddle' without loss of time." More panic ensued when a terse telegram arrived at the CVRR depot from the operator at Hagerstown, "The rebels are in town, I am off." At least, the message indicated that the Rebels were most likely still in Maryland and had not yet entered Pennsylvania. The trouble was that it was now clear they were not riding to West Virginia, Ohio, or Pittsburgh. They were clearly headed through the Cumberland Valley toward Harrisburg. "And so the preparations for their reception were continued," the reporter added. "It was too late to prepare for defense against such a large body as was reported

17 "Pennsylvania Employees Hear History of the Old C. V. Road," CVRR files, FCHS; Baer, 1863 *PRR Chronology*. In the early 1900s, Bard, then a Republican U. S. senator from California, appointed George S. Patton to West Point.

advancing, and all who remained in town resolved to make their property as secure as possible, and then calmly submit to their fate."

"The vicinity of the Cumberland Valley depot presented a scene of lively interest," the *Valley Spirit* man went on to say. "The Railroad Company were preparing to remove their rolling stock and the machinery from the shops; and almost every family had some valuables they wished transported to places of greater safety, while many were anxious to go themselves. Those who had horses and cattle were startling them down the eastern turnpike or running them off to the mountains. Our colored populations, and particularly the 'contrabands,' were alarmed beyond measure. Some fled to the woods, others sought protection in the houses of the citizens, and others succeeded in getting charge of some of the 'skedaddling' horses, and thus made good their own escape and, at the same time, conveyed the hors[e] flesh to a place of safety."[18]

Canadian-born Rachel Cormany recorded, "This morning pretty early Gen Milroy's wagon train (so we were told) came. Contrabands on ahead coming as fast as they could on all & any kind of horses, their eyes fairly protruding with fear—teams coming at the same rate—come with the covers half off—some lost—men without hats or coats—some lost their coats as they were flying, one darky woman astride of a horse going what she could. There really was a real panic. All reported that the rebels were just on their heels."[19]

The panic grew worse as the day wore on and reports arrived that the Rebels had reached Greencastle, some 13 miles south of Chambersburg along the line of the Franklin Railroad. "In a few minutes, Gen. Jenkins' Western Virginia Cavalry dashed into town," recalled resident William A. Reid, "and finding the coast clear, commenced their pleasant task of searching stables, and taking therefrom all the horses they could find." The Rebels, according to the Reverend J. C. Smith of the United Brethren Church, were "in the prime of health, boasting of the exploits they would do." Despite Jenkins' bragging that he had come "to burn and destroy," his men stayed in town less than an hour. However, they "immediately commenced to empty stables and capture every article within his reach that seemed to fit the fancy of his men." Although Jenkins threatened to burn and destroy the town, the only major damage occurred when his horsemen partially burned down the Franklin Railroad's station. Even so, the blaze created quite a

18 "The Rebel Invasion," *Valley Spirit*, July 8, 1863.

19 Samuel Cormany and Rachel Cormany, James C. Mohr, ed., *The Cormany Diaries: A Northern Family in the Civil War* (University of Pittsburgh Press, 1982), 328-29.

stir. "The fire could be seen for miles," a resident informed a newspaper in New York. "Only three buildings were destroyed, together with some wood and a water tank."[20]

The troopers cut the telegraph wires and resumed their twilight advance to Chambersburg. Greencastle residents breathed a little easier; they "were confident then that it was only a raid for plunder," according to a New York newsman. "We lay down to sleep, and our slumbers were disturbed by visions of Jenkins and his men." Jenkins left a small detachment in Greencastle to maintain order and protect his line of communication. Meanwhile, Union Lt. Charles Palmer with a small force of Maryland cavalry raced ahead of the Confederate column north to Chambersburg. About 8:00 p.m., he breathlessly entered the CVRR telegraph office and reported the Rebel presence at Greencastle. Youthful operator W. Blair Gilmore of the Atlantic and Ohio Telegraph Company dutifully tapped out the message to officials in Harrisburg.[21]

Word soon spread throughout the Chambersburg area, further alarming the nervous populace. Guilford Township farmer Amos Stouffer noted, "A warm day. The excitement is very great about the rebs. No one is at work about here except to hide their valuables. It is reported that they are in Greencastle. Self & Andy in town this evening. The Provost guard came in while we were there. They had a skirmish with them at Green Castle. They are coming for sure. Andy and James took the horses to the mountains."[22]

Rachel Cormany related, "For awhile before dark the excitement abated a little—but it was only like the calm before a great storm. At dusk or a little before the news came that the rebels were in Greencastle & that said town was on fire. Soon after some of our guard came in reporting that they had a skirmish with them. Soon followed 100-200 cavalry men—the guard. Such a skedaddling as their [sic] was among the women & children to get into the houses. All thought the Rebels had really come. The report now is that they will be here in an hour. If I could only hear of My Samuels safety—Many have packed nearly all of their packable goods—I have packed nothing. I do not think that we will be disturbed even should they come. I will trust in God even in the midst of flying shells—but of course shall seek the safest place possible in that case—which I hope will not

20 "Our Greencastle Correspondence," June 17, 1863, *New York Herald*, June 20, 1863.

21 Ibid.; Franklin Repository, July 8, 1863; "Rebel Invasion of Pennsylvania," *Greencastle* (PA) *Pilot*, July 28, 1863; OR 27, pt. 3, 161.

22 Stouffer diary, June 15, 1863, "The Rebs Are Yet Thick About Us."

come to us. I have just put my baby to sleep & will now sit at the front door awhile yet—then retire, knowing all will be well."

Cormany did not sleep long. "At 11 ½ I heard the clattering of hoofs," she penned. "I hopped out of bed & ran to the front window & sure enough the Grey backs were going by as fast as their horses could take them down to the Diamond." But after a short time the whole body came," she added. "The front ones with their hands on the gun triggers ready to fire & calling out as they passed along that they would lay the town in ashes if fired on again. It took a long time for them all to pass, but I could not judge how many there were—not being accustomed to seeing troops in such a body."[23]

Jenkins' men camped northeast of town on the sprawling farm of abolitionist newspaper editor Alexander K. McClure, the same place that many of Stuart's men had camped the previous October. This time, McClure had taken his horses to safety and was not home, but his wife Matilda was present. Rousted in the middle of the night, she served the general and his staff a bountiful supper. McClure later mentioned in his *Franklin Repository*, "However earnest an enemy Jenkins may be, he don't seem to keep spite, but is capable of being very jolly and sociable when he is treated hospitably. For prudential reasons, the Editor was not at home to do the honors at his own table; but Jenkins was not particular, nor was his appetite impaired thereby. He called upon the ladies of the house, shared their hospitality, behaved in all respects like a gentleman, and expressed very earnest regrets that he had not been able to make the personal acquaintance of the Editor."[24]

Accompanied by CVRR superintendent O. N. Lull and director D. Ott Gehr, telegraph operator W. Blair Gilmore fled town on a hand car. When they arrived at Scotland, Lull and Gehr continued to Shippensburg, while Gilmore stayed behind and reestablished telegraphic communications. Governor Andrew Curtin learned that, scarcely eight months after Stuart's troopers had visited McClure's farm, the Rebels had returned to Chambersburg. In Harrisburg, "Governor Curtin and General Couch are working night and day," wrote a newsman. "On the receipt of this news the Governor ordered the bells rung, and the people assembled en

23 Cormany and Mohr, *The Cormany Diaries*, 329. Samuel Cormany served in the 16th Pennsylvania Cavalry, Army of the Potomac.

24 "Invasion of Pennsylvania!" Franklin Repository, July 8, 1863.

Confederate Cavalry burning the Cumberland Valley Railroad Bridge at Scotland, Pennsylvania, in June 1863. *House Divided Project at Dickinson College*

masse at the Court-house to devise means to defend the city. It is evident that something must be done immediately, or the State capital will be invaded."[25]

Quickly, Jenkins set about securing the area and cutting off Carlisle and Harrisburg from Chambersburg. The Confederate troopers "threw out their pickets towards Green Village and Scotland, a portion of whom proceeded to burn the railroad bridge over the Conococheague, at the latter place, as a precaution against an advance of the federal forces," a local newsman mentioned, "The timbers being wet, they failed in their attempt, and then proceeded to destroy it, as far as they were able, by cutting and sawing the timbers." Eighteen-year-old Lizzie Wolf of Shippensburg later sent a letter to a cousin in Pittsburgh in which she mentioned the Scotland bridge. "They could not burn it as the timber was water soaked. I think it is too bad that they can just do exactly as they please, but I hope there is a day of retribution coming."[26]

25 *Daily National Intelligencer,* June 17, 1863; *Philadelphia Press,* June 17, 1863; "The Rebel Advance," *Columbia* (PA) *Spy,* June 20, 1863, quoting a Harrisburg correspondent writing at midnight on June 15.

26 "The Rebel Invasion," *Valley Spirit,* July 8, 1863; Lizzie F. Wolfe to Agnes M. Wolfe, Shippensburg, PA, July 1863, Civil War files, FCHS.

The frequent rumors that "The Rebels were coming; The Rebels are coming!" had, unfortunately, again come true for the war-weary residents of the Cumberland Valley. Repairs were still underway from the enemy cavalry's last visit, and many feared that, this time, the infantry would march into town on the heels of the vanguard cavalry.

Chambersburg under the Rebel Flag, Again

By the morning of Tuesday, June 16, Jenkins' brigade had firmly secured control of Chambersburg, even as some of Couch's Yankee militia scouted the outskirts of town. The long-bearded General Jenkins established his headquarters in Dr. John Montgomery's hotel. "Early in the morning our pickets were attacked by the Federals," the 14th Virginia Cavalry's Hermann Schuricht recorded in his diary, "but the enemy was repulsed, and we made some prisoners. A railroad bridge and telegraph connections were destroyed by our men. General Jenkins ordered the storekeepers to open their establishments, and we purchased what we needed, paying in Confederate money. The inhabitants had to provide rations for the troops and we fared very well, but their feelings toward us were very adverse. However, a number of them, belonging to the peace-party, treated us kindly, especially were the Germans in favor of peace. Many inhabitants had fled in haste from the city, but owing to the suddenness of our approach, clothes and household utensils were left scattered in the streets. I was ordered, with part of my company, to move this unprotected property safely into the houses of its probable owners."[27]

A detachment of Rebels headed to the railroad yard and nearby warehouses to apply the torch. Upon receiving assurances that Criswell's warehouse on Railroad Street and several loaded freight cars on the CVRR siding were private property and the contents were not destined for the military, the soldiers spared them. "A warm day," wrote youthful farmer Amos Stouffer, "The Rebs are in town. The great body have followed Milroy's wagon trains which went through town yesterday. About 500 wagons and 2,000 horses—a very valuable train. The rebs are mannerly yet and do not disturb private property. They have their pickets all around us. Our news is cut off and we are under rebel rule."[28]

---

27 Schuricht diary entry for June 16, 1863, *Richmond Dispatch*, April 5, 1896.

28 "Scotland Bridge Burned," Franklin Repository, July 8, 1863; Stouffer diary entry for June 16, 1863, "The Rebs are Thick Yet About Us."

Fresh mounts and food were not all that Jenkins' Virginians sought in Franklin County. "One of the exciting features of the day," recalled Greencastle resident Charles Hartman, "was the scouring of the fields about town and searching of houses for Negroes. These poor creatures, those of them who had not fled upon the approach of the foe, concealed in wheat fields around the town. Cavalrymen rode in search of them and many of them were caught after a desperate chase and being fired at. In some cases, the Negroes were rescued from the guards. Squire Kaufman and Tom Pauling did this, and if they had been caught, the rebels would have killed them." Soldiers escorted the captive blacks to Maryland. William A. Reid elaborated in the pages of the *Greencastle Pilot*: "In the afternoon of this day, a lot of 'contrabands,' about thirty in number, under charge of a Chaplain and three or four other soldiers, on their way to Hagerstown, were captured by a crowd of people near East Baltimore Street. The darkies were liberated, and the Chaplain and soldiers sent to Waynesboro'. This created a wonderful excitement."[29]

The slave hunt stretched from the border north to Chambersburg. There, housewife Jemima Cree mailed a letter to her husband John in Pittsburgh, telling him, "They took up all they could find, even little children, whom they had to carry on horseback before them… This morning among the first news I heard was that they had been scouting around, gathering up our Darkies, and that they had Mag down on the court house pavement. I got my fixens on, and started down, and there were about 25 women and children, with Mag and Fannie. I interceded for Mag, told them she was free born, etc. The man said he could do nothing, he was acting according to orders. As they were just ready to start, I had to leave; if I could have had time to have seen the General, I might have got her off. Fannie being contraband, we could do nothing for her. I went over to the Gilmores and we all stood and saw them march up the street, like so many cattle, poor Mag and Fannie in the first line." To many residents, it seemed to matter not to the Rebels if their captives were fugitives or free.[30]

"O!" Rachel Cormany mourned, "How it grated on our hearts to have to sit quietly & look at such brutal deeds. I saw no men among the contrabands all women & children. Some of the colored who were raised here were taken along. I

29 Hoke, *The Great Invasion of 1863*, 97-99. See also, Conrad and Alexander, *When War Passed This Way*; *Greencastle* (Pa.) *Pilot*, July 28, 1863. Reid added, "In the evening a number of citizens signed a paper, and presented it to a Rebel Colonel (———), who desired to know what had become of the missing men."

30 Jemima K. Cree letter, "Jenkins' Raid," *Kittochtinny Historical Society Papers*, 1908, 94.

sat on the front step as they were driven by just like we would drive cattle… One woman was pleading wonderfully with her driver for her children but all the sympathy she received from him was a rough March along at which she would quicken her pace again. It is a query what they want with those little babies whole families were taken." She added, "I suppose the men left thinking the women & children would not be disturbed."[31]

Storekeeper Jacob Hoke recorded, "Among their captures was that well and favorably known colored man, Esque Hall. A rebel rode past our store with this poor frightened man on behind him. I went immediately for Dr. [Benjamin S.] Schneck, who went to Jenkins' headquarters, and after assuring Jenkins that Hall was long a resident of this place, and not a fugitive slave, he was released." Schneck was soon pressed into service again to vouch for the identity of free blacks. Rebels had seized Henry Deitrick and Samuel Claudy, two of the Cumberland Valley Railroad's repair gang. They had been pumping a hand car on the line from Scotland to Chambersburg when cavalrymen accosted and seized them. Upon Dr. Schneck's affirmation of their identity, the two railroad employees were released and allowed to go on their way.[32]

As a result, many African-Americans concealed themselves, or left their homes altogether for safer surroundings. "All who could get there fled to the woods," wrote Jemima Cree, "and many who were wise are hid in the houses of their employers." Businessman William Heyser, traveling through Carlisle, "encountered many colored people fleeing the Rebels[.]" He sympathized with "[t]hese poor people," who "are completely worn out, carrying their families on their backs. Saw some twenty from Chambersburg that I recognized." Some travelled as far as Philadelphia, where the "colored refugees from Chambersburg, Carlisle, and Gettysburg" appeared "with their small effects in every variety of package and bundle that could be carried by hand[.]"[33]

Meanwhile, some local whites tried appeasing the invaders by expressing pro-Southern sentiments and offering assistance. "When Jenkins was at

---

31 Cormany diary entry for June 16, 1863, Cormany and Mohr, *The Cormany Diaries*, 330. For more on the seizure of free blacks, see Ted Alexander, "A Regular Slave Hunt: The Army of Northern Virginia and Black Civilians in the Gettysburg Campaign," in *North and South*, Vol. 4, No. 7 (September 2001), 82-89.

32 Hoke, *Historical Reminiscences of the War*, 38.

33 Heyser Diary, June 18, 1863, Valley of the Shadow Project, UVA; M. Brainerd, *Life of Rev. Thomas Brainerd, D.D., for Thirty Years Pastor of Old Pine Street Church, Philadelphia* (J. B. Lippincott & Co., 1870), 303, Cree letter, "Jenkins' Raid," 94.

Chambersburgh [sic]," the *New York Times* reported, "he engaged in conversation with a Union man. As the former was speaking a Copperhead stepped up, made himself and his sentiments known, and very obligingly offered to impart any information which might be desired. Jenkins glanced at him for a moment, and then, with an expression of countenance that nearly frightened the skulking vagabond out of his wits, ordered him to leave his presence, remarking that if he had him on the other side, he should adorn the first tall tree they came to."[34]

"Jenkins' Guerilla Brigade is in rule over us," lamented Reformed Mennonite farmer Jacob Stouffer. "They want everything—butter, milk, eggs, chicken, cheese, bread, etc." After losing all of his grain, oats, tools, and salt, Marion farmer Henry B. Hege wrote to a relative, "I tell you [the] greatest portion of them are nothing but thieves and robbers and some murderers."[35]

A. K. McClure, who with neighbors and friends were keeping tabs on Rebel movements in the Cumberland Valley and reporting to Governor Curtin and General Couch, recalled, "Jenkins' command did not destroy much property. There was little left in the country that was useful to the army, as stores were empty of goods, banks without money, and farmers generally without horses or cattle. His first order required all persons in the town possessing arms, whether guns or pistols, to bring them to the front of the court house within two hours, and the penalty for disobedience was that all who refused would expose their houses to search, and make them lawful objects of plunder."[36]

"Early in the morning," wrote Lt. Hermann Schuricht of the 14th Virginia Cavalry, "the citizens were ordered by the general to give up all weapons, and we received about 500 guns of all sorts, sabres, pistols, etc." A staff officer, Adjutant Henry Fitzhugh, sorted through the confiscated weapons and instructed troopers to load those of military value into wagons. He ordered the remainder destroyed. "This he did by striking them over the stone steps in front of the Court House," mentioned Chambersburg merchant Jacob Hoke, "or twisting them out of shape in the ornamental attachments of the iron gas posts. When Dr. W. H. Boyle

34 *New York Times*, June 24, 1863, dateline June 22.

35 Helen Binkley Green, ed., *Pages from a Diary, 1843-1880: Excerpts from the Diaries of Jacob Stouffer and Eliza Rider Stouffer* (s. n., 1966), 21; Henry B. Hege to Henry G. Hege, July 12, 1863, Lancaster County, PA, Mennonite Historical Society of the Cumberland Valley, Chambersburg, PA, as paraphrased in James O. Lehman and Steven M. Nolt, *Mennonites, Amish, and the American Civil War* (Johns Hopkins University Press, 2007), 134.

36 Alexander K. McClure, *Old Time Notes of Pennsylvania*, 2 vols. (John C. Winston Co., 1905), 2:92.

brought in a beautiful silver mounted Sharp's rifle, Capt. Fitzhugh appropriated it to his own use."[37]

The Virginians spread throughout town to "purchase" supplies and personal items. Jenkins ordered Chambersburg's shopkeepers to open their establishments from 8:00 until 10:00 a.m. to sell goods to his soldiers in exchange for Confederate money. "Business for about an hour was very brisk," reported dry goods merchant Jacob Hoke, "and to avoid giving offense they patronized all. Fortunately for us and many others, stocks of goods were generally sent away or hid, but what little we had was bought up and paid for in Confederate scrip and shin plasters issued by the City of Richmond and other Southern corporations." Jenkins instructed the townspeople to provide rations for his hungry troopers, who fared well despite the residents' adverse feelings.[38]

McClure sneered, "True, the system of Jenkins would be considered a little informal in business circles; but it's his way, and our people agreed to it perhaps to some extent because of the novelty, but mainly because of the necessity of the thing… Jenkins was liberal—eminently liberal. He didn't stoop to haggle about a few odd pennies in making a bargain, and to avoid the jealousies growing out of rivalry in business, he patronised all the merchants, and bought pretty much everything he could conveniently use and carry. Some people, with the antiquated ideas of business, might call it stealing to take goods and pay for them in bogus money; but Jenkins calls it business, and for the time being what Jenkins called business, was business. In this way he robbed all the stores; drug stores, &c., more or less, and supplied himself with many articles of great value to him."[39]

Jacob Hoke added, "While this traffic was in progress a rebel soldier seized a number of remnants of ladies' dress goods, which we did not think worth hiding, and putting them under his arm walked out and down past Jenkins' headquarters. Jenkins came quickly out and caught the fellow and pushed him back on the double quick into the store, and said: 'Did this man get these things here, and did he pay for them?' Upon being told that he took them without paying for them, he drew his sword and flourishing it above the man's head and swearing terribly, he declared that he had a mind to cut his head off. Turning to us he said, 'Sell my men

---

37 Schuricht diary entry for June 17, 1863, *Richmond Dispatch*, April 5, 1896; Hoke, *Historical Reminiscences of the War*, 34. Other accounts suggest the gun collection took place on June 16.

38 *Richmond Daily Dispatch*, April 5, 1896; Stoner, *History of Franklin County*, 369; Hoke, *Historical Reminiscences of the War*, 38.

39 *Franklin County Repository and Transcript*, July 8, 1863.

all the goods they want, but if anyone attempts to take anything without paying for it, report to me at my headquarters. We are not thieves."[40]

One concern was the Franklin Railroad's former engine house, which was no longer in use. The sturdy brick structure was packed full of hay, with another large stack just outside of the building. Several townsmen who owned nearby property asked the Reverend Schneck to go to Jenkins and ask him not to burn this hay. If it had to be burned as a military precaution, they requested permission to move the hay to another location farther from their houses and businesses. The Rebel general replied that it was not his intention to burn it, because "Lee and his whole army was coming to Chambersburg and would want the hay for their own needs."[41]

Later that morning, a Confederate officer galloped into downtown and sought out General Jenkins. Hoke chronicled, "Jenkins came out in haste and mounting his horse he, in a voice of great power, ordered the men to the field. A rush was made down Main street and out to what is known as Geisinger's hill, a few miles below the town, on the Harrisburg pike, where a line of battle was formed. In a short time a number of men returned leading the horses, the soldiers dismounting and preparing to fight as infantry. They were all armed with carbines as well as pistols and sabres. After an hour or two they fell back through the town and out where their horses were taken and rode back beyond Greencastle… As the last of these soldiers were leaving the lower end of the town, they set fire to the warehouse of Messrs. Oaks & Linn, but it was speedily extinguished." The warehouse contained 500 barrels of flour and other valuable property. Several citizens rushed into the burning structure as flames approached the roof. Only twelve barrels were destroyed.[42]

The 14th Virginia Cavalry's Lieutenant Schuricht wrote, "About 11 o'clock news reached headquarters of the advance of a strong Yankee force, and consequently we evacuated the city and fell back upon Hagerstown, Md." Chambersburg-area farmer Amos Stouffer noted in his diary, "2 O'clock A.M. The Rebs are just leaving town." However, no one was certain if their withdrawal meant the end of a relatively minor, yet annoying cavalry raid, or if it was the

---

40 Hoke, *Historical Reminiscences of the War*, 38.

41 Ibid.

42 Ibid.; "The Foray on Chambersburg," *Daily Alta California* (San Francisco), July 15, 1863, citing the *New York Tribune*. Other accounts give the name of the eminence where Jenkins posted his pickets as Shirk's Hill. It was along the turnpike near Scotland, about two miles south of Green Village. It commanded the relatively flat terrain surrounding it.

precursor to a much larger and longer incursion. Gettysburg resident Sarah Broadhead noted, "Today passed without much excitement, though rumors of all kinds were going."[43]

Farther north along the line of the Cumberland Valley Railroad, Carlisle's citizens had taken several precautions, especially after Milroy's fleeing wagon train passed through town on June 15 and reported the initial Rebel incursion. "Very little apprehension was felt by this portion of the Valley," wrote Cumberland County deputy sheriff Simpson K. Donavin, a former West Virginia newsman. "Most of the community believed it was a mere raid, such as been made by Stuart last fall. Measures of precaution, however, were taken by our merchants and tradesmen, who immediately commenced packing their goods, and a number of them sent them to the Eastern cities."[44]

A youth named James W. Sullivan watched the seemingly endless parade of refugees passing through Carlisle toward Harrisburg. "The men and boys pegged along like tramps," he recalled years later. "The women and children, peering from their poor vehicles, seemed frightened dumb. They rarely took up talk with the townspeople, who gazed at them. I remember them as never singing, or calling, cheerily or otherwise, to one another, or shouting at the animals. The small children neither laughed nor cried. All, plainly, were bewildered… I imagine they were mostly of the class of tenant farmers or 'workers on shares" (metairistes), whose few possessions were for the most part transportable. Solid property holders had [railroad] car fare."[45]

To the southwest in Greencastle, reports circulated that Jenkins' main body had retreated to Hagerstown "with a large number of horses, wagons and plunder," according to William Reid. "We congratulated ourselves that evening upon the termination of the 'raid.'" The *New York Herald* announced, "It is now believed that the raid will be extended no further than Chambersburg, and by

---

43 Schuricht diary entry for June 17, 1863, *Richmond Dispatch*, April 5, 1896; Stouffer diary entry for June 17, 1863, "The Rebs are Thick Yet About Us"; Broadhead diary entry for June 17, 1863, vertical files, library of the Gettysburg National Military Park.

44 S. K. Donavin, "The Invasion," *Carlisle American Volunteer*, July 9, 1863. Donavin had witnessed John Brown's Harpers Ferry raid and subsequent trial and execution.

45 James W. Sullivan, *Boyhood Memories of the Civil War, 1861-'65* (Hamilton Library Association, 1933), 14. Métairie was a French term for a small tenant farm where the landlord received a pre-set share of the produce.

to-morrow the rebel cavalry will probably be rushing back to their infantry supports."[46]

As dawn broke on Wednesday, June 17, Greencastle residents believed that Jenkins' threat was over with his retreat into Maryland. However, according to a newsman, "about 10 o'clock, A.M., as some hands were employed in repairing the telegraph line, a sudden dash was made into town, and the hand car and hands captured, but were soon released. Capturing horses was all the go. Indeed, it seemed as if these men possessed some sort of peculiar instinct in finding horses which were concealed in the most secret places. They found thickets, dales and secret places which few of our people could find without being shown thither. Yet these men had no guides, at least none of the citizens of this township. The success of these horse dealers was amazing."[47]

In Guilford Township near Chambersburg, Amos Stouffer wrote in his diary, "A warm day. The Rebs have all left Chambersburg and it is quiet again, but the horses have not come home yet. They would not be very safe yet. 1 O'clock A.M. Another wild report that the Rebs are coming. Men & women running away from town. A great excitement. The Rebs hold Hagerstown in strong force. Self on picket all night between Greencastle and town."[48]

With Jenkins gone, Judge Frederick Watts, the officials of the Cumberland Valley Railroad, and the residents of Chambersburg and Carlisle breathed a little easier. However, there remained the troubling issue of the long columns of Rebel infantry possibly also heading their way. No one was quite certain where Jenkins had gone, or when or if his men would return. For now, several farmers brought their horses back from hiding and began working their fields, harvesting crops or cutting hay. Some merchants began bringing their inventory back and restocking their shelves. However, nerves remained on edge among the Valley folk.

Stunning news stoked their anxiety. A CVRR employee (likely Thomas Bard, ending his all-night hand car journey) had managed to slip through the Rebel pickets surrounding Hagerstown and make it to Chambersburg the next morning. He reported that 4,000 Rebels, including infantry and artillery, now occupied Hagerstown. An additional 4,000 to 6,000 enemy soldiers were on the road between Williamsport and Hagerstown. Jenkins and his men were encamped at Middleburg, "and were plundering and driving off the horses and cattle from that

46 *Greencastle* (PA) *Pilot*, July 28, 1863; *New York Herald*, June 17, 1863.

47 *Greencastle* (PA) *Pilot*, July 28, 1863.

48 Stouffer diary entry for June 18, 1863, "The Rebs are Thick Yet About Us."

section." The informant also "saw several squads of cavalry at different points on the line of the railroad, but avoided them." Another report soon came in that Rebel horse soldiers had passed through Greencastle and were heading toward Waynesboro. That same June 17, a CVRR train left Harrisburg and traveled as far south as Shippensburg. The crew "saw no rebels, notwithstanding reports to the contrary."[49]

Couch's Militia Arrives in Chambersburg

Temporary relief came in the form of Brig. Gen. Joseph F. Knipe's brigade of untested militia. A veteran commander in the Army of the Potomac, Knipe had been recuperating from battlefield wounds and a bout with malaria when the invasion had sparked his return to service. Given a command by General Couch, Knipe hurried to overtake his men, who had already entrained on a rainy June 19 when reports arrived that Jenkins had returned to Greencastle. Knipe's "brigade" consisted of the 8th and 71st New York State National Guard and E. Spencer Miller's Philadelphia battery—all in all, some 1,000 men. They had taken a CVRR train south from Fort Washington, the Union redoubt being erected opposite Harrisburg in the panic over the Rebel invasion, some forty miles south to Shippensburg, where Knipe caught up with them. Their orders from Couch were to act as a deterrent, keeping the advancing Rebels in check but under all circumstances avoiding an engagement. If pressed too hard, Knipe and his men were to retire slowly and harass Jenkins as much as possible, providing the Federal forces at Harrisburg enough time to finish the fort and other defenses.[50]

A Shippensburg resident recorded the militiamen's arrival in his nightly diary entry for June 19. "Several car loads of lumber were passed through to build the Scotland bridge. A train load of New York militia and [a] battery from Philadelphia encamped on [the] Samuel Nevin farm." That the New Yorkers could only reach Shippensburg is indicative of the damage already done to the CVRR line throughout Franklin County. Jenkins' destruction of the Scotland Bridge on June

49 "America," *The Times* (London, England), July 2, 1863; "Telegraphic Accounts, Harrisburg, June 17, 1863," *The Daily True Delta* (New Orleans), June 27, 1863. Middleburg is now known as State Line, PA.

50 Augustus Theodore Francis (compiler), George Edward Lowen (ed.), *History of the 71st Regiment, N.G., N.Y., American Guard* (Eastman Publishing, 1919), 258-260; Henry Whittemore, *History of the Seventy-First Regiment, N.G.S.N.Y.* (W. McDonald & Co., 1886), 75; Colonel Joshua Varian's report, quoted in John Lockwood, *Our Campaign Around Gettysburg* (A. H. Rome & Brothers, 1864), 37-38.

16 was already frustrating the Union war effort. Much to their dismay, Knipe's men would cover the additional eight miles to Scotland on foot. It was "a march over the worst road I ever saw," penned Captain William Robinson of the 8th NYSNG. Although the regiments arrived separately, they both observed the ruins of the Scotland Bridge, and some locals assumed that the New Yorkers had been sent to repair it. Grateful, and also relieved at seeming deliverance from the hands of the enemy, residents of Scotland lavished the men with sandwiches, pies, cakes, and coffee.[51]

While Knipe's men were more eager to fill their stomachs, work rebuilding the bridge did begin, going through the night. Nevertheless, CVRR officials were hardly sanguine about prospects for the imminent future. When Capt. E. Spencer Miller, a Philadelphia law professor leading a militia artillery outfit, requested further rail service from Shippensburg on the afternoon of Sunday, June 21, he was refused. However, Miller, who had 100 men, four navy 12-pounder howitzers and two rifled pieces in tow, was determined, and wired Knipe with the simple message: "The Rail Road refuses transportation[.]"[52]

In the meantime, with the railroad still not functional to Chambersburg, Shippensburg became the main Union concentration point. Two glistening field pieces sat unlimbered on top of Cemetery Hill, with hundreds of well-equipped troops camped nearby. "Soldiers and citizens in commotion, moving to and fro," the diarist recorded that day. "New York soldiers and a battery came today. Mysterious movements of cars—a very long train of empty cars from Harrisburg."[53]

By late Sunday evening, the Scotland Bridge had been sufficiently repaired to allow passage directly to Chambersburg, where Captain Miller finally arrived on Monday morning with his men, guns, and equipment. They joined Capt. Thomas S. McGowan's Patapsco Guards, a Maryland company that had for some time been guarding the sprawling U. S. Army General Hospital complex in York. They

---

51 "Effects of War News," *Shippensburg* (PA) *Chronicle*, July 3, 1913; William Robinson Diary, June 19-21, 1863, Civil War Miscellaneous Collection, USAHEC; Jacob Hoke, *The Great Invasion of 1863: Or, General Lee in Pennsylvania* (W. J. Shuey, 1887), 120.

52 George W. Ashenfelter to Joseph F. Knipe, June 21, 1863; E. Spencer Miller to Joseph F. Knipe, June 21, 1863, Telegraphs, Caspar Dull Papers, HSDC; A. J. Pleasonton, *Third Annual Report of Brigadier General A.J. Pleasonton, Commanding the Home Guard of the City of Philadelphia, to the Hon. Alexander Henry, Mayor for 1863* (King & Baird, 1864), 69.

53 "Effects of War News," *Shippensburg* (PA) *Chronicle*, July 3, 1913.

had arrived via rail from York on June 20 to protect the repair crews from any further Rebel raids.[54]

While the inexperienced Federals slowly congregated in Chambersburg and the railroads worked to protect the river crossings, General Jenkins, urged on by impatient superiors frustrated at his recent timidity, had again crossed the Mason-Dixon Line and was returning to Franklin County. On Monday, June 22, some of Jenkins' men engaged Capt. William L. Boyd and a small detachment of the 1st New York (Lincoln) Cavalry at the William Fleming farm, situated just north of Greencastle not far from the railroad tracks. There, Cpl. William H. Rihl—a Philadelphia native serving under Boyd—became the first Union soldier killed in action on Pennsylvania soil. When news of the scuffle reached Chambersburg, the militiamen assembled there grew uneasy. "About two P.M. word came in that our cavalry were skirmishing... but holding their own," recorded one man. "This caused some excitement," and the exhausted New Yorkers "suddenly became very fresh to march." The veteran General Knipe, however, was not eager to bring about a conflict. He had orders to fall back slowly upon Carlisle and resolved to do so about dark because the enemy was in considerable force. Knipe deemed the Rebels as "sassy."[55]

The angst only grew when a woman entered the Union camp that afternoon. "She was attired in mourning apparel," recorded Chambersburg resident Jacob Hoke, "with her face almost concealed in a black bonnet of somewhat antiquated style. She went about the camp pretending to be silly, and inquired where a certain farmer lived whom no one knew." While some suspected that the visitor was really a male Confederate soldier in disguise, the colonel of the 8th NYSNG dismissed her as "a silly woman, and must not be disturbed." Man or woman, spy or not, the rumor mill was ablaze as the visitor disappeared at a brisk pace southward on the railroad tracks in the direction of the Rebel lines.[56]

While his men debated the identity of the mysterious stranger, General Knipe questioned a local resident, who indicated there were not less than one thousand

54 Pleasonton, *Third Annual Report*, 69. On the 22nd, the Patapsco Guards withdrew to Carlisle and then headed back to York on a Northern Central train.

55 Isaac Harris Diary, June 22, 1863, Civil War Document Collection, USAHEC; William Harrison Beach, *The First New York (Lincoln) Cavalry, From April 19, 1861, to July 7, 1865* (Lincoln Cavalry Association, 1902), 248; Hoke, *The Great Invasion*, 125-126.

56 Hoke, *The Great Invasion*, 123. This encounter bears a striking resemblance to another incident a week later from Oyster's Point, just outside of Harrisburg, where Jenkins' brigade was also reconnoitering the area. See the John Mater Narrative, Caspar Dull Papers, HSDC.

Confederates concentrated near Greencastle. Turning to his staff, Knipe declared: "Men, we cannot hold a point this far out." He immediately began preparations for as orderly a withdrawal as could be managed. Simultaneously, he tried to temper the anxious New Yorkers, some of whom had declared themselves to be ready to set fire to their tents and leave. The anxiety reached a new high when rumors spread that General Couch was more concerned with keeping CVRR's rolling stock out of Rebel hands. The alleged order—several versions were circulating through the ranks—supposedly instructed Knipe to withdraw "the cars to the other side of Scotland bridge regardless of what became of the men and stores."[57]

By 5:00 p.m., disorder reigned supreme, and the militiamen made a mad dash towards the CVRR depot on North Second Street. They paid no heed to their officers, who "were running around and in an excited manner giving commands," but streamed through town, "leaving guns, tents, and other camp equipage standing." Miller's Philadelphia artillerymen abandoned two brass howitzers (later retrieved by members of Chambersburg's home guard company, placed on the CVRR, and transported safely out of Confederate hands). Shortly before 7:00 p.m., the men of the 8th NYSNG and Miller's battery began boarding the trains which would take them to Shippensburg.[58]

This came as quite a shock to several companies of the 71st NYSNG, then deployed southeast of town. Apparently having been isolated from the earlier panic, they learned of the withdrawal only when they saw their comrades nearly all entrained. After an understandably sour exchange with Knipe, their commander, Col. Benjamin L. Trafford, sent four companies to the depot, while personally deploying another as a picket guard to cover the retreat. However, unfamiliar with the locale, he had put his men on the wrong road, and they were still struggling to reach the depot as the trains departed at 7:00 p.m.

Judge Frederick Watts later told a friend about an incident as the Rebel horsemen approached Chambersburg for the second time in a week. The Confederates had a particular interest in appropriating as many maps of the Cumberland Valley as they could find to distribute to their officers. Watts mentioned that the farmers in the region had hastily torn their personal maps from the walls of their homes and sent them with their horses and other valuables to

---

57 Hoke, *The Great Invasion*, 126-128; Whittemore, *History of the Seventy-First Regiment*, 75; Francis, *History of the 71st Regiment*, 261.

58 Hoke, *The Great Invasion*, 128-130.

safety. According to his friend, R. Pearsall Smith of Philadelphia, "The rebel visitation was very complete; [Watts] thought it likely that not a single house had been overlooked. The sack of the Valley would have been most disastrous, but for the want of rolling stock on the railroad. What they carried off was on their backs." The two trains which had brought the New York militiamen to Chambersburg departed just in the nick of time. They passed through the CVRR's Scotland station only four minutes before Jenkins' Rebel cavalry dashed in from the south to cut them off.[59]

The Rev. Benjamin S. Schneck was the editor of the German Reformed Church's books and religious materials, which were printed at the denomination's publication office on the southeastern side of Chambersburg's town square. He was not charitable toward the New Yorkers who had fled at the first sign of trouble. "The border was known to be imperiled a second time, and a large portion of our citizens were armed and marched out with these regiments." During the night, a scout had arrived with the news the Rebels were on their way. "In the greatest conceivable consternation, these 'defenders' made for Chambersburg in 'double-quick,' took seats in the cars, 'homeward bound.'" Schneck claimed that the Empire State militiamen made sure to keep the citizen-soldiers between them and the Rebels, "to assure themselves as safe a retreat as possible." They had even abandoned their camp equipage to the invaders. The retreating soldiers had no right later to boast of their bravery, in Schneck's biased opinion.[60]

Confederate Infantry Enters the Cumberland Valley

Meanwhile, while Knipe's New Yorkers headed rearward, Lt. Gen. Richard S. Ewell's Second Corps of the oncoming Army of Northern Virginia continued to march north through the Cumberland Valley toward Chambersburg. The pioneer corps was ready to catch any oversights Jenkins' men may have made in the destruction of rail lines and railroad bridges. "On our whole way up the Valley," proudly recalled Capt. John Gorman of the 2nd North Carolina, "all railroad bridges were burnt[.]"[61]

---

59 "Stated Meeting, March 18, 1864," *Proceedings of the American Philosophical Society*, vol. 9, no. 70 (June 1863), 350.

60 Rev. B. S. Schneck, D. D., *The Burning of Chambersburg, Pennsylvania* (Lindsay & Blakiston, 1864), 10-13.

61 John Gorman to Dear Mother and Wife, July 8, 1863, *Raleigh Daily Progress*, July 22, 1863.

The advance of the Rebel infantry and artillery brought fresh fears of another attempt to sever the CVRR by destroying the vital Scotland bridge. Many locals depended on the railroad for both personal and trade necessities. Consequently, its safety loomed heavily in their thoughts. Shippensburg merchant John Stumbaugh had already heard of the damage wrought by Jenkins' men in Franklin County. The Confederates had "cut down all the railroad shops and torn down the depot foundation walls that had just [been] put up," he wrote despairingly. If residents at all doubted the rumors swirling about them, they only had to glance at the lines of the CVRR. On the evening of June 21, druggist J. C. Altick recorded "a large train of empty cars" passing through town—confirming the CVRR was indeed evacuating its rolling stock. Two counties to the east, officials of the Northern Central Railway, fearful the Rebels might head into York County to disrupt their line, sent almost all of their locomotives well north of Harrisburg to Sunbury for protection.[62]

On the following day, Rodes' division of Ewell's Second Corps reached Greencastle at 1:30 p.m. "The people seemed downhearted," Pvt. Louis Leon of the 53rd North Carolina Infantry recalled, "and showed their hatred to us by their glum looks and silence, and I am willing to swear that no prayers will be offered in this town for us poor, ragged rebels." The division lingered in the Greencastle area until June 23, when the men resumed their northerly trek through the Cumberland Valley. Leon and a companion went in search of food and supplies, but "when we came to a house, they would close their doors in our faces, or let us knock and not open. We got the ear of one or two ladies, and after proving to them that we were not wild animals nor thieves, they gave us what we wanted, but would not take pay for anything."[63]

"The R.R. runs down main street," Pvt. Thomas Ware of the 15th Georgia Infantry mentioned in his diary when Brig. Gen. George Doles' brigade later marched through Greencastle. He marveled at the beauty of the town: "Houses large and fine. Shady streets. This town like others in this State have never felt the affect of war." The people were strong Unionists, in his opinion, and they looked "mad & sullen at our appearance." The stores were closed and many of the people had shut their doors. He noted the presence of many young men of military age and "some nice looking girls dressed very fine as every thing is cheap." After

62 John Stumbaugh to My Dear Son, July 9, 1863, Harrisburg Civil War Round Table Collection, USAHEC; J. C. Altick Diary, Transcript, June 21, 1863, Civil War Times Illustrated Collection, USAHEC.

63 Louis Leon, *Diary of a Tar Heel Confederate Soldier* (Stone Publishing, 1913), 32.

marching through town at quick time to music from the regimental band, the regiment passed the Franklin Railroad station and surveyed the damage left by Jenkins' earlier foray through Greencastle. "The depot on the north side of town was burned," Ware noted, "& R.R. in several places."[64]

As news spread that the Rebels had reached Greencastle, hundreds of anxious Valley residents packed up and left for safer environs. Many of them crowded into trains headed for Harrisburg. On Tuesday, June 23, a reporter with the *New York Times* mentioned the arrival in the state capital of one such train, "packed with citizens escaping from the Rebels." Men, women, and children were arriving in droves, often on foot or horseback, with some riding in vehicles of all sorts. Many of the new arrivals were glad to have put the Susquehanna River between themselves and the Confederates, thankful that they had reached the presumed safety of the East Shore. Ironically, at the same time, terrified Harrisburg residents flocked to the depot to board trains heading out of Harrisburg. Reports came in that night that Governor Curtin had received a telegram that 1,000 enemy cavalrymen had arrived in Scotland. The reporter conjectured that the bridge had likely been destroyed, if the report was accurate.[65]

That same day, a riot among the remaining residents of Chambersburg broke out near the line of the Cumberland Valley Railroad on the north side of town. According to Jacob Hoke, several residents who had "no scruples against taking anything from Uncle Sam they could," headed for one of the warehouses of a private freight forwarder. It contained large quantities of government stores, including hardtack crackers, beans, and bacon, all commodities the crowd wanted for themselves rather than allow the food to fall into the clutches of the Confederates. In a short time, they had all but cleaned out the warehouse. "Men, women and children came running in crowds," Hoke related, "and a general scramble took place, and upon every street and alley leading from the warehouse persons were seen carrying bacon and rolling barrels of crackers and beans." One man made several return trips, collecting four barrels that he put into his cellar for safekeeping. Some of the wayward townspeople, in their haste to gather what they could, began scolding and chiding one another. Soon, the bickering led to kicking and fighting. A reliable eyewitness told Hoke that two women were rolling barrels of crackers down a street when one of them crowded the other too much. The

---

64 Thomas Ware diary entry for June 27,1863, Greencastle, PA, Louis Round Wilson Special Collections Library, University of North Carolina at Chapel Hill.

65 "Our Harrisburg Correspondence," *New York Times*, June 25, 1863.

second woman turned around and angrily tried to kick the offender, but missed and went sprawling over her own barrel. By the time she picked herself up, someone else had rolled it away. A general fistfight soon ensued. Hoke deemed the whole sordid affair as "a raid of a most shameful and yet ludicrous character."[66]

To the north in Shippensburg, the citizens also scrambled to safeguard their valuables. "If you could see the excitement in Shippensburg at this time you would wonder that I could be sufficiently composed to sit down and write a letter to you," teenager Lizzie Wolf wrote in a letter on June 23 to her cousin in Pittsburgh, "but you know I do not belong to that excitable class of persons who are always ready to catch up and believe every report they hear." The Rebel cavalrymen reportedly were only five miles away, in Greenvillage, and continuing to advance. All the stores in town were closed, and Lizzie's family had hidden their valuables and the tinware from her father's shop in the garret of their home upon hearing that the Rebels had taken clothing from private homes in Waynesboro.[67]

That same day, the Cumberland Valley Railroad took the last of its scheduled trains out of service, fearful that the Rebels intended to march all the way to the river. In Mechanicsburg, work crews gathered up all of the rolling stock they could find, attached them to the few remaining locomotives, and hauled everything beyond the Susquehanna River to Harrisburg and safety. With that act, the CVRR was officially out of business, at least until the Rebel threat subsided and normal operations could be resumed. General Couch made plans to burn the CVRR bridge and the adjacent Theodore Burr-designed Camelback highway bridge. "Rebels are coming. New York soldiers retreating towards Harrisburg. Bad sign," an unknown Shippensburg diarist recorded, "Refugees coming in to report the Rebels in force in Chambersburg. Their pickets extend to Greenvillage. We feel more alarmed this evening than any time yet."[68]

With General Jenkins' saddle soldiers heading north through the Valley with the apparent intent of reaching Harrisburg, the telegraph operator at Shippensburg packed up his instrument and key on June 24, and skedaddled to Newville to avoid capture. He reported that the Rebels had a supply train three

---

66 Hoke, *Historical Reminiscences of the War*, 47.

67 Lizzie F. Wolfe to Agnes M. Wolfe, Shippensburg, PA, July 1863, Civil War files, FCHS.

68 *Mechanicsburg Civil War Centennial* (Mechanicsburg Centennial Committee, 1963), 11; "Effects of War News," *Shippensburg (PA) Chronicle*, July 3, 1913; "Effects of War News," *Shippensburg (PA) Chronicle*, July 3, 1913.

miles long, the bridge at Scotland had been burned, and the telegraph lines destroyed for miles. He did not tarry. From there, the operator quickly headed east to Greason's Station, five miles from Carlisle. He told the locals the Rebels had halted eight miles west of the railroad, at Palmstown in West Pennsboro Township. Union cavalry was a mile from the Rebels, but they were too few to block the route to Carlisle for any length of time.[69]

The next day, June 24, Albert Jenkins' mounted brigade arrived in Shippensburg after easily driving in the few remaining Union defenders. "At 10 o'clock a.m. our cavalry rear guard are coming in retreating," the unknown local diarist noted. "Rebels came in through our town at 1 o'clock p.m. yelling like so many demons. Stores have all been pilfered. General Jenkins ordered the citizens to prepare and deliver to [the] old post office building 500 loaves of bread and other provisions for his cavalry."[70]

The road-weary Confederate horsemen enjoyed a momentary respite from their northward trek. Washington Hands, a Maryland artilleryman attached to Jenkins' command, recalled partaking "the delicious apple butter, ham, bread &c. furnished them in abundance by the startled inhabitants." Their feast was disrupted when Boyd's cavalrymen reappeared, but the cautious New Yorkers "could not be induced to come within range of Griffin's Parrotts"—the Baltimore artillery outfit serving with Jenkins' brigade—instead falling back towards Carlisle. Six-year-old J. W. McPherson, clinging to his father's hand, went to Shippensburg's town square. His father brought a basket of food, as the Rebels demanded. The soldiers ate well. McPherson later recalled "that loyal people were very mad, one man who was a notorious tobacco user, expressing it forcibly by spitting in the pies that he was compelled to furnish."[71]

Jenkins and his men soon left Shippensburg and rode to Carlisle, where they found the Yankee flag defiantly flying from the public buildings. Believing the town to be heavily defended, the Virginia native prepared to attack. Jenkins placed two pieces of artillery in a position to rake the main street (High Street) and

---

69 *Buffalo Daily Courier*, June 25, 1863. John Greason owned a tavern along the turnpike near the railroad station at Woodhope. He laid out a station on his farm in 1856. In the newspaper accounts, the site is misspelled as Gleason's Station. See Durant, *History of Cumberland County*, 363.

70 "Effects of War News," *Shippensburg* (PA) *Chronicle*, July 3, 1913.

71 Ibid.; Washington Hands, "Civil War Memoirs," 88-103, Special Collections, Alderman Library, University of Virginia.

deployed his troops around town before demanding to see a deputation of Carlisle's leading citizens and municipal authorities.[72]

While Jenkins' horsemen continued their advance, Rodes' division and its batteries and wagons were still in tow several miles behind them. The infantrymen passed through Marion and entered Chambersburg about noon on June 24, and the vanguard marched three miles north to camp near the railroad. "Chambersburg is a very fine place, 10,000 inhabitants, but nary a smile greeted us as we marched through town," the 53rd North Carolina's Pvt. Louis Leon related. "There are a plenty of men here—a pity they are not rebels, and in our ranks." In several places in Pennsylvania, the Confederates marveled at how many healthy-looking males were in civilian garb and not in the Federal army. For some Rebels, it was disheartening to learn how many potential reserves the Union could muster if needed.[73]

The Free South, a partisan newspaper in Beaufort, South Carolina, mocked the efforts of "the whole grand army of the Potomac to resist and thwart" Lee's invasion of Pennsylvania. The editors bragged about some of the accomplishments in recent weeks, including "the rich Cumberland Valley penetrated, the fat and sleek horses of the old Dutch farmers dragged from their cool stalls in the big barns, or taken from the plows in the field, and transferred to the ranks of the redoubtable rebel Stuart; the whole population along the Cumberland Valley Railroad sent flying in consternation to the north of the Susquehanna; the city of Harrisburg deserted by its original inhabitants and occupied with troops from almost every northern state."[74]

As the Rebels neared, the citizens of Carlisle weighed their options. Beyond personal safety, most were concerned with removing whatever property they could before the enemy columns swept through. "We were drove out of Carlisle by the rebels," recorded George Chenoweth. On June 25, he and his family bundled what they could in a single trunk, leaving every thing else to the mercy of the enemy. They boarded the CVRR at 7:00 p.m. that evening, taking the last train that left Carlisle before the Rebels arrived.[75]

72 Hands, "Civil War Memoirs," 88-103, University of Virginia' "Effects of War News," *Shippensburg (PA) Chronicle*, July 3, 1913.

73 Leon, *Diary of a Tar Heel Confederate Soldier*, 33.

74 "The Late News from the North," *The Free South* (Beaufort, SC), June 27, 1863.

75 George D. Chenoweth to Prof. James W. Marshall, July 15, 1863, Dickinson College Archives & Special Collections, Carlisle, PA.

The annual commencement of Dickinson College took place in Carlisle as scheduled that day. The next morning, June 26, the diplomas were distributed. As the Confederates came closer that day, "the negro population were impressed to dig rifle pits & make barricades about a mile west of the town, & the citizenry soldiery went out to man the fortifications supported by two N. York militia regts," as Charles F. Himes, a wealthy businessman and amatuer photographer from New Oxford, recalled. "Prof. Wilson & I walked out to inspect the defences & came in to town, & in a few minutes the rebels were announced within sight of the fortifications, & the train was standing with steam up ready to leave on sight." Himes was carrying $10,000 in cash that he had recently withdrawn from the bank. He was concerned the Rebels might capture him and take it, but he was determined to get home. He and his brother started over the mountains and made it back to New Oxford without incident.[76]

That same rainy Friday, the Confederates of Jubal Early's division occupied Mummasburg and Gettysburg after marching across South Mountain from their campsites east of Chambersburg. Behind them, the First and Third Corps began filing through Chambersburg and setting up their own camps east and northeast of town. Robert E. Lee established his headquarters in Messersmith's Woods on the east side of Chambersburg along the turnpike to Gettysburg. Lee soon had his entire Army of Northern Virginia in Pennsylvania when his rear guard—the division of the ringleted, charismatic Maj. Gen. George E. Pickett—marched through Hagerstown and crossed the Mason-Dixon Line.

After entering the Cumberland Valley, Pvt. David E. Johnston of the 7th Virginia deemed it a "magnificent land, the counterpart of the lovely valley of Virginia, the sight bringing homesickness to the heart of not a few Virginia boys." He added, "Nothing was seen indicating that these people knew that a terrible war had been raging for two years, only a few miles away; certain it is they had felt little of its effect, either upon their population or resources. At Greencastle was noted among the people defiance and vindictive mien; while not speaking out, their looks indicated that deep down in their bosoms was rancor and the wish that all the rebel hosts were dead and corralled by the devil." Fear spread that the Rebels intended to pillage the Valley and torch private property. According to Dr. Charles E. Lippitt, the surgeon of the 57th Virginia in Pickett's division, "The Dutch

---

76 Charles F. Himes to Ogden N. Rood, New Oxford, PA, October 2, 1863, Dickinson College Archives & Special Collections. Himes, a member of one of the earliest amateur photography clubs in America, traveled extensively.

farmers say Take de horses take de cattle take eberyting put don't purn de parn don't purn de house & don't hurt de wife & leetle one."[77]

The following day, Saturday, June 27, Jubal Early's soldiers departed Gettysburg and Mummasburg, and pushed eastward through Adams County. They passed through New Oxford on their way toward York, with the goal of pushing on to the great covered bridge over the Susquehanna River at Wrightsville. Pickett's men arrived in the Chambersburg area that same day, putting the town under martial law with the Henry Guards of the 24th Virginia serving as the provost force.[78]

By now, throngs of frightened refugees had fled the Valley in seach of safety across the broad Susquehanna. "Each train that arrives at Harrisburg from the south on the North[ern] Central and the Cumberland Valley road brings its load of fugitives," a reporter noted. "There are congregated at the depot the old and the young, mistress and man, strong men and weak children, white and black, all commingled in one common mass, panic stricken, weary, hungry and exhausted. Baggage is piled up like huge stacks," he wrote, "trunks and carpet sacks are continually accumulating." Many of the refugees had no destination in mind, other than to reach Harrisburg.[79]

Meanwhile, General Jenkins continued his steady push northward, screening the advance of Ewell's two powerful divisions led by Maj. Gens. Robert E. Rodes and Edward Johnson. "At Shippensburg the track of the railroad was torn up and a bridge burned," a Confederate officer related. "The citizens, who turned out in large numbers to witness the passage of the rebels, were generally quiet Occasionally you found a spirited girl, or a spunky person... That portion of Pennsylvania which our army occupied, was completely subjugated; very few having the courage to raise their heads. Foraging thrived. For a little Confederate note, and often for nothing, a soldier could get quantities of every delightful thing in the grand category of the productions of the great Cumberland Valley." Rodes' column, in the wake of Jenkins' cavalry screen, entered Carlisle on Saturday

77 David E. Johnston, *The Story of a Confederate Boy in the Civil War* (Glass & Prudhomme, 1914), 196-97; Charles Edward Lippitt Diary and Medical Record Book (#3157) Southern Historical Collection, Manuscripts Department, Wilson Library, UNC Chapel Hill.

78 Ralph White Gunn, *24th Virginia Infantry* (H. E. Howard, 1987), 43; Johnston, *The Story of a Confederate Boy in the Civil War*, 191-92. See Mingus, *Flames Beyond Gettysburg*, for the definitive account of Early's ill-fated expedition to the river.

79 "Latest News," *Union County Star and Lewisburg (PA) Chronicle*, June 26, 1863.

The Railroad Hotel, which no longer stands, was located near the town square in Mechanicsburg, Pennsylvania. With the town lacking a formal depot until after the war, the hotel served as a boarding spot for CVRR passengers. On June 28, 1863, it played host to General Jenkins, who stopped for a brief respite with his staff, allowing him to scan Northern newspapers for any useful intelligence. *Mechanicsburg Museum Association*

evening and camped in and around the town, while "Allegheny" Johnson's division camped at Plainfield.[80]

As Jenkins approached Mechanicsburg on June 28, a small detachment of Union militia—the 100 or so men of Capt. Frank Murray's "Curtin Guards"—were arrayed to contest the Confederate cavalrymen. However patriotic, Murray's men were no match for Jenkins' brigade, in either experience or numbers. Some accounts suggest that Jenkins and Murray may have met one another under a flag of truce. Eager to dispatch what he saw more as a nuisance than a real threat,

80 "The Great Pennsylvania Campaign," *Hillsborough* (NC) *Recorder*, July 29, 1863. For more, see Cooper H. Wingert, *The Confederate Approach on Harrisburg: The Gettysburg Campaign's Northernmost Reaches* (The History Press, 2012).

Jenkins ordered one of Capt. Wiley Griffin's Parrott rifles to unlimber and take aim. Washington Hands later recalled with amusement, "a shot from Griffin caused them to beat a hasty retreat." About 8:30 a.m., Murray "dashed into town," bound directly for the telegraph office, where he wired news of Mechanicsburg's impending capture. The telegraph operators quickly grabbed their instruments and headed on a hand car toward Bridgeport and Harrisburg.[81]

Several days earlier, Mechanicsburg had been deprived of 64 of its own able-bodied men. The Russell Light Cavalry, a militia outfit recruited from the area in and around Mechanicsburg, had taken the CVRR to Harrisburg on June 23. What set the Russell Light Cavalry apart was its captain, 18-year-old Theodore F. Singiser. A native of nearby Churchtown, he had learned the art of printing before enlisting in 1861 at age 16. He fought at Antietam before being discharged for disability in February 1863. Singiser returned to the military in June 1863 as captain of the 64-man squad. As their town lay vulnerable to rebel forces, members of the company helped to build Fort Washington just miles away.[82]

Local politician George Hummel, faced with Jenkins' threat to bombard the town, had no choice except to surrender to the Rebels. Riding into town, Jenkins led his staff to the Ashland House Tavern at the Railroad Hotel, situated alongside the CVRR tracks. There Jenkins reclined, poring over Northern papers, gathering information just steps away from the railroad he had already damaged severely.[83]

With the loss of Mechanicsburg, nearly the entire length of the Cumberland Valley Railroad and Franklin Railroad was now under Confederate control or left in ruins in their wake. Department of the Susquehanna officials across the river in Harrisburg eyed the enemy advance with mounting concern. On Sunday, orders came for the 22nd New York State National Guard to "barricade several buildings

81 *Harrisburg Daily Telegraph*, June 15, 1863; Hands, "Civil War Memoirs," 88-103; *Cumberland Valley Journal*, quoted in *Miniatures of Mechanicsburg* (J. A. Bushman, 1928), 130. Frank Murray operated a livery stable on Fourth and Walnut streets in Harrisburg.

82 H. H. Snavely, "Personal War Sketch," Col. H. I. Zinn Post No. 415 Papers, Simpson Public Library, Mechanicsburg, PA; *OR* 27, pt. 3, 563, 622; "From Mechanicsburg," *Harrisburg Evening Telegraph*, June 23, 1863; "Russell Light Cavalry," *Daily Patriot and Union*, June 24, 1863; U. S. Congress, *A Biographical Congressional Directory 1774 to 1903* (Government Printing Office, 1903), 800; Janet B. Hewett, ed., *Supplement to the Official Records of the Union and Confederate Armies*, 100 vols. (Broadfoot, 1994-2004), 57:2, 626-627. Shortly after their arrival in Harrisburg, Singiser and his company mustered into service for six months (most would later reenlist and serve through 1865) and eventually assigned to the 20th Pennsylvania Cavalry.

83 *Cumberland Valley Journal*, quoted in *Miniatures of Mechanicsburg*, 130; A. J. Hauck, *Hauck's Centennial Directory of the Borough of Mechanicsburg* (Thomas & Demming, 1876), Mechanicsburg Museum Association.

George W. Wingate's drawing of his fellow New Yorkers beginning to fortify the CVRR's engine house at Bridgeport, PA (modern-day Lemoyne). *History of the Twenty-Second Regiment of the National Guard of the State of New York, From its Organization to 1895*

commanding the approaches to the important" CVRR bridge. Companies A and I, with assistance from local African-Americans who had been at work on Fort Washington, hauled "beams, barrels of earth, bundles of lath, railroad sleepers and sand-bags[.]" By nightfall, they had successfully converted the CVRR engine house into "a loop-holed and casemented battery[.]" A barricade of railroad ties and sandbags fronted the open doors, with a pair of embrasures for artillery pieces. Two howitzers of E. Spencer Miller's Philadelphia battery (the same outfit that had been at Chambersburg with General Knipe) would have a commanding line of fire to protect the railroad from attacks. Companies of the 22nd were posted in nearby buildings. Other men dug rifle pits and erected temporary low fortifications to protect key spots along the West Shore's railroads, including barricading a rock cut and putting rifle pits overlooking the Northern Central tracks near Bridgeport. They were finished by 10:00 p.m. Well into the night, with rumors of approaching Rebels, the 22nd and the nearby 37th NYSNG formed a battle line, whispering commands to one another. When nothing transpired, they marched back to the riverfront and camped along the NCRY tracks.[84]

---

84 George Wood Wingate, *History of the Twenty-Second Regiment of the National Guard of the State of New York, From its Organization to 1895* (Edwin W. Dayton, 1896), 180-181; J. R. Schwarz and J. Zeamer, *The Cumberland Blue Book: A Compendium of Information of Lower Cumberland County* (J. Robley Schwarz, 1903), 93.

Sketch of the fortified CVRR engine house at Bridgeport, Pennsylvania, June 30, 1863. *History of the 22nd NYSM*

That same night, just outside of Frederick, Maryland, the oncoming Army of the Potomac welcomed a new commander, Maj. Gen. George Gordon Meade. The Spanish-born Philadelphian had capably led the Fifth Army Corps, but was promoted to command of the army after General Hooker, frustrated with the War Department over multiple disagreements, submitted his resignation. The often dour Meade, widely known as "Old Goggle Eyes" or "Old Snapping Turtle," wasted little time. He had his army back on the road early on June 29, headed for south-central Pennsylvania and a planned rendezvous with the Rebels.[85]

On Monday morning, June 29, in Carlisle, Confederate Maj. Gen. Robert E. Rodes set about destroying the infrastructure of the Cumberland Valley Railroad, paying particular attention to the Main Street/CVRR bridge and 600-foot-long wooden trestle over Letort Spring Run on the eastern edge of the town. About 10:00 a.m., between 100 and 200 soldiers, armed with axes, crowbars, and fire-brands, congregated at the bridge as a crowd of residents gathered in horror to watch the spectacle. "Track rails were ripped up and thrown down to the surface

85 For more, see Tom Huntington, *Searching for George Gordon Meade: The Forgotten Victor of Gettysburg* (Stackpole Books, 2013).

George W. Wingate's depiction of the 22nd NYSNG's bivouac beneath the CVRR bridge at Bridgeport. The regiment, under Col. Lloyd Aspinwall, served in the 4th Brigade, 1st Division, Department Susquehanna, during the Gettysburg Campaign. *History of the 22nd NYSM*

road," young resident James Sullivan recounted. "Next came ties, which were set on fire, and then all the 15 or 20 piers were stripped of their half-dozen upper courses of heavy stone." A newsman believed, "From the manner in which they worked it it was apparent that they were new hands at the business, but the earnestness which they exhibited showed that their hearts were in the work, and that it was only necessary to take off the restraint which was held over them, and they would carry fire and sword into every dwelling." Hundreds of concerned, or merely curious, citizens jammed the nearby streets to gain a vantage point.[86]

"The sleepers and ties of the bridge were fired at every pier and soon the entire structure was in flames," the *Carlisle Herald* reporter added. "The iron rails were thrown across the burning timber, and as soon as heated were warped. At the same time parties were engaged in tearing up the track below the bridge... About a quarter of a mile of the track was torn up and destryed. The timber burnt slowly, and when night came there was a stream of fire stretching down the track lighting

86 "The Destruction of the Railroad Bridge," Carlisle Weekly Herald, July 31, 1863; James W. Sullivan, Boyhood Memories of the Civil War, 1861-'65: Invasion of Carlisle (Hamilton Library Association, 1933), 19; Gorman to Mother and Wife, July 8, 1863, Raleigh Daily Progress, July 22, 1863.

up the neighborhood, which attracted crowds of our citizens to the scene." Some of the Confederates approached the work with zeal, drawing the ire and contempt of onlookers. Other soldiers severed telegraph lines throughout the area.[87]

To the south, at Chambersburg, General Pickett's men paid particular attention to the Franklin Railroad and the CVRR tracks snaking out from the town. Soldiers pried up the wooden crossties and burned them. They lifted the heavy T-iron rails onto the bonfires, which caused them to sag and warp under their own weight. Soldiers bent some of the heated rails around nearby trees. Switches, signals, culverts, etc. also became targets for destruction. Confederate staff officer Launcelot M. Blackford, with Pickett's division, mentioned visiting A. K. McClure's Norland estate just north of Chambersburg: "One I saw, on the premises of a Mr., or Judge McClure, this side of Chambersburg, which was not only of very large size, but really elegant: painted snow-white, with ornamented eaves, pendants. The house and whole property of this individual however are beautiful and complete beyond description."[88]

Pickett's division stayed in Chambersburg for several days, awaiting the arrival of Brig. Gen. John D. Imboden's cavalry brigade to assume the role as the army's rear guard. The Virginia infantrymen continued their destruction of the railroad, and bonfires at night marked their destruction of rails as far as the eye could see. "The Rebs are still about doing all the mischief they can," housewife Rachel Cormany penned in her diary on June 30. "They have everything ready to set fire to the warehouses & machine shops—Tore up the railroad track & burned the crossties—They have cleared out nearly every store so they cannot rob much more."[89]

To the northeast, Jenkins' Rebel cavalrymen and mounted infantrymen were camped on the eastern outskirts of Mechanicsburg. On the morning of June 30, a courier summoned Lt. Hermann Schuricht of the 14th Virginia Cavalry to General Jenkins' headquarters. There, the long-bearded brigadier ordered Schuricht to ride into town with his Company D and a piece from Jackson's Kanawha Horse Artillery, hold the town "until ordered otherwise," and "destroy the railroad track

87 "The Destruction of the Railroad Bridge," *Carlisle Weekly Herald*, July 31, 1863.

88 Ralph White Gunn, *24th Virginia Infantry* (H. E. Howard, 1987), 43; Johnston, *The Story of a Confederate Boy*, 191-92; L. M. Blackford to My Dear Father, Chambersburg, PA, June 28, 1863, Valley of the Shadow website, UVA. http://valley.lib.virginia.edu/papers/A0001. Accessed February 3, 2018. Original in Blackford Family Letters, Accession #6403, Albert and Shirley Small Special Collections Library, University of Virginia, Charlottesville.

89 Cormany and Mohr, *The Cormany Diaries*, 331.

as far as possible." Upon arrival, the lieutenant found Capt. Frank Murray's Curtin Guards had returned to the vicinity. Murray's men fell back as Schuricht arrived, but did not vanish entirely. As Schuricht set to work tearing up the CVRR tracks, he found his progress hampered by Murray's lingering presence. The Harrisburg cavalrymen had fallen back to woods near Shiremanstown (east of Mechanicsburg) and from there kept up a sporadic fire. "We were repeatedly interrupted… by the reappearance of Yankees," moaned Schuricht in his diary. Distracted from tearing up the tracks, Schuricht and his men were forced "to keep up a lively skirmish all day."[90]

In harassing the Virginians, Murray's men were preventing the destruction of a vital resource for the Department of the Susquehanna. Although Schuricht remained in Mechanicsburg until sunset, his destruction of the rail lines had been severely impeded. In part thanks to Murray's harassment, the CVRR between Harrisburg and Carlisle would be operational again within three days.

The same was not true to the southwest in Chambersburg and Scotland, where matters were about to get much worse for the beleaguered Cumberland Valley Railroad. First, late on June 30, Edward Johnson's Confederate division camped near Scotland on their way toward Gettysburg. The engineers, including Lt. Henry H. Harris, dismantled the CVRR bridge over Conococheague Creek. Harris noted in his diary that the pioneers quickly "completed the destruction of the rail road bridge."[91]

Then, on Wednesday, July 1, in Chambersburg, General Pickett made good on his threat to burn the warehouses and destroy the railroad infrastructure. According to merchant William Heyser, at 9:00 a.m. a large train of supply wagons began rumbling through town, headed east toward Gettysburg. It took four hours until the final one passed by. Meanwhile, Pickett's men were busy destroying the Franklin Railroad both north and south of town. "Along with sills [cross-ties] of the road," Heyser wrote, "they pile on all the fence they can find to heat and twist the rails. Another force of about 500 men have been sent to destroy the railroad depot and buildings, starting with the large turntable. It is so soundly built of iron castings, their fires had little effect on it. The engine house was pulled down after an immense amount of work."

90 Schuricht Diary, *SHSP*, 343-44.

91 Henry H. Harris diary entry for June 30, 1863, in W. Harrison Daniel, ed., "H. H. Harris' Civil War Diary, 1863-1865," *Virginia Baptist Register*, No. 35, 1996, Part 1, 1771.

Confederate soldiers went from building to building, burning them. To Heyser, it was "a senseless thing to do, as the structures were of no importance to us as we could not use them." He tried to reason with a nearby officer about the wanton destruction, but was told, "This is in retaliation for your troops' work on the South, particularly Fredericksburg." Other officers repeated the refrain. Leaving the scene of destruction, he climbed into the belfry of the German Reformed Church and peered toward his distant farm, fearing he might see signs of damage. However, intervening timberland blocked his view. The railroad, however, was another matter. "You could mark the line of the railroad by the smoke of the burning ties. From what I can see, there is little damage to crops and grassland.[92]

Pickett had ordered the destruction of the machine shops (the CVRR's were located on the northern side of Chambersburg and the Franklin Railroad's on the eastern edge) and nearby railroad property. "I did not wish to use fire for fear of injuring private property," Maj. Edmund Berkeley of the 8th Virginia recounted, "and as the shops were in a large brick building I made some of the men take… heavy railroad rails." He put six men to a rail and soon had them battering down the walls "as easily as a needle through a piece of cloth, and after making a slit some twenty feet or more, down would come the wall." The massive iron turntable, however, proved much more of a challenge, defying "the efforts of some of my strongest men with heavy sledge hammers to break it." Spotting some nearby cords of wood at the carpenter shop, Berkeley had his soldiers pile it onto the turntable. He ordered a fire set, which heated the iron "red hot. When it cooled, it warped out of shape and was useless." To lessen the danger to nearby private property, the major had his men keep buckets of water handy.[93]

Berkeley's superior officer, Col. Eppa Hunton, added his own twist to the story: "I was assigned the duty of tearing up the road, destroying the turntable, and battering down the railroad houses. While I was engaged in this work, a man came out to me and asked me if I would spare his property, which was in one of the cars. I told him certainly, that we were not there to make war on private individuals. He was very grateful, and invited me and half a dozen others into his house to take a drink. While we were in the dining-room taking a drink, his wife came in, in a perfect fury, and said to him, 'How dare you to bring rebels into my house to take a

92 Jane Dice Stone, ed., "Dairy of William Heyser," *Papers Read Before the Kittochtinny Historical Society*, vol. 1 (Mercersburg Printing, 1978), 54-58.

93 Edmund Berkeley to the Mayor of Chambersburg, August 1914, cited by Westhaeffer, *History of the CVRR*, 82.

drink? I will see that you are punished for this.' But notwithstanding her rage, we all took our drink."[94]

"The rebs have stripped this valley of everything," Dr. William H. Boyle later complained. "All the Stores—Book, Dry Goods, Groceries, Mills and Warehouses have been emptied. There is not enough left for the people to live on for two weeks. Both railroads are destroyed. All the new depot building[s] are down. Many farms are destroyed by roads over them and encampments upon them. The telegraph lines are all destroyed." The Irish-born Boyle, a former editor of the *Valley Sentinel*, bemoaned the sudden lack of communications and news, "We are completely cut off from the outside world."[95]

In the confusion and excitement, at least one Confederate decided it was a good time to desert. During the evening, he called at the residence of H. E. Hoke and declared his desire to escape from the army and remain in the North. Hoke, after being satisfied the man was being sincere, arranged to bring a suit of clothes and meet him the next morning in the first woods north of town along the Cumberland Valley Railroad. Early on July 2, Hoke met the soldier there and gave him the suit. The Rebel took off his uniform, handed Hoke his musket and accoutrements, and donned the civilian garb. He told Hoke that many in the army were disheartened because, while the South had put its entire manpower in the field, the soldiers had encountered so many able-bodied Pennsylvanians who could join the Federal forces that "few of their army had any hope of success." The deserter bade farewell to his benefactor, put his hand on top of a nearby fence, and sprang over, saying, "Farewell to Jeff Davis and the Southern Confederacy."[96]

Jeb Stuart's Attack on Carlisle

Just days after Albert Jenkins' Virginia cavalry and mounted infantry passed through Carlisle on their way to Mechanicsburg, the inhabitants of the Cumberland County seat soon faced a fresh Rebel threat. Jeb Stuart was again riding around the Federal army, this time not intentionally. He had broken camp on June 24 and taken three brigades of veteran cavalry, numbering more than

---

94 Eppa Hunton, *Autobiography of Eppa Hunton* (The William Byrd Press, 1933), 87.

95 Dr. William H. Boyle to Isaac McCauley, July 5, 1863, Gilder Lehrman Collection. www.gilderlehrman.org/content/civilian-describes-pillaging-near-gettysburg-1863. Accessed January 8, 2018.

96 Hoke, *Historical Reminiscences of the War*, 58.

5,000 men, eastward. He planned to turn to the north, cross the Potomac River while screening the right flank of Ewell's Second Corps, and then connect with Ewell somewhere near the Susquehanna River. However, when he found the northward-moving Union Second Corps blocking his intended path near Thoroughfare Gap, Stuart swung farther east, 50 miles from Lee's army. His column approached Rockville, Maryland, where he captured a lengthy Union supply train. Taking 125 loaded wagons in tow, his column turned northward, damaging the Baltimore & Ohio Railroad line at Cooksville. They lost almost a full day at Westminster, where they fought a small but time-consuming engagement on June 29.[97]

The next day, Stuart clashed for several hours with the Federal cavalry division of Brig. Gen. Judson Kilpatrick at Hanover, Pennsylvania, before withdrawing and heading toward the important industrial and railroad town of York. He expected to rendezvous there with Maj. Gen. Jubal Early's division of Ewell's corps but learned from civilians that Early had already left York after three days of occupation. Stuart instead headed for Dover in west-central York County, where he camped overnight. He resumed his northerly march on July 1— concurrent with the first day of the battle of Gettysburg—and sent Wade Hampton's brigade and the captured Union wagons to Dillsburg while taking the rest of the cavalry toward Carlisle.[98]

Stuart just missed intercepting a valuable prize. A CVRR repair train with tools, machinery, and twenty to thirty workmen had departed Harrisburg at 8:00 a.m. on the morning of July 1 to repair the road. The train returned to the capital that evening "with all on board in a high state of excitement," a reporter mentioned. The train had proceeded slowly and cautiously, while the work gang repaired slight injuries to the track as they advanced until they reached Mechanicsburg, nine miles west of Harrisburg. There, about 5:00 p.m., the train encountered a group of farmers and refugees, who informed the workers that enemy cavalry was approached from Dillsburg. They advised the railroaders to turn back and return to Harrisburg, which was quickly done. "The possession of a locomotive and rolling stock would be invaluable to the enemy," the reporter

97 For more on Stuart's march, see Eric J. Wittenberg and J. David Petruzzi, *Plenty of Blame to Go Around: Jeb Stuart's Controversial Ride to Gettysburg* (Savas Beatie, 2006).

98 See Scott Mingus, *Confederate Calamity: J.E.B. Stuart's Cavalry Ride Through York County, Pa.* (Amazon CreateSpace, 2015).

opined. He believed it would have given the Rebels a great resource to transport confiscated property up the Valley, "with the speed of steam," to the main army.[99]

Late that night, Stuart, finding that Maj. Gen. William F. "Baldy" Smith's militia guarded Carlisle, demanded their surrender. When Smith refused, Stuart ordered his horse artillery to shell the town. Although Ewell's infantrymen had already destroyed the CVRR tracks in Carlisle, during the bombardment the townhouse of President Frederick Watts became part of the battlefield. Watts and his family had already vacated their 20 East High Street residence, but Capt. Robert F. Clark and his company of the 28th Pennsylvania Volunteer Militia occupied the home during the cannonade. Anticipating a cavalry charge down the main thoroughfare, at the orders of Capt. C. P. F. West of Smith's staff, they felled Watts's shade trees, "to give us a fair chance to fire and to make an obstruction in the street." However, these precautions proved unnecessary. Word soon came that Lee had engaged the Army of the Potomac in battle at Gettysburg, and Stuart broke away and rode overnight toward that place.[100]

On the morning of July 2, Smith moved the 33rd Pennsylvania Volunteer Militia east of Carlisle, near Stuart's position from the previous night. From their new vantage point, Pvt. Joseph Boggs Beale described the calculated destruction of the Cumberland Valley Railroad line. "The rails were bent, the wood work burned & the masonry knocked down," he wrote home. In Lebanon that same day, a wagon train loaded with fresh produce arrived from the Cumberland Valley, seeking safety. "The farmers report that the enemy compelled them to grind corn and haul it to them," a newsman noted, "and plundered them extensively." He went on to say, "Some of the rolling stock of the Cumberland Valley Railroad is reported to be returning here."[101]

---

99 "Our Harrisburg Letter," *Philadelphia Inquirer*, July 4, 1863.

100 Robert F. Clark to Dear Sir, July 2, 1863, *Columbia Democrat and Bloomsburg General Advertiser*, July 18, 1863; Joseph F. Culver to My Dear Wife, October 19, 1863, Nashville, TN, Joseph F. Culver Civil War Letters, University of Iowa Libraries, Ames. Culver encountered Captain West on a train in Alabama in the fall of 1863. West told him that he "was in Carlisle at the time the Rebels were throwing shells into the town. He says that it was him who cut those fine shade trees down in front of Judge Hepburn's, Martin's [Farmer's] Hotel, and Judge Watts'."

101 Joseph Boggs Beale to Dear Pa, Ma, Aunty, Sisters & Brothers, July 3, 1863, Joseph Boggs Beale Papers, Historical Society of Pennsylvania; "The Philadelphia Blue Reserves in Action," *Philadelphia Public Ledger*, July 17, 1863; "From the Cumberland Valley," *New York Herald*, July 2, 1863, and *Baltimore Sun*, July 3, 1863.

Repairing the Railroad

With Stuart's withdrawal, the line running between Carlisle and Harrisburg was rapidly repaired, with "[l]arge numbers of men at work on the Cumberland Valley Railroad." According to A. J. Gerritson of the 28th Pennsylvania Volunteer Militia, a "train of cars came up from Harrisburg" and arrived in Carlisle as soon as July 2. It is not clear who or what was on that train, nor is it clear who was active in repairing the tracks. As of July 1, the tracks were still deemed unserviceable, because Brig. Gen. Joseph F. Knipe's brigade received orders to march on foot from Fort Washington to Carlisle. However, by the evening of July 3, the tracks were back and serviceable, the telegraph lines restored, and several freight cars arrived carrying supplies for Smith's men. Within several hours, the line was transporting Brig. Gen. Philip Schuyler Crooke's brigade of New York National Guardsmen, who arrived in Carlisle during the pre-dawn hours of July 4. There, Crooke eyed "the ruins of the barracks and the railroad bridge outside, destroyed by the rebels."[102]

In Shippensburg after the battle of Gettysburg, with reports that the Rebels were again coming their way, merchants packed up their goods and sent them via wagon or train to safety. "Our town in pandemonium; intense excitement," a resident scribbled in his diary on the evening of July 4, "our streets are filled with fleeing wagons, horses, cattle and negroes. Two trains of soldiers hurriedly passed up the road to Chambersburg. General Couch telegraphed, 'No Rebels this side of the Potomac river.'"[103]

Union Capt. Ulric Dahlgren, the dashing son of famed U. S. Navy Admiral John Dahlgren, led a squadron of cavalry on a reconnaissance west and south of Chambersburg on July 4, and, according to the reporter, "paid a flying visit to the town of Greencastle, on the Cumberland Valley road." They captured several Rebels there. It was Dahlgren's second visit to Greencastle in three days, having led ten men into town on the 2nd. Then, they had secreted themselves in the southeastern corner of the town square, not far from the railroad, hoping to intercept any Rebels that passed by. They fired on a small group of Rebels and took almost two dozen men, including two couriers, as prisoners. One of them carried a valise that contained, among other items, a message from Jefferson Davis

102 "Other Dispatches," *Hartford* (CT) *Courant*, July 6, 1863; "Editorial Correspondence," *Montrose Democrat*, July 9, 1863; OR 27:2, 224-225, 241-242.

103 "Effects of War News," *Shippensburg* (PA) *Chronicle*, July 17, 1913.

to Robert E. Lee, informing him that he would not be receiving any fresh troops to reinforce his army at Gettysburg. The captured message was rushed to General Meade for his reference.[104]

On July 4, Confederate cavalry under Brig. Gen. John D. Imboden escorted a 17-mile-long wagon train of wounded men west from Gettysburg toward the Cumberland Valley. They took the Pine Stump Road to Marion (six miles south of Chambersburg on the way to Greencastle). A few of them made a wrong turn and wound up in Chambersburg and were made prisoners. Some of the soldiers straggled from the main column in the driving rain and become lost, wandering from the road. According to George Myers, who lived near the railroad tracks at Marion, some of the weary teamsters tried to take short-cuts across the muddy fields. The wagon wheels cut into the soft mud up to their axles. "Some of the cavalrymen," he added, "having lost the road went along the railroad, jumping their tired horses over the cattle guards." The groans of the wounded men as they passed by could be heard all night long, and Myers' water pump was in constant use for water to "bathe the wounded [and] quench the thirst of the wretched inmates of the wagons…" Another group of wagons also made a wrong turn and wound up in Chambersburg, where they were captured.[105]

On July 6, with Imboden and the remaining wagons gone from Franklin County, Thomas R. Bard, the CVRR station agent who had fled Hagerstown when the Rebels arrived, took a train from Harrisburg to Carlisle. From there, he pumped a hand car to Scotland. With the bridge out, he walked along the tracks to Chambersburg, where he found the track had been torn up for five miles on either side of town. In addition, the railroad facilities lay in ruins.[106]

The following day, a CVRR train brought 160 Rebel prisoners down the Valley into Harrisburg. They had been out foraging when Union troops captured them. "Some of them will take the oath," the *Patriot and Union* believed, "but the majority will be sent east to camps for paroled prisoners. Their appearance was

---

104 "A Raid on Greencastle, the Enemy's Rear," *Philadelphia Inquirer*, July 6, 1863; "Captain Ulric Dahlgren and the famous 'Dahlgren Incident' in Greencastle, PA," web page, Allison-Antrim Museum, Greencastle, PA. www.greencastlemuseum.org/dahlgren-incident.html. Accessed February 1, 2018.

105 Hoke, *Reminiscences*, 88.

106 Baer, *1863 PRR Chronology*. Bard moved to California in 1864 and later became a U. S. senator. See William Henry Hutchinson, *Oil, Land, and Politics: The California Career of Thomas R. Bard*. 2 vols. (University of Oklahoma Press, 1965).

suggestive of hard times. A very curious crowd collected in front of the Marshal's office to make a close inspection of the piebald tatterdemalions."[107]

In the following days and weeks, army engineers continued their grueling work in the summer heat as they repaired large sections of the CVRR. There was a military motive in hastening the railroad's repair—some Union commanders hoped that the thousands of militiamen then assembled in Harrisburg could be hastened to the front to cut off Lee's retreat. While "Baldy" Smith's command trudged south from Carlisle over the South Mountain passes, slowed by a drenching rain storm, Couch hoped to speed the process by sending other units via the CVRR. He was hurried by an impatient President Lincoln, who personally wired Harrisburg to express his displeasure with the militia's slow pace. "Lee is now passing the Potomac faster than the forces you mention are passing Carlisle," Lincoln wrote. At their current rate, he sneered, the militia were "as likely to capture the 'man in the moon' as any part of Lee's army."[108]

Urged on by Lincoln's critiques, temporary repairs made under Col. Thomas A. Scott's personal direction gradually restored rail service. Regiments were regularly transported from Fort Washington to Carlisle, but beyond there, problems still lingered. Brigadier General Charles Yates's 5th and 12th New York State National Guard rode the CVRR to Carlisle on July 7, but had to march the remaining distance to Shippensburg. Later, they moved to Chambersburg.[109]

A report from Carlisle on July 8 mentioned, "The railroad bridge was finished yesterday. The Cumberland Valley Railroad is now open to Scotland creek bridge, this side of Chambersburg. Between these points, about three miles of the road is destroyed, and also about the same distance between Chambersburg and Hagerstown." He added, "It is believed that there is now no enemy in this State." At the same time, Brig. Gen. Herman Haupt's crews from the U. S. Military Railroad were busy in York County rebuilding more than a dozen bridges on the Northern Central Railway and Hanover Branch Railroad to allow the evacuation of more than 11,000 wounded soldiers from Gettysburg to military hospitals in York, Baltimore, Harrisburg, Philadelphia, and New York City.[110]

Also on July 8, Haupt decided to pay another personal visit to Cumberland and Franklin counties. He informed Secretary of War Stanton, "I am on my way to

---

107 "More Rebs," *Harrisburg Patriot and Union*, July 7, 1863.

108 *OR* 27:3, 612.

109 Ibid., 27:2, 230.

110 *Chicago Tribune*, July 9, 1863.

Harrisburg to open the Cumberland Valley Railroad, which is now very necessary for army operations." He also told Quartermaster General Montgomery C. Meigs, "I will return immediately to Harrisburg and pass through the line to Hagerstown as fast as possible to gain possession." He added some personal commentary, with a touch of braggadocio: "We should be able to capture as many prisoners and take wagons and ambulances and perhaps artillery before the enemy can cross the river. The late rains and bad roads will help us, but I do not believe we can prevent Lee's army from crossing. I could build trestle-bridges of round sticks and floor with fence rails. It is too much to assume the rebels cannot do the same."[111]

Urgent requests came in to Haupt soliciting his crews to rebuild the CVRR, but "as the Construction Corps had more on hand than could possibly be managed," Haupt contacted Col. Thomas A. Scott of the PRR and asked for his assistance. He wanted Scott to "take men from the shops under his control, until I could relieve a portion of my own forces from other duties. Colonel Scott promptly responded to this request and, for several days, superintended the work in person."[112]

Throughout early July 1863, militia regiments continued to filter into Harrisburg. Those soldiers who moved across the river to Fort Washington had ample opportunity to observe the destruction of the CVRR wrought by Confederates. "[T]he rebles [sic] tore up the track here and robbed the store houses," Arthur Martin of the 45th Pennsylvania Volunteer Militia wrote to his siblings.[113]

Finally, by Friday, July 10, rail service between Harrisburg and Shippensburg was effectively restored, with Scott's and Haupt's assistance. Work continued to the south at Chambersburg. The 47th Pennsylvania Volunteer Militia was among the first units to travel along the track, then repaired to within half a mile of Shippensburg. There, the men of the 47th were forced to disembark and march into town.[114]

Another train that same day brought the newly raised 51st Pennsylvania Volunteer Militia to Chambersburg. They left West Philadelphia at 6:00 p.m. and

---

111 Haupt, *Reminiscences*, 238.

112 Ibid., 276.

113 Arthur Martin to My dear brothers and sisters, July 9, 1863, Bond-Martin Papers, USAHEC.

114 Robert J. Forrest Diary, July 10-11, 1863, Box 7, Harrisburg Civil War Round Table Collection, USAHEC.

traveled through the night on a train to Harrisburg, arriving at four o'clock on Saturday morning, July 11. After a three-hour layover the soldiers transferred to a CVRR train, crossed the Susquehanna to Bridgeport, and made it to Shippensburg without incident—but hit an unscheduled three-hour delay. "And we must say here," a militiaman recalled with appreciation, "that we received from the people of that place much kindness in food and drink." Their appetites sated during their detention, they finally reboarded the train and left at 2:00 p.m. for Chambersburg, which was reached at 4:30 p.m. They had been on the road almost a 24 hours since leaving Philadelphia. The men camped a mile north of the town.[115]

On July 13, the indefatigable Governor Curtin arrived in Shippensburg on his way to Hagerstown to be at the front. That same day, the 26th Pennsylvania Volunteer Militia left Fort Washington and took the CVRR, destined to join a force of state militia massing in an attempt to cut off Lee's escape. Traveling along the newly repaired tracks from Bridgeport to Shippensburg, an enlisted man described the view: "Mechanicsburg was the first place we came to of any importance it is a real pretty place at least as much of it as could be seen from the cars." He went on to say, "The Cumberland valley is a magnificent piece of country—The farms are of the very best kind, the land all level or slightly rolling and the crops in fine condition—hardly any of the grain has been harvested—We passed thro Carlisle which was a much handsomer town than I expected to see— It is really a beautiful place—We saw traces of the rebels along the road at several places, but the Farms were very little impaired—not nearly so much as there in the vicinity of Harrisburg, by our troops."[116]

According to another militiaman, as of July 13 the railroad had only been repaired a short distance beyond Shippensburg, so he and his comrades disembarked there. Finished with the repairs to the Northern Central and Hanover Branch, General Haupt had the previous day sent 180 men with four wagons of equipment from Gettysburg some 25 miles west across South Mountain to Chambersburg. They soon began working southward on the Franklin Railroad. Progress was slowed by continual rain showers. "We have a sweet time reconstructing the Hagerstown road," Haupt later reported. "Rain or drizzle all the time; men work but accomplish very little[.]" He obtained the use of a steam-driven sawmill to facilitate the process. It ran day and night.[117]

115 "Second Coal Regiment, Fifty-First P. V. M.," *Philadelphia Inquirer*, August 4, 1863.

116 Shriver to Frederick Augustus Shriver, July 13, 1863, Shriver Family Papers, MDHS.

117 Pennypacker Anonymous Correspondence, July 20; Haupt, *Reminiscences*, 240, 243.

One of the issues was replacing the thousands of ties that Pickett's men had burned. That same Monday, July 13, was "a cloudy rainy day" with "heavy showers," according to Guilford Township farmer Amos Stouffer. "They are busy working on the rail road. Brigadier Gen. Haupt came here to day and pressed our teams to haul slabs and some joists from the saw mill. They must have the road done in two days. He says it is torn up or 8 or 10 miles." The following day, young Stouffer noted, "We are all working in the saw mill getting out slabs and sawing railroad ties. Henry Ryder's team is hauling too. There are a great many reports from the front. The rebs are crossing their [supply] trains and plunder [across the Potomac River] as fast as they can. Most likely Lee will get his army over yet, though people think his annihilation or capture [is] certain."[118]

Haupt also requisitioned 400 tons of fresh iron from the Cambria Iron Company of Johnstown to replace the rails. In the meantime, he set about reusing the ones ruined by the Rebels. His men used the saw mill to straighten the rails bent by the Rebels. Three-fourths of them appeared salvageable. Draft horses were now scarce in the region following the Rebel acquisitions, so Haupt resorted to sending a USMRR train from Alexandria, Virginia, north via the B&O and Northern Central. The cargo included 25 pairs of oxen, along with the requisite yokes and harness, as well as drivers and attendants. The work stopped, however, on the 15th when Haupt received orders from Quartermaster General Montgomery C. Meigs to return to Alexandria and send the replacement T-iron back to the Cambria Iron Works. Lee's army and the Federal Army of the Potomac had retired to Northern Virginia, and supplies would henceforth be sent on the Federally-controlled railroads in that region.[119]

On July 15, Haupt paid a personal visit to the civilians who were helping to resupply the railroad. They included Amos Stouffer, who recorded, "Gen. Haupt came this morning to tell us that we need not saw any more railroad stuff as the Rebs are all across the river and the road will be left as he and his men are ordered to Alexandria."[120]

Haupt's sudden withdrawal from the Cumberland Valley left Judge Watts and the CVRR/FRR with the task of finishing the job. Still recovering from the

---

118 Amos Stouffer diary entries for July 13 and 14, 1863, Valley of the Shadow website, UVA. http://valley.lib.virginia.edu/papers/FD5500. Accessed February 3, 2018.

119 Westhaeffer, *History of the CVRR*, 82-83.

120 Amos Stouffer diary entry for July 15, 1863, Valley of the Shadow website, UVA. http://valley.lib.virginia.edu/papers/FD5500. Accessed February 3, 2018.

damages incurred during Stuart's raid the previous autumn, now the CVRR faced more than $53,000 in temporary repairs to resume full operations to Hagerstown. Five miles of the Franklin Railroad line were gone, as was an equal amount of CVRR trackage. The water station at Greencastle was in ruins, as were other buildings on the FRR. The largest expenditure, $34,000, was to rebuild the Scotland bridge permanently. It would take $7,000 to rebuild the buildings and machine shops at Chambersburg and another $10,000 to lay new T-iron and white oak sills to restore the road. The railroad filed a claim with the U. S. government, but only received $23,800 in compensation for the losses, with the authorities countering that Haupt had expended $24,000 himself for repairs. Watts argued that the USMRR repairs had only been temporary and insufficient for regular railroad traffic. Likewise, net damage to the subsidiary Franklin Railroad had been $15,000, of which the government only paid a little more than a thousand dollars.[121]

A disconcerted Judge Watts wanted more attention and consideration from Washington. While the U. S. Military Railroad had constructed a temporary bridge at Carlisle at government expense, the other losses along the line were "destroyed because it was in the service of the country, and rendering a service, too, so essential to its protection and safety," he wrote in his annual report. "Justice would seem to require, that the Government should replace that which was lost in its service and on its account." However, he rued, "With the Government it is extremely difficult to attain the settlement of any amount." Some of the Federal agents appeared unwilling to cooperate. "We have not yet complained," he warned, "but patience, even by a Company, may be exhausted."[122]

On July 20, the first passenger train left Harrisburg at 4:00 p.m., bound for Chambersburg. That same day, Governor Curtin left for Philadelphia and General Couch returned to his temporary headquarters in Chambersburg. The War Department relieved General Knipe from duty and sent him to Washington to await further orders. "The cars have resumed their regular trips" through Shippensburg, its unknown diarist recorded. Three days later, "the first regular freight train for Chambersburg to-day" passed through Shippensburg. Unfounded rumors the next day that the Rebels were coming back caused great concern until they were disproved. For the next few days, several trains with

121 CVRR Files, FCHS; *Twenty-Ninth Annual Report of the Cumberland Valley Railroad Company, to the Stockholders, Made October 1, 1863* (The Herald Office, 1863), 5-7.

122 Ibid.

infantry and cavalry chugged through through Shippensburg headed for Harrisburg.[123]

The CVRR Begins to Recover

While permanent repairs proceeded over the summer and early autumn, the CVRR slowly returned to normalcy. On Saturday morning, August 1, a massive train of 200 passenger and freight cars, with three locomotives providing the motive power, went up the Cumberland Valley Railroad to Chambersburg to pick up emergency militiamen whose term of service was over, now that Robert E. Lee and the Army of Northern Virginia was long gone from Pennsylvania soil. The last regiment of emergency men departed Chambersburg that afternoon.[124]

Occasionally, the military sent special trains back and forth on the Cumberland Valley Railroad. Their mission was not always evident to the populace. "A passenger car and engine passed through at a furious rate of speed," a Shippensburg man penned in his diary on the evening of August 10. No one could determine the need for such excessive haste, because all the other trains that summer passed through town at a normal rate of speed.[125]

Needing far more troops for the war effort, the U. S. Congress in March had passed the Enrollment Act, which paved the way for the first major military draft in the country's history. Men in the North between the ages of 20 and 45 were eligible to be drafted to fulfill specific quotas established for each congressional district. As the summer progressed and the draft began, protest riots occurred in New York City, necessitating the need to send Federal troops to restore order. The Federal government contracted with the railroads to take the draftees to the nearest place of rendezvous. In Cumberland County, farmer Jesse O'Hara of West Pennsboro Township received a draft notice on August 20 instructing him to report to Carlisle on or before September 22. He was to present the document to the CVRR agent at Alterton Station for free transportation to Carlisle, where he was to report to army officials to begin his three-year term of service. If he did not

123 "Mr. C. N. Graffun's Despatch," *New York Herald*, July 26, 1863; "Effects of War News," *Shippensburg* (PA) *Chronicle*, July 3, 1913.

124 "Another Long Train," *Harrisburg Evening Telegraph*, August 3, 1863.

125 "Effects of War News," *Shippensburg* (PA) *Chronicle*, July 10, 1913.

FORM 39.

Provost Marshal's Office,

15th District, State of Pennsylvania

Carlisle Aug 26th 1863

To *Jesse O'hara*

West Pennsboro Twp

SIR:

You are hereby notified that you were, on the *14th* day of *August*, 1863, legally drafted in the service of the United States for the period of *Three years*, in accordance with the provisions of the act of Congress, "for enrolling and calling out the national forces, and for other purposes," approved March 3, 1863. You will accordingly report, on or before the *22nd of September 1863*, at the place of rendezvous, in *Carlisle Penna*, or be deemed a deserter, and be subject to the penalty prescribed therefor by the Rules and Articles of War.

Transportation will be furnished you on presenting this notification at *Alterton Penna*, on the *Cumberland Valley R Road*, or at the station nearest your place of residence.

R M Henderson

Capt. & Provost Marshal,

15th Dist. of Penna

Jos M Patton Deputy

This August 1863 draft notice assures recipient Jesse O'Hara that "[t]ransportation will be furnished you on presenting this notification" at the nearest CVRR station. O'Hara resided in West Pennsboro township, Cumberland County. *Cumberland County Historical Society*

show up by the appointed time, he would "be deemed a deserter, and be subject to the penalty prescribed therefor by the Rules and Articles of War."[126]

Advertisements cropped up in the Valley's papers for social excursions, including trains that left Newville on September 28, 29, and 30 to take sightseers to Philadelphia for the day. The special fare was $4.55 each way. Similar notices appeared in other papers along the line. For those heading south to Chambersburg or Hagerstown, the view of the cars was disconcerting. "The destruction made by the rebel invaders is to be seen all along the road, after you leave Carlisle," observed the Pennsylvania state school superintendent as he headed to Chambersburg in November to attend the Franklin County Teachers' Institute. The Cumberland was "one of the finest valleys in the state," he wrote, "and is remarkably rich in agricultural products. . . . These fertile plains were covered with growing grain, or fed large herds of cattle, and the rebel army needed both. Noble horses were to be found in abundance, and the rebel cavalry could not do well without them; hence the raid along the line of the Cumberland Valley rail road."[127]

In mid-November, scores of Cumberland Valley residents traveled to Gettysburg to attend the dedication of the new Soldiers National Cemetery on a small portion of the battlefield. There, on November 19, overlooking more than 3,500 fresh graves on Cemetery Hill, famed orator Edward Everett spoke for more than two hours as the featured speaker. President Lincoln, invited to give a few dedicatory remarks, then delivered a two-minute speech that has come down in history as the Gettysburg Address. The throng included Guilford County farmer Amos Stouffer, who traveled in a two-horse buggy with four kinsmen and friends to be at the ceremonies. "A very fine fall day," he penned in his diary. "The day opened with the booming of cannon. Abe Lincoln, Gov. Curtin, Gov. Seymour, Gov. Todd, Gov. Brough, Maj. Gen Schneck, Maj. Gen Couch, Gen. Stoneman & several other Maj. Gens. were there and about a doz. Brigadier Gens. Shook hands with Old Abe & Curtin. Everet[t] delivered the oration. The dead of the different states are all kept separate. It was a grand affair. About 30,000 people here. We came home in the evening."[128]

126 Files of the Cumberland County Historical Society. The Alterton station was eight miles west of Carlisle on the east side of what is now Kerrsville Road. John and David Alter had established the stop in 1839.

127 "Excursion Tickets," *Newville Star and Enterprise*, September 24, 1863; *Pennsylvania School Journal* (Lancaster, PA), vol. XII, no. 7, January 1864, 205.

128 Amos Stouffer diary entry for November 19, 1863, Valley of the Shadow website, UVA. http://valley.lib.virginia.edu/papers/FD5500. Accessed February 3, 2018.

"Yesterday was a great day at Gettysburg," editor A. K. Rheem of the *Carlisle Herald* simply remarked. "Thousands upon thousands were there." He spent far more time on an item of greater local interest: the state government had authorized the formation of a special three-man board of appraisers "to investigate the claims for damages in Fulton and Franklin counties, occasioned by Stuart's [October 1862] raid." That was "all right and proper," but Rheem reminded his readers that the people of Cumberland and Adams counties had suffered as much, or more, during the past summer's "depradations" and "are certainly entitled to compensation... If the citizens of Franklin and Fulton counties are entitled to indemnity, so also are the people of Cumberland and Adams. We trust the next Legislature will take immediate action on the subject."[129]

As the year ended, the frustration in Carlisle and Gettysburg over compensation continued, while in Chambersburg, residents who had lost horses or property to Stuart's cavaliers eagerly followed the news to learn the particulars of the proposed claims process. They could not know that the lingering bitterness over Stuart's raid would soon give way to a deeper grief over their beloved town's fate.

---

129 "Military Claims," *Carlisle Weekly Herald*, November 20, 1863.

Chapter 6

1864: The Rebels' Revenge

With the advent of the new year, the Cumberland Valley Railroad and its partner Franklin Railroad announced a new and higher fare structure. It now cost $2.45 to ride from Hagerstown all the way through the Cumberland Valley to Harrisburg, reported Superintendent O. N. Lull. Almost 12,000 people had purchased tickets in Hagerstown the previous year. For riders embarking at Chambersburg (27,500 the previous year), it would be $1.70 to the state capital. The company charged an additional ten cents for those passengers who got on board at stops without a depot or ticket office and needed to purchase their tickets on board from the conductor. The goal was to match revenues to the railroad's recent higher expenses to maintain profitability. Skilled labor rates had increased as an inducement to keep mechanics and other vital employees from joining the army or taking positions with other companies or industries. In addition, there was the towering $53,000 in costs to repair the damage the Rebels had inflicted in their July operations against the railroad. On the plus side of the ledger, the Franklin RR/CVRR had transported 34,305 soldiers northward and 32,252 southward. Freight tonnage, a good amount related to the military, exceeded 30 million pounds.[1]

---

1 "The Franklin Railroad," *Pittsburgh Daily Commercial*, February 15, 1864; "Cumberland Valley Railroad," *Carlisle Weekly Herald*, January 8, 1864.

"The Cumberland Valley Railroad is perhaps the most carefully and economically managed road in the State," the *Carlisle Weekly Herald* declared in mid-January. "We believe that since it was relaid there has not been a single fatal accident on the road to a single passenger, excepting only the collision when the Corn Exchange regiment was being transported, and when the road was in the hands of the military employees. Had it been under the immediate management of the Superintendent, Col. O. N. Lull, we hazard little in saying that no such accident would have happened." The editor also had kind words for the railroad's guiding executive and visionary: "Judge Watts has been the President for many years, and has administered its affairs with great skill and success." The majority of the board of directors returned for another term, including Watts, Col. Thomas A. Scott, Pennsylvania Railroad President J. Edgar Thomson, and Thomas B. Kennedy. Prominent Philadelphia financier Edward M. Biddle, Judge Watts' brother-in-law, continued effectively in his role as secretary and treasurer.[2]

Not everyone shared the *Weekly Herald's* rosy view of the CVRR. Reacting to an article in the *Shippensburg News* that the railroad company was selecting a site in that town to erect a suitable building as a ticket office and reception room, the *Greencastle Pilot*, with more than a touch of jealousy and anger, railed against the CVRR. It reminded its readers that Jenkins' Rebels had burned the water house in their town, and no one was doing anything to replace it. At the same time the water house had been torched, the sawmill belonging to the railroad's sawyer had burned. "The sawyer is a poor man," the *Pilot's* editor complained, "and can but illy bear the loss, which is over $100. With the littleness of soul, which had always characterized the Cumberland Valley [Railroad] Company in its operations at this end of the road, no attempt had been made by this company to furnish the sawyer with another apparatus. We suppose there is not another railroad company in the country, that would not have been more generous to its employees."[3]

While the CVRR worked to recover its profitability and restore its reputation, the citizens of the Cumberland Valley who had been victimized by the Rebels and/or the Pennsylvania state militia during the past two years continued to try to get compensation. During state legislature's winter session, J. McDowell Sharpe, who, along with A. K. McClure represented Perry and Franklin counties, introduced a bill to indemnify the citizens of the border counties for their losses.

2 "Cumberland Valley Railroad," *Carlisle Weekly Herald*, January 15, 1864. The highly capable Biddle served as the CVRR's treasurer for more than 50 years.

3 "Railroad Matters," *Greencastle Pilot*, January 19, 1864.

Sharpe, and others who supported the proposed act, used "every legitimate argument" to secure its passage, according to a reporter. "But the Republican party holding a majority in both branches of the legislature fought the measure with a vindictiveness that seemed more akin to personal animosity against our people than fair and manly opposition. Every parliamentary trick was resorted to for the purpose of embarrassing the passage of the bill. The result is too well known to require further exposition."[4]

In March, another old topic—connecting the railroad to resources outside of the Cumberland Valley—returned, with a new twist. In the 1850s, the goal has been to construct a line across the mountains from Chambersburg to Pittsburgh. Now, it was a shorter, more practical objective, connecting the CVRR with the Connellsville Railroad and the extensive Broad Top bituminous coal fields in Bedford, Fulton, and Huntingdon counties to the west. Separate groups from New York and Pittsburgh, as well as the local Southern Pennsylvania Railroad Company, were contemplating such an undertaking, but with competing interests and plans. One of the proposed routes was from Greencastle through Cowan's Gap. Others wanted the line to connect in Chambersburg. "We fear that the enterprise must fail unless there can be some concentration of our energies and capital," a Chambersburg newsman reported. He insisted, "The Cumberland Valley must get direct communication with Broad Top at an early day. It has become a necessity; and the growing trade of the country clearly points to another great Pathway to the West through this region. The Southern counties should lose no time in making common cause in this important movement, and secure the priceless advantages it offers us."[5]

While war raged in northern Virginia, memories of the various Rebel incursions into the Cumberland Valley the previous two years remained fresh, even as the citizens and local businessmen tried to resume their normal routines. In Carlisle, F. Gardner & Company, operating a door and sash factory, took out several advertisements in the *Herald* throughout the winter and spring notifying the public, "We are also prepared, as heretofore, to build and repair burden cars for transportation on the railroad, with promptness and reasonable terms."[6]

The firm of Weaver & Bricker announced the recent acquisition of the Carlisle Forge from its previous owner, Jacob Goodyear. "We have commenced

---

4 "The Fate of the Chambersburg Relief Bill," *Valley Spirit*, August 31, 1864.

5 "Our Railroad Connection," *Franklin Repository*, March 23, 1864.

6 "Carlisle Foundry," *Carlisle Weekly Herald*, March 4, 1864.

the manufacture and will keep constantly on hand all sizes of the best quality of bar iron," they advertised. "We will give prompt attention to all orders, whether from a distance or at hours." The company needed a steady supply of raw materials for the facility on Boiling Springs and Yellow Breeches Creek some four-and-a-half miles southeast of Carlisle. "The highest cash prices paid for old wrought iron scraps, delivered at the Forge, at the railroad bridge, in Carlisle," the new owners added. Scrap iron, particularly in the wake of General Rodes' systematic destruction of the railroad tracks the previous summer, was still plentiful in the region.[7]

A group of investors in the Cumberland Valley were planning to develop a new railroad to bring iron products from the blast furnaces near Mont Alto in southern Franklin County to a planned connection with the Cumberland Valley Railroad at an undetermined point to the north near Scotland. Incorporated on May 3 as the Scotland and Mont Alto Railroad Company, the new enterprise planned to raise $500,000 in capital through the sale of stock. It had to be started within five years and completed within ten. However, the line would not be constructed and opened until October 1872. By then, the terminus had been changed from Scotland to outside of Chambersburg and the company had changed its name to the Mont Alto Railroad.[8]

In wartime, however, commercial projects were overshadowed by the progress of the armies. In early May, the powerful Union Army of the Potomac, accompanied in person by General-in-chief Ulysses S. Grant, stubbornly pushed south toward Richmond in what became popularly known as the Overland Campaign. Unlike past battles in Northern Virginia which his predecessors had lost or failed to follow through on early gains, Grant was determined to keep driving, no matter the cost. He wanted to force Robert E. Lee into a prolonged war of attrition that the South could ill afford, not being able to readily replenish its battlefield losses. Fighting raged in the Wilderness and later at Spotsylvania Courthouse, where tens of thousands of soldiers fell in the twin battles. A few weeks later, veteran employees of the CVRR learned that one of their former colleagues based in Chambersburg was numbered among the dead. "Mr. John Buxton, of the 7th Maryland Regiment, Infantry, was among the killed in the eight days' fight in the Wilderness," A. K. McClure's *Franklin Repository* reported. "He

7 "Carlisle Forge," *Carlisle Weekly Herald*, May 13, 1864.

8 *Laws of the Commonwealth of Pennsylvania Passed at the Session of 1864, in the Eighty-eighth Year of Independence* (Singerly & Myers, 1864), 730. For more on the proposed railroad spur, see Thomas T. Traber, III, *Railroads of Pennsylvania Encyclopedia and Atlas* (s. n., 1987).

was from Hagerstown. For many years he resided in this place, and for a long time was a Baggage Master on the Cumberland Valley Railroad."[9]

As the spring of 1864 ripened into summer, war news dominated the papers in the Cumberland Valley. In the west, Maj. Gen. William T. Sherman's Union armies were pushing southward from Tennessee through northern Georgia, aiming at the vital railroad town of Atlanta. In northern Virginia, General Grant, undeterred by massive casualties at the Wilderness and Spotsylvania Courthouse in May, continued to sidestep Lee and force the Rebels to withdraw ever closer to Richmond. German-born Maj. Gen. Franz Sigel moved southward up the Shenandoah Valley, hoping to take the railroad center at Lynchburg. Intercepted on May 15 at New Market by 4,000 Confederates, including much of the student body of the Virginia Military Institute, Sigel withdrew to Strasburg. His abject failure cost him his command, and Maj. Gen. David Hunter replaced the politically-connected but militarily-challenged Sigel.

In mid-June, the CVRR again temporarily replaced war news in the headlines when it suffered a rare accident—something it was not known for, the 1862 Bridgeport disaster notwithstanding. "On Thursday last a collision occurred on the Cumberland Valley Railroad," the *Franklin Repository* informed its readership, "near Alterton, between the Accommodation Passenger Train going down and the Freight Train coming in this direction. Several cars were considerably damaged, and the Baggage-Master, Engineer, Fireman and one or two others were badly, though not dangerously injured on the passenger train."[10]

The Burning of Chambersburg

To the south, in the Shenandoah Valley of Virginia, the war raged on with a new fury. Union Maj. Gen. David Hunter, a native Virginian, was proving to be one of the South's worst enemies. On June 11, 1864, Hunter reached Lexington, Virginia, where he burned the famed Virginia Military Institute, as well torching as the home of the commonwealth's former governor, John Letcher, and a few other private residences. To relieve the "breadbasket of the Confederacy," Lee dispatched Lt. Gen. Jubal A. Early and his Confederate Second Corps. Early, an

9 "Mr. John Buxton," *Franklin Repository*, June 8, 1864. McClure purchased the paper in 1863 and infused his Republican and pro-Lincoln beliefs.

10 "Collision," *Franklin Repository*, June 22, 1864.

irascible and unabashed Southerner, quickly put Union forces on the retreat, and began moving north toward Maryland.[11]

As Early garnered headlines with his march, in south-central Pennsylvania, Governor Curtin, General Couch, and the senior officers of the CVRR took several precautionary steps to protect the railroad. As during the Gettysburg Campaign, the Department of the Susquehanna again dispatched the Patapsco Guards from the York U. S. Army Hospital to the Cumberland Valley. The 60 or so Marylanders traveled on the Northern Central to Harrisburg and then took a train to Chambersburg, where Capt. Thomas McGowan took charge of the small garrison there. He brought with him a field piece and crew from Battery A, 1st New York Light Artillery.[12]

On the morning of July 6, when Brig. Gen. John McCausland and his Confederate cavalrymen rode into Hagerstown, things started looking ominous for the CVRR. The 26-year-old VMI graduate demanded that the town councilmen provide $20,000 in cash, as well as 1,500 suits, shoes, shirts, and pantaloons for their "Southern brethren" within three hours. If not, he would burn the town. After some intense negotiations, the red-bearded general agreed to spare the town from the torch in exchange for the cash and whatever clothing could quickly be collected. After loading wagons with barrels of wheat, 400 cavalry saddles, and other equipment and articles, the horsemen departed at 1:00 a.m. for Boonsboro.[13]

Other Rebel bands continued to roam Maryland over the next few days. Some of them did not honor McCausland's previous agreement not to burn Hagerstown or private property. On July 7, about 180 men of the 23rd Virginia Cavalry rode into town and began looting any stores with goods left after McCausland's visit. When informed of the agreement, their commander, Capt. Thomas S. Davis, ordered the thievery stopped and they rode off. Not long afterward, another band, looking rougher and more menacing, arrived. They planned to burn a pair of warehouses, but agreed not to do so when given $500 in cash and a $1,000 promissory note signed by Hagerstown's leading citizens. However, the Rebels forced the townspeople to burn the contents of the two storage facilities. The

11 Alexander, *When War Passed This Way*, 94-95.

12 Daniel Carroll Toomey, *The Patapsco Guards: Independent Company of Maryland Volunteer Infantry* (Toomey Press, 1993), 14.

13 Joseph V. Collins, *Battle of West Frederick, July 7, 1864: Prelude to Battle of Monocacy* (Xlibris Corporation, 2011), 136-39.

irregulars also torched several bales of hay and, to the local railroad officials' dismay, the engine house. A detachment of the 6th U. S. Cavalry suddenly rode into town, scattering the Rebels before they could do any more mischief.[14]

After two successive years of invasions and damage, the railroad was now better prepared to handle Rebel raids, particularly when they received adequate warning. On July 11, 1864, Early's men reached the outskirts of Washington, sending a clear message that Confederate armies still posed a threat to Northern border communities. That same day, Maj. John S. Schultze, the assistant adjutant general of the Department of the Susquehanna, notified all telegraph stations on the CVRR that Early's Confederates were making demonstrations on Baltimore and Washington, at the same time casting doubt on rumors of another incursion into Pennsylvania. Nevertheless, in mid-July, the CVRR moved its shop machinery onto rail cars for safekeeping.[15]

With the rumors of another Rebel invasion, many of the remaining black residents of the Cumberland Valley fled northward, often by rail. Almost four decades later, a Newville resident recalled that, "Methinks we can still hear the whistle of some of these engines drawing their living freight of soldiers up and down the valley, and also those who were trying to get away from the rebels. We suppose we all remember the July of 1864, when a train of open cars arrived at this place, literally alive with colored people, and which was placed on the siding here and remained from Saturday until the next Thursday, and upon one of the cars, in the hot sun, two infants were born: also during the same month we were surprised one morning to find the wood house, at the depot, occupied by some soldiers who mysteriously arrived during the night, and all thought they were rebels, but they turned out to be union soldiers."[16]

A reporter echoed the plight of the numerous black refugees who streamed into Harrisburg on incoming CVRR trains. "The rolling stock of the Cumberland Valley Railroad is being removed to this point. Large numbers of fugitive colored people accompany this stock, and present a most deplorable condition as they are huddled on the hot side walks around the railroad depot."[17]

---

14 Ibid., 140-41.

15 "Latest Telegraphic News!" *Valley Spirit*, July 13, 1864; Westhaeffer, *History of the CVRR*, 83.

16 "More Reminiscences," *Newville Star and Enterprise*, November 20, 1901.

17 *Baltimore Sun*, August 1, 1864, citing a conversation in Harrisburg with a Chambersburg newsman who had arrived on the morning train.

Meanwhile, General Early had continued his practice of levying ransoms on Yankee towns, including Frederick, Middletown, and Hagerstown in early July. He ordered Brig. Gen. John McCausland and his 2,800 mounted men to cross the Mason-Dixon Line and ride to Chambersburg, where they were to demand "100,000 in gold; or in lieu thereof 500,000 in greenbacks," as "retaliation of the depredations committed by Major-General Hunter[.]" If the residents did not comply, McCausland should warn them that their town would be laid to ashes within three hours. Early expected them to capitulate, as had other communities, including York, Pennsylvania, the previous summer when he had demanded $100,000 in cash, more than a thousand shoes and boots, and three days of supplies and food for his men.[18]

McCausland, a Missouri-born former mathematics professor known to his men as "Tiger John," soon set out with his own brigade and that of Brig. Gen. Bradley T. Johnson, as well as two batteries of horse artillery. Johnson, a native Marylander and an 1849 graduate of Princeton, was no stranger to raids into enemy territory, having earlier that month led a daring raid on the lines near Baltimore that resulted in the destruction of several key railroad bridges. Midday on Friday, July 29, W. Blair Gilmore received a message at the Atlantic and Ohio Telegraph office at Chambersburg, confirming that Rebel cavalry had crossed the Potomac at McCoy's Ford. At least one detachment reportedly had headed through Clear Spring to Mercersburg, with the apparent intention of riding into Chambersburg. As the frightening news spread through Chambersburg, townspeople reacted with "indescribable confusion, such as had occurred several times previously during the war," merchant Jacob Hoke recounted.[19]

By now, the residents had plenty of experience—most of it bad—in dealing with the Confederate visitors. The merchants and other businessmen feverishly began preparations to hide their valuables or remove them to safety. Most chose to take them into their basements or store them in outbuildings away from their main places of business. Hoke remembered a warning from a friend that the next time the Rebels came calling, it would be to plunder and burn, and that he should get everything that he could out of town. Accordingly, he ran to the CVRR depot on the north side of Chambersburg to secure transportation for the inventory of

18 Orders of Jubal Early, quoted in, Edward L. Ayers, *The Thin Light of Freedom* (W.W. Norton, 2017), 204.

19 *Hoke, Historical Reminiscences of the War*, 110; OR 19, 353-54. Small patrols of Rebels also crossed the Potomac at Cherry Run and Back Creek near Williamsport, but the main body used McCoy's Ford.

his store. He learned from freight forwarder Oaks & Linn that they had one empty car that he could use. Hoke made the necessary arrangements and hastily packed as much of his stock of merchandise into what boxes he could find. Fortunately, he had sent a considerable part of his inventory to Philadelphia a few weeks previously upon the last rumors of approaching Rebels. He loaded everything in a wagon and sent it to the warehouse, where an Oaks & Linn conductor supervised the loading process onto the burden car. Hoke hid the remainder of his merchandise—mostly hosiery, gloves, and other small articles—in the beer vault under a neighboring business's outbuilding. Other people soon put their items in the vault and it was walled in.[20]

That evening, in a scene that recalled Milroy's wagons racing through town the previous year, fifty or more supply wagons from Brig. Gen. George Crook's command passed through Chambersburg and headed down the Valley toward Harrisburg. Behind them came "large numbers of straggling and demoralized soldiers—infantry and cavalry—from the same command," all intent on reaching safety before the Rebels could catch them. Hoke estimated the throng as a thousand or more men, "weary, hungry and greatly demoralized." He and his family took several of them into their home and fed them.[21]

Late at night, a train passed through Chambersburg on its way to Harrisburg. With long-time engineer Jacob Sweitzer at the controls of the locomotive, the cars were returning from Hagerstown. Earlier in the day, the train had passed through Chambersburg heading the other way, carrying a New York regiment. It had arrived in Hagerstown at 7:30 p.m. and the soldiers disembarked and marched away. The conductor, Jacob H. Fosnot, received orders from the CVRR superintendent, Col. O. N. Lull in Chambersburg, to collect all of the cars in Hagerstown and leave for Chambersburg at once, with reports of Rebels between Williamsport and Hagerstown. A few army officers refused to allow Fosnot to take several cars there on the siding that were loaded with forage, commissary stores, and other military supplies. Fosnot, a CVRR employee less than a year, quickly wired Lull with the news of the officers' refusal. Soon, he received a reply to leave at once with what cars he could.

Fosnot, Sweitzer, fireman P. Zeigler, and brakeman Andrew Stepler quickly hooked all the rest of the cars they could find onto the train and, about 9:00 p.m., it

---

20 Ibid.

21 Ibid., 110-11. Crook crossed the Potomac River at Williamsport on July 26. He was part of Maj. Gen. David Hunter's command.

slowly began chugging from Franklin Street out of town. Just then, fifteen to twenty Rebels rode up to the passenger depot. Spotting the slow-moving train heading up a heavy grade, they started after it. Fosnot was standing on the platform of one of the cars near the end of the train, ready to uncouple the last four or five cars in an attempt to impede the oncoming enemy riders. Fortunately for he and the crew, the cattle guard at the engine house arrested the Confederates' pursuit and the train headed off to Chambersburg. The Rebels, frustrated that they could not catch the train, rode back to the railyard and burned all the cars left at the Hagerstown siding, including the ones the army officers had refused to allow to be coupled to the train. Meanwhile, Sweitzer, glad to be out of Hagerstown with his train and crew, highballed it through the night to Harrisburg.[22]

Preparations were being made that same day, July 29, all along the line of the Cumberland Valley Railroad. The local agent of the Adams Express Company in Harrisburg refused to accept any freight for shipment anywhere south of Chambersburg, and to that point only at the risk of the shipper. The CVRR only ran their trains to Carlisle, and evacuated almost everything from Chambersburg. Where the Rebels were ultimately headed was anyone's guess. A *Philadelphia Bulletin* correspondent in Harrisburg speculated that "in official circles here it is believed that it is their intention to go to Bedford county and the mountains adjacent, a sort of general rendezvous." No one in the state capital knew Jubal Early's real reason for sending John McCausland and Bradley Johnson into the Cumberland Valley. However, the newsman noted, "the most experienced men at this post are now convinced that the invasion of the State is by a large force, composed of some of the best troops of General Lee's army." Major General Darius N. Couch, commander of the Department of the Susquehanna, withdrew from Chambersburg to Carlisle, after ordering the removal of all military supplies and his headquarters papers. Colonel Thomas Scott took a train to Bedford, where he met with Governor Curtin to discuss the situation. The two of them then returned to Harrisburg. Trouble loomed late that night when the telegraph lines south of Chambersburg stopped working. The Rebels were at hand.[23]

---

22 Ibid., 111. Fosnot joined the CVRR in July 1863 as a freight brakeman and worked his way up the ladder. "Captain" Fosnot, as he was affectionately known during his 50+ years on the line, died at home in Chambersburg in 1918. His son George worked for many years as the chief clerk in the office of the Master Mechanic of the CVRR (obituary in the *Waynesboro Record*, April 3, 1918).

23 "Invasion of Pennsylvania," *Alexandria (VA) Gazette*, July 30, 1864, citing the *Philadelphia Bulletin*; "The Harrisburg Telegrams," *New York Herald*, July 31, 1864.

About 3:00 a.m., Lt. Hancock T. McClean and 45 men of the 6th U. S. Cavalry from the Carlisle Barracks, joined by Captain McGowan and 35 soldiers from the Patapsco Guards and the lone New York cannon, took up position on a hill along the turnpike west to Pittsburgh. Not long afterward, they contested the advance of roughly 200 men of the 36th Battalion, Virginia Cavalry, riding toward Chambersburg from the west. The Union men delayed the Virginians for a full two hours before withdrawing through town. That bought just enough time to get the last trainload of military goods out of Chambersburg before the Rebels arrived.[24]

At the same time McClean's and McGowan's handful were making their desperate defense, CVRR employee Thomas Bard, the assistant to the superintendent, was scrambling aboard a hand car. He headed south to Greencastle, where he sought Union Brig. Gen. William W. Averell, the commander of a division of 2,500 cavalrymen camped near town. "Where is the general?" Bard demanded. No one knew his whereabouts, however. Eventually, Bard and an officer located Averell sleeping by a fence and woke him. Bard explained that General Couch needed him to take his troops to Chambersburg, because Rebels were approaching. "Tell Couch I'll be there in the morning," the groggy Averell reportedly responded. In fact, Averell would be tardy, with tragic results.[25]

July 30 dawned bright and warm in Chambersburg, with the promise that the mid-summer sultry heat would intensify as the day progressed. McClean and McGowan had finally withdrawn under pressure, clearing the way for the Rebels. Firing artillery from a high hill a mile west of town to announce their arrival, more than 800 of McCausland's men galloped into the square around 5:30 a.m. Leaving the rest of his troops with the field guns for the time being, McCausland rode into town and rang the courthouse bell to summon the civil leaders to the Diamond. McCausland demanded $100,000 in gold or $500,000 in U. S. funds, or else he would apply the torch to the town. Much to his dismay, the locals scoffed at his ransom, confident the Rebels would never burn a defenseless town. They were also reassured by the presence of Averell's division in Greencastle, only about ten miles south of Chambersburg; many assumed the Federal troopers would soon

---

24 Toomey, *The Patapsco Guards*, 14-15; Ted Alexander, et al, *Southern Revenge: Civil War History of Chambersburg, Pennsylvania* (Chambersburg Chamber of Commerce and White Mane Publishing, 1989), 116-17.

25 Catherine Henderson, "Brigadier General John McCausland: 'The Man Who Never Knew Defeat,'" *Civil War Times Illustrated*, vol. XXIII, no. 4, June 1984, 36-45.

ride to their rescue. McCausland ordered the seizure of eight citizens, including J. McDowell Sharpe and CVRR director Thomas B. Kennedy, as hostages to ransom for the requisitioned money. When it was clear he would not receive any money, he reluctantly released them. Unable to impress residents with the seriousness of his orders, at 9:00 a.m. McCausland ordered the town fired and gave the task to Lt. Col. Harry W. Gilmor and his veteran Maryland cavalrymen.[26]

Gilmor and his men had been part of Bradley Johnson's recent raid on the railroads near Baltimore. On July 11, they had captured and burned a pair of passenger trains of the Philadelphia, Wilmington and Baltimore Railroad, as well as a depot and several outbuildings at Magnolia Station in eastern Harford County. Soldiers had pushed one of the blazing trains onto the long bridge spanning the Gunpowder River, catching the draw section on fire. Rumors later spread that the Rebels had robbed several frightened passengers, some of whom were Union soldiers or medical personnel heading to Pennsylvania and safety. Taking Union Maj. Gen. William B. Franklin and other Federal officers as prisoners, Gilmor's horse soldiers rode away without losing a man. No strangers to the torch, they now set about their grim business at Chambersburg.[27]

Soldiers rolled two or three barrels of kerosene taken from a neighborhood grocery across the Diamond to the courthouse to set it on fire. Flaming embers soon landed on other nearby buildings, and the resulting conflagration began spreading within ten minutes, eventually forming a cone-shaped "whirlwind" of fire. Jacob Hoke's business and home soon burned; his brother Henry's dwelling in another part of town was spared. Jacob's wife emerged from their home carrying a precious photograph of her late father; little else was saved. Homes on both sides of Market Street were soon blazing, "and the street was filled with the drunken and infuriated soldiers," Hoke recalled. "They seemed to be as demons from the infernal pit." Residents were running wild in the streets, carrying what little clothing and valuables they could carry. "Children were screaming after their parents," wrote Hoke, "and parents were frantic after children. The feeble efforts of the aged and infirm to carry with them some valued articles from their burning homes, were deeply distressing." The scene was vividly etched into his mind. "The roaring and crackling of the flames, the falling walls, the blinding smoke, the intense heat intensified by the scorching sun, all united to form a picture of the

---

26 Ibid., *Richmond Daily Dispatch*, May 11, 1864. McCausland later stated that he gave the town six hours to comply with his demands, but Chambersburg accounts say the torch was applied three hours after the proclamation.

27 Mingus, *"This Trying Hour,"* 188-92.

terrible which no pen can describe nor painter portray. It was such a sight as no one would desire to witness but once in a lifetime."[28]

McCausland sent several four- or six-man detachments throughout the doomed town to set additional fires, carrying axes, heavy planks, and iron crow-bars to break into locked structures. They smashed furniture and belongings and poured oil on them before lighting them on fire. Carrying out their business in what one eyewitness called "a most ruthless and unrelenting manner," the soldiers deliberately burned one or two buildings on eleven blocks and allowed the resulting whirlwind and flying embers to spread the conflagration. Confederate accounts suggest they made sure all of the dwellings and businesses were empty before applying the firebrands. Several accounts from residents disagree, reporting that they saw citizens fleeing from the flaming buildings. To some observers, it appeared the officers had very specific targets in mind. Four refugees later told a Pittsburgh newspaper, "The rebels came prepared with a list and seemed to be well posted [about] persons and localities." In a few cases, angry citizens fought back, reportedly killing a Rebel officer. In another case, according to the Rev. B. S. Schneck, an elderly woman "of true Spartan grit, gave one of the house-burners such a sound drubbing with a heavy broom, that the invader retreated, to leave the work of destruction to be performed by another party, after the woman had left to escape the approaching flames of the adjoining buildings."[29]

"After it began, it was quickly done," 1st Maryland cavalryman Fielder C. Slingluff later wrote. "Men pleaded to have their houses saved; but the women acted in a much calmer manner after they understood the thing was inevitable, and in some cases excited our admiration by their courage and defiance… The most usual method of burning was to break the furniture into splinters, pile it in the middle of the floor, and then fire it. This was done in the beginning; but as the fire became general it was not necessary, as one house set fire to another. Most of the houses were vacant when fired, the occupants having fled."[30]

28 Hoke, *Historical Reminiscences of the War*, 115. Market Street ran east-west; it was part of the turnpike from Pittsburgh to Gettysburg, York, Lancaster, and Philadelphia. Main Street, the turnpike through the Shenandoah and Cumberland valleys, ran north-south.

29 *Pittsburgh Gazette*, October 2, 1864; Schneck, *The Burning of Chambersburg, Pennsylvania*, 14-16, 29, 44.

30 Fielder C. Slingluff, "Burning of Chambersburg-Retaliatory," *Confederate Veteran*, vol. XVII, no. 11 (November, 1909), 559-61. Slingluff wrote a letter in August 1864 to Chambersburg resident Ephraim Hiteshew, which was reprinted in a Baltimore newspaper in 1906 and in *Confederate Veteran* in 1909.

Spectators survey the charred ruins of the Bank of Chambersburg and the adjacent Franklin House following McCausland's devastating raid. *Library of Congress*

Sometimes, desperate inhabitants used bribes or gifts to convince the cavalrymen to spare their homes. Margaret McDowell, the "mother of the late Captain McDowell, a distinguished cavalry [artillery] officer killed at the battle of Marietta, had her house saved by making presents of preserves to the soldiers." Another woman, the wife of a clergyman, recognized a Confederate officer as the same man she had fed during Stuart's raid and tended when he stayed at her house-turned-hospital after being wounded and captured at Gettysburg the following year. Elsewhere, there was no stopping the wanton arson. Only four houses along Main Street escaped the unfolding disaster; most of those on Market Street were also consumed, along with the public buildings, two paper mills, a brewery, several factories and machine shops, the local academy, the bank, hotels, stores, livery stables, and other businesses. Horses, cows, hogs, cows, dogs, cats, and other animals perished.[31]

Captain Frederick W. Smith, one of McCausland's staff officers, was sent to the northern outskirts of town with a half-dozen troopers to burn "Norland," the comfortable residence of Republican stalwart Alexander K. McClure. Some of Jeb Stuart's men had camped on the sprawling farm during their raid in 1862 and then Albert Jenkins' soldiers again in 1863. Smith's aged father, William Smith, was the current governor of Virginia, a role he had also held during the Mexican War before going off to California during the Gold Rush and then serving five consecutive terms in the U. S. congress. "It doesn't make any difference to me who you are," an ill Matilda McClure reportedly scolded him after learning his identity. "If you are ordered to burn my house, the sooner you do it the better." She managed to save a few items, and a few sympathetic soldiers carried many of her husband's books from his extensive library outside to spare them. McClure's nearby bank barn, filled with freshly-harvested wheat, also was burned, but the raiders missed several nearby farms that he also owned. Young Fred Smith was apparently quite active with the torch that fateful day. Charles H. Taylor, a Chambersburg banker, later remembered that "Not the least active among the incendiaries was Captain Smith, son of Ex-Governor Smith, better known as Extra Billy Smith. He was observed by many people, going from house to house, applying the match, and scoffing at defenceless [sic] and homeless women, as they passed him in search of a retreat from the flames. It will be remembered that his father's property has always been protected by the Union troops."[32]

Chaos soon overran the doomed town. "Armed men marched through the streets breaking into the houses, going into cellars, capturing old wines and liquors of many years ripening, drinking heavily and leaving a line of fire behind," wrote Nathaniel Harris of the 16th Virginia Cavalry, with remorse. Indeed, Harris claimed to overhear an argument between McCausland and Col. William E. Peters of the 21st Virginia Cavalry, who vehemently protested that he had "not joined the

31 Ibid. Captain Samuel M. McDowell, the commander of Independent Battery B, Pennsylvania Light Artillery, perished during the Atlanta Campaign at Kennesaw Mountain just a month before the burning of Chambersburg. He was a cousin of merchant Jacob Hoke's wife.

32 Ibid.; Charles H. Taylor, "The Burning of Chambersburg," in Thomas L. Wilson's *Sufferings Endured for a Free Government: A History of the Cruelties and Atrocities of the Rebellion* (King & Baird, 1865), 252; Schneck, *The Burning of Chambersburg*, 25-27. For more on Smith, the oldest general in either army at the battle of Gettysburg, see Scott L. Mingus, Sr.'s award-winning *Confederate General William "Extra Billy" Smith: From Virginia's Statehouse to Gettysburg Scapegoat* (Savas Beatie, 2013). McClure moved in with relatives in Shippensburg until he could rebuild.

Confederate Army to burn houses over the heads of helpless women and children." McCausland instead turned to more willing subordinates, relieving Peters of his command. Harris was in moral agony as he "saw the flames and heard the roar of the awful conflagration as it followed the shouting and frenzied troops through the city." As he left the town three hours after he and his fellow troopers arrived, Harris fell back on his faith, confident God would not allow such an act to go unpunished. With McCausland's riders finally gone on the turnpike westward toward McConnellsburg, Averell and his Union cavalrymen, who residents had believed would save them from peril, did not show themselves until 2:00 p.m. that afternoon, in time only to see the smoldering ruins of downtown Chambersburg.[33]

Chambersburg resident Emma V. Stouffer later sent a brief letter to her brother Amos, mentioning that it was "thanks to a kind Providence that we still retain our home. That old scoundrel Mcclausland [sic]... fired the Companies ware house, Court-house-Hall, Academy and then carried fire in the private houses. There is nothing but ruins from the Depot up till Dr Sueserott's house Eysters mill the paper mill and everything is gone. There is nothing left but the superbs [suburbs] of the place... The Citizens Killed a Rebel Major who was drunk & had straggled back and was burning buildings... Once while the fire was raging and again when it was pretty well over, from the mill we could see the Cupola of the Academy, Benjn Franklin &c. fall over it looked very hard."[34]

Telegraph operator W. Blair Gilmore had fled a few miles outside of Chambersburg to avoid capture. From the field that night, he managed to send off a quick wire to Col. Alexander McClure in Harrisburg to inform him that the Rebels had fired Chambersburg. McClure would later learn that his own farmhouse was gone, as well as almost 11 blocks (then called squares) of the town. The extent of the damage to Chambersburg, once the queen of the Cumberland Valley, was horrible, yet at the same time awe-inspiring. At least 500 buildings lay in ruins, 278 of them homes and shops. Among the structures obliterated from the landscape were the court house, the banks and even churches. Only one fatality was reported—an elderly former slave, who died the next day of a heart attack.[35]

---

33 Union prisoner quoted in Ayers, *The Thin Light of Freedom*, 204-208; Nathaniel E. Harris, *Autobiography: The Story of an Old Man's Life with Reminiscences of Seventy-Five Years* (J. W. Burke Co., 1925), 93-94.

34 Emma V. Stouffer to Amos Stouffer, Chambersburg, Pa., August 1, 1864, Valley of the Shadow, UVA. http://valley.lib.virginia.edu/papers/F6508. Accessed February 3, 2018.

35 Ayers, *The Thin Light of Freedom*, 212. In 1871, the state border claims commission set the tally of losses at $1.6 million. Merchant Jacob Hoke placed his damages at $5,500.

Many residents would find themselves "safe, though homeless and with only some clothing left," as the Rev. Benjamin S. Schneck wrote to his sister Margaretta. Most people no longer had "even a single change of clothing. But blessed be God, there are those who were spared, + their hearts + houses are open to the rest. Help in the way of provisions + clothing is coming in. None need to starve. But such a scene of Ruin! No imagination can conceive it. Gov. Curtin came up last evening and said to me: 'The reality is fearfully beyond all my conceptions.' He requested us to try + keep the people in heart, for many have left, + more do not know what to do here now." Fortunately, most of the churches of the town had been spared, and several threw open their doors to the refugees. His two-story stone-and-brick house on East Market Street was gone, as well as almost all of the contents including his impressive library of theological and history books and his wife's "nearly new" seven-octave piano. The Mansion House, the publication office and printing facility for the German Reformed Church, was also destroyed, taking with it the printing press, bindery, inventory of books, etc. Schneck had been the editor.[36]

Some of the Confederates expressed sympathy with the residents and spared parts of the town, or individual buildings such as the Masonic Lodge and several churches. At least one soldier had lived in the Cumberland Valley not far from the line of the CVRR. Brice Blair, the youthful Presbyterian chaplain of the 37th Battalion, Virginia Cavalry, hastily penciled a note on an envelope and handed it to an acquaintance, the Reverend S. J. Nicolls of the town's Presbyterian Church. "Please write my father and give him my love," the note read. "Tell him, too, as Mrs. Shoemaker will tell you, that I was most strenuously opposed to the burning of the town." He signed the message, "B. B. Blair, Chaplain, and son of Thomas P. Blair, Shippensburg, Pa."[37]

The damage to the CVRR was less drastic than with Lee's occupation of Chambersburg during the Gettysburg Campaign or with Jeb Stuart's October 1862 raid. In years past, the railroad had borne the brunt of Confederate destruction, while civilian property had gone relatively untouched. This time, it

36 Benjamin S. Schneck to My Dear Sister + Brother, August 3, 1864, Valley of the Shadow Project, University of Virginia, http://valley.lib.virginia.edu/papers/F6084. Accessed January 5, 2018. B. S. Schneck Claim, RG-2, Records Relating to the Civil War Border Claims, Franklin County Damage Claims, Records of the Department of the Adjutant General, Pennsylvania State Archives, Harrisburg.

37 Schneck, *The Burning of Chambersburg*, 28. Blair was a native of Dillsburg in northwestern York County.

was the opposite. A modern historian has postulated the railroad likely suffered "little real loss" from the burning, because Watts had been reluctant to rebuild "to any considerable extent," after the previous two invasions. It also helped that the critical shop machinery had been removed and held on cars at a safe distance from McCausland's raiders. Unlike the Rebels' 1863 visit, the tracks and ties were still intact and the railroad could still move its trains into and out of Chambersburg. McCausland, unlike Stuart and Jenkins, had not tried to destroy the bridge at Scotland or wreck the railroad infrastructure.[38]

Soon, the retrospectives began, with a focus on who was to blame for the fiasco. "On the morning of the 30th of July our beautiful town was laid in ashes by the vandalism and barbarity of a desperate band of freebooters, commanded, by the infamous McCausland," the *Valley Spirit* cried, despite its previous openly Southern sympathies. "Two hundred and sixty-five dwelling houses were consumed by fire. Over three thousand people [more than half the population] were pecuniarily ruined, and the greater part of them rendered houseless and homeless. The destruction of the town was in obedience to the command of General Early, and was justified by him as a retaliatory act for the atrocities committed by General Hunter in the Valley of the Shenandoah."[39]

If the departed McCausland was despised, then Averell's late-arriving troops were by no means welcomed as heroes. "[S]ome attach great blame to Gens Couch and Averel[l]," wrote resident Emma Stouffer, reporting rumors that Averell "was so drunk in GreenCastle that he could not write an answer to a dispatch sent him by Couch[.]" Whether true or fabricated, the rumors spoke to the incredible anger and abandonment felt by Chambersburg's populace. For herself, Stouffer admitted that it was "hard to tell where the blame rests," but lamented "that so few should come in & do so much damage."[40]

Others, including former Secretary of War Simon Cameron, blamed the Department of the Susquehanna's long-time commander, Maj. Gen. Darius Couch, for failing to protect the border with more troops and for failing to rouse Averell. Cameron deemed Couch "inefficient" in a telegram he sent to President Lincoln. In his opinion, "The Burning of Chambersburg has created great excitement & indignation & whether right or wrong so much has centered on

---

38 Westhaeffer, *History of the CVRR*, 83.

39 "The Fate of the Chambersburg Relief Bill," *Valley Spirit*, August 31, 1864.

40 Emma V. Stouffer to Amos Stauffer, August 1, 1864, Valley of the Shadow Project, University of Virginia, http://valley.lib.virginia.edu/papers/F6508, accessed January 5, 2018.

Genl. Couch as to utterly destroy his usefulness." He asked Lincoln to replace Couch with George Cadwalader, a native Pennsylvanian who had the confidence of the people of the state, and he predicted, "troops will at once rally to his command. I believe he will be able to get troops enough not only for the defense of this Valley but to greatly assist in defending Washington. Give him the command and you will not only satisfy your friends but do your Country an essential Service."[41]

Jacob Hoke, after surveying the charred ruins of his home and business, had no qualms in assigning the blame solely on Confederate Maj. Gen. Jubal Early. The "dastardly villain" had ordered the destruction of Chambersburg, much as he had the previous year burned Congressman Thaddeus Stevens' Caledonia Iron Works in eastern Franklin County. McCausland's "vandal horde" had applied the torch to Chambersburg at Early's command. His men were nothing more than a "band of cut-throats, thieves, and incendiaries," in Hoke's opinion.[42]

Many of the leading participants, of course, had different viewpoints, insisting they acted within the accepted laws of war concerning retaliation. One of McCausland's chief subordinates later claimed he tried to keep order, but found it impossible. "After the order was given to burn the town of Chambersburg," Brig. Gen. Bradley T. Johnson explained, "and before drunken soldiers paraded the streets in every possible disguise and paraphernalia… I tried, and was seconded by almost every officer of my command, but in vain, to preserve the discipline of this brigade, but it was impossible; not only the license afforded was too great, but actual example gave them excuse and justification." "Tiger John" McCausland, in mid-June 1872, wrote to a Philadelphia newspaper that "by Early's orders, I burned Chambersburg. I have no apology to make. My conscience is clear." Nevertheless, he became anathema to the residents of southern Pennsylvania and, after the war, a warrant would be issued for his arrest, as well as for Johnson's. McCausland spent several years in self-exile until he received assurances the government would not pursue the charges.[43]

Years later, Jubal Early hinted that Chambersburg's residents should have taken McCausland's warning much more seriously, writing in his memoirs, "The

41 Simon Cameron to Abraham Lincoln, August 1, 1864, http://valley.lib.virginia.edu/papers/F1401. Accessed February 3, 2018. Cadwalader, a Philadelphian, had commanded a division in Patterson's army in 1861.

42 Hoke, *Historical Reminiscences of the War*, Introduction, 53, 116.

43 OR 62, part 1, 7-8; G. L. Eskew, "They Called Him 'Town Burner,'" *West Virginia Review*, vol. XVI, 62.

policy pursued by our army on former occasions had been so lenient, that they did not suppose the threat was in earnest this time, and they hoped for speedy relief." He, at least, took full responsibility for his decision. "I would have been fully justified, by the laws of retaliation in war, in burning the town without giving the inhabitants the opportunity of redeeming it. For this act I alone am responsible, as the officers engaged in it were simply executing my orders, and had no discretion left them. Notwithstanding the lapse of time which has occurred, and the result of the war, I am perfectly satisfied with my conduct on this occasion, and see no reason to regret it." McCausland believed "Early's idea was sensible and justified. Fair retaliation."[44]

Reaction to the burning of Chambersburg, of course, varied greatly between the North and South. Several Northern papers vilified McCausland and Early for their "fiendish act." In North Carolina, the *State Journal* bragged that "our boys *Hunterized* the place and it is now ashes," referring to the destruction that Union General David Hunter had recently wrought in the Shenandoah Valley. "This is but the beginning," the editor warned. "We expected daily to hear from Early's boys again, and now we expect to hear, amid the shouts of triumph, the crackling flames making merry over the sufferings of the Yankee race; while the dense columns of smoke shall tell of our whereabouts, and the heaps of ashes and of ruins mark the track of our men. We believe the Almighty will look approvingly upon these acts of retribution for the foes' inhuman and barbarious [sic] conduct towards us. We have cried 'mercy' long enough; now let our watchward [sic] be eyes for an eye, teeth for a tooth."[45]

Similar, though toned-down, rhetoric filled several other papers in Dixie. In South Carolina, the *Camden Daily Journal* commented that Early's destruction of Chambersburg was "in earnest that some portion of the devastation which has marked the track of the Yankee armies on Confederate soil is to be henceforth retorted upon the dwellers of Yankeedom." The editor took special delight in republishing an article from a Democratic New Jersey paper that claimed that recent Rebel retaliation in Maryland was justified as mild compared with "the unnumbered outrages and crimes which have been committed against the

44 Jubal Early, *A Memoir of the Last Year of the War for Independence in the Confederate States of America* (Lovell & Gibson, 1866), 74; Henderson, "Brigadier General John McCausland," 44.

45 "The Very Latest," *New York Herald*, July 31, 1864; "Destruction of Chambersburg by Our Troops," *Western Sentinel* (Winston, NC), August 11, 1864, citing the *State Journal*.

defenceless [sic], unprotected women and children in the South by our armies during the last three years of terror and blood."[46]

One of McCausland's troopers, J. Kelley Bennette of the medical staff of the 8th Virginia Cavalry, upon reflection, decided that the arson was indeed justified: "The burning of Chambersburg was generally condemned by our Regt. at first when all the sympathies were all aroused, but when reason had time to regain her seat I believe that they all thought as I thought at first; that it was Justice & Justice tempered with Mercy. That burning per se is wrong no one can deny; and the bare idea of turning out of doors upon the cold charities of the world unprotected women & unoffending children is sufficient to cause the feelings to rebel. But there may be circumstances under which it is not only justifiable but becomes a duty—stern it is true but nevertheless binding." Captain A. J. Tynes of the 5th Virginia Cavalry was worried about what was to come, correctly judging that the burning had ushered in a terrible new phase in the increasingly bitter war: "City fired about noon. Saddest spectacle I ever witnessed to see the women and children. This inaugurates a terrible system of retalliation [sic], devastation and rapine."[47]

Chambersburg's residents rebuilt or planned to leave. Their city had become political fodder in an ongoing war of words, as well as an excuse for vengeful Union soldiers who began burning buildings in the Southern states in retaliation for the devastation in Pennsylvania.

The Aftermath

Within days of the burning, the Cumberland Valley Railroad offered free transportation for any citizens who wished to leave town. Hundreds of displaced residents took advantage of the company's generosity and boarded outgoing trains in the week immediately following McCausland's painful visit. Many went to stay with family or friends in distant towns. Some never returned. For example,

46 "Retaliation," *Camden* (SC) *Daily Journal*, August 11, 1864.

47 J. Kelly Bennette diary entry for July 30, 1864, Valley of the Shadow website, UVA. http://valley.lib.virginia.edu/papers/FD4501, accessed February 3, 2018. Original in the J. Kelly Bennette Papers, #886, Southern Historical Collection, The Wilson Library, UNC Chapel Hill; A. J. Tynes to Harriet "Hattie" F. Tynes, July 29, 1864, Valley of the Shadow website, UVA. http://valley.lib.virginia.edu/papers/FD4507. Accessed February 8, 2018. Original in Achilles James Tynes Papers #1874, Southern Historical Collection, The Wilson Library, UNC Chapel Hill.

attorney Jeremiah Cook soon moved to the Montana Territory, taking advantage of the government's offer of free land to homestead.[48]

"The excitement in our town beggars description," a Shippensburg resident noted in his diary on the evening of July 30. "All classes of citizens of Chambersburg and surrounding country are flocking in and through our town by the thousands. The Rebels are burning Chambersburg and people are fleeing for their lives with only the clothing on their backs. Their homes and possessions laid in ashes. The crying of the children and the distress of the women is awful." The local telegraph officer, unsure if McCausland was heading his way, packed his instrument and fled on the presumption "the enemy has thrown out a strong advanced position in that direction," a Philadelphia reporter commented. General Couch established his headquarters in Carlisle, from which he was busy "directing the necessary means of defense, the details of which cannot be alluded to now. The presumption is, however, that he will be able to offer a stern resistance to any advance that may be made in this direction." As the day progressed, it became evident that the Rebels were not threatening Shippensburg, and, in fact, had withdrawn, their task of burning Chambersburg accomplished.[49]

On Sunday, July 31, with the Rebels gone for sure, a special train came up the Valley from Harrisburg. All along the line of the CVRR, it stopped to pick up supplies of bread and other provisions donated for the relief of Chambersburg's remaining residents. The train also brought a large congregation of passengers from all points in the Valley. Some had come to minister to the suffering populace. Others were mere curiosity seekers, who came to town strictly to see the ruins. Major General Couch sent provisions daily for more than a week. Workers unloaded them from the burden cars and stored them in an undamaged Wunderlich & Nead warehouse.[50]

That same day, Captain McGowan and the Patapsco Guards returned to Chambersburg to serve as the military provost. He and his men would remain for two full months, keeping order and assisting the public where possible. "A relief train sent to Chambersburg with assistance and provisions," the Shippensburg diarist noted on July 31. "Contributions pouring in. Oh, what a horrible sight to behold. The demons have laid most of the town in ashes, and insulted the wives,

---

48 Hoke, *Historical Reminiscences of the War*, 127; *Franklin Repository*, August 21, 1864.

49 "Effects of War News," *Shippensburg* (PA) *Chronicle*, July 17, 1913; "The Invasion," *Philadelphia Age*, August 1, 1864.

50 Hoke, *Historical Reminiscences of the War*, 128.

mothers and children in their distress. A pitiful sight as they strayed into our town more dead than alive. Our citizens made them as comfortable as possible." The following day, August 1, the writer noted, "Seven Rebels who helped to burn Chambersburg were taken through as prisoners." Businesses were suspended on the 2nd and, the following day, "We arrested a Rebel today and a man was kicked out of town for uttering treasonable talk."[51]

New misery soon came for the beleaguered townspeople of Chambersburg. Rumors spread on August 6 that Rebels were "hovering about the Potomac, threatening to return and complete the destruction of the town in retaliation for the killing of one or two of their number here on their retreat here and along the road," according to Jacob Hoke. "Rebels entered Hagerstown at 9 o'clock this morning, at which time Wm. B. Wilson left," the *Philadelphia Inquirer* informed its readers. "Mr. Wilson is a reliable operator belonging to the Pennsylvania Railroad Company." Later that day, the paper reported it was "still in telegraphic communication with State Line, a station on the Franklin Railroad, seven miles north of Hagerstown. The operator there states that the Rebels in Hagerstown have thrown out pickets, but as yet have made no further advance movements."[52]

Soon, the seemingly endless reports that "the Rebels are coming!" were repeated. It was the final straw for many war-weary Valley residents. "The railroad company placed a large train of cars at the disposal of the people, and all who desired to go away were permitted to do so," Hoke noted. Most of the people whose homes had been destroyed who had remained in town now flocked to the depot. Others, fortunate that their dwellings were intact, but terrified at the prospects of yet another Rebel raid, joined them. "The people cane bearing heavy burdens," Hoke reported, "panting under the heat of the day and trembling with excitement. The cars were packed with a mass of frightened humanity. Many could not get seats." Hopeful of another train in the morning, people slept that night in and around the depot. Few wanted to stay to face another group of Rebels with torches.[53]

A Harrisburg reporter noted that the CVRR trains brought large numbers of black people to join "the party of negro refugees for several days past quartered in

---

51 Toomey, *The Patapsco Guards*, 15; OR 43, part 2, 141, 216; "Effects of War News," *Shippensburg* (PA) *Chronicle*, July 17, 1913.

52 Hoke, *Historical Reminiscences of the War*, 129; "The Rebel Invasion," *Philadelphia Evening Bulletin*, August 6, 1864.

53 Ibid.

the Pennsylvania railroad depot. They came from Chambersburg, Shippensburg and Carlisle, frightened away from their homes by rumors of another rebel invasion." He went on to say, "A number of white people, equally alarmed, arrived on the same trains from the above mentioned towns. The farmers are again on the move, and we may soon expect to see long wagon processions from the Cumberland Valley passing through our city, should the reports now current be confirmed."[54]

Those refugees soon became a source of considerable consternation. "From two to three thousand negro refugees, of both sexes and all ages, are now quartered in the Pennsylvania railroad depot," another reporter commented, "crowded together promiscuously upon the platforms. Nearly all of these poor creatures are in a destitute condition, ragged and penniless paupers upon the bounty of our citizens, who are obligated to subsist them. They occupy a large portion of the depot, to the great annoyance of travelers and the inconvenience of the railroad company." He speculated, "How these people are to be disposed of is a matter of serious consideration. The probability is that many of them will find their way to the poor-houses of this and neighboring counties."[55]

Over the next few days, the entire rolling stock of the CVRR was engaged in taking refugees from the Cumberland Valley to Harrisburg to avoid the Rebels. In a single evening, more than 2,400 women and children arrived in the state capital. Many of them were from burned-out Chambersburg. "It was a pitiful sight to behold these standing in groups, strangers as it were, in a strange city, pilgrims from their once happy homes, which but yesterday were turned to ashes by the torches of the invading traitors," a reporter wrote. "Old women, who had never expected to be borne away from their homes until they were carried to their graves; matrons in the prime of life, with their families of half-grown children clustering, affrighted, around them; and the young mother with her infant at her breast, all alone, with tearful eyes, and blanched cheeks, made up a picture of distress such as we have seldom before beheld, and such as we do not again desire to gaze upon." The appearance of a party of Rebels at Hagerstown the previous morning caused the panicky exodus. The newsman was certain the women of Harrisburg would kindly welcome and hospitably treat the refugees, remembering that many of these very same huddled masses had fed and welcomed their

54 "More Refugees," *Pittsburgh Daily Commercial*, August 8, 1864.

55 "Refugees at Harrisburg, PA," *Baltimore Sun*, August 9, 1864, citing the *Harrisburg Union*.

husbands and loved ones in the army during their sojourns into the Valley over the course of the war.[56]

Within a few days, it became evident that the Rebels were not returning to Chambersburg, or any other town in the Cumberland Valley. People slowly began returning home, with the exception of those in the Franklin County seat whose houses were no more. In the ruined town, crowds of men and boys tore down free-standing walls and cleared away rubble in preparation to rebuild their dwellings and businesses. "You can hardly see for the dust, so great is the crowd of returning refugees," the Shippensburg diarist penned on August 8. Two nights later, he noted, "General Averil's [sic] wagon train, with a regiment of soldiers, passed up to Chambersburg." They would help clear the rubble.[57]

A few weeks after Chambersburg burned, the state legislature, at the initiative of Governor Curtin, met in special session to discuss a proposed relief bill to help the victims recover some of their losses. It was, like previous debates over past border claims from 1862 and 1863, at times a spirited disagreement. A committee of the ruined town's leading citizens invited the politicians to visit Chambersburg to see the extent of the destruction for themselves. The Cumberland Valley Railroad's superintendent, Col. O. N. Lull, whose own dwelling place was now gone, arranged for an excursion train to bring the legislators, free of charge, from Harrisburg on the morning of August 11. "The august body visited the ruins and departed, carrying the hopes and fears of our distressed people," the *Valley Spirit* noted in anticipation of a favorable ruling. However, the relief bill continued to be under discussion for some time.[58]

The victims who filed for compensation included several CVRR employees and those men who worked in the supporting industries, including the freight warehouses. Ticket agent and accountant Alexander H. McCulloh (kinsman of former CVRR president Thomas G. McCulloh) asked for $2,000 in compensation for his lost two-story brick house, stone stable, and personal property. Engineer James Adams and brakeman Jacob Keller were more fortunate; their residences had escaped the flames, as had that of George W. Rice, a freight conductor since 1861. Atlantic and Ohio telegrapher W. Blair Gilmore lost some personal property left behind when he wisely fled with his telegraph instrument; he later filed a claim

---

56 *The Jeffersonian* (Stroudsburg, PA), August 11, 1864, citing the *Harrisburg Telegraph*.

57 "Effects of War News," *Shippensburg* (PA) *Chronicle*, July 17, 1913.

58 "The Fate of the Chambersburg Relief Bill," *Valley Spirit*, August 31, 1864; "Pennsylvania Legislature," *Evening Star* (Washington, DC), August 13, 1864.

that was adjudicated to $53.50. The newspaper offices of archrivals *Franklin Repository* and *Valley Spirit* both were now gone; their respective owners filed claims. More than 30 claimants were African-Americans.[59]

Those unfortunate men who lost their homes included Joseph Deckelmayer, who had been one of three Chambersburg residents arrested in October 1862 for openly sympathizing with Jeb Stuart's raiders. Back then, the German-born merchant had supposedly congratulated the Confederates on their visit this far north. This time, he was not as excited about McCausland's visit. Deckelmayer lost his two-story brick front and rear buildings in the conflagration, as well as his one-story bakery/confectionary shop on East Main Street. His initial claim was for $3,000. It was not the first time he had experienced a significant loss from fire. In the middle of July 1860, less than a year before the war, his house and store had been destroyed and needed to be replaced. In that earlier inferno, he had lost "a large amount of goods—barrels of Crackers, bags of nuts, boxes of figs and raisins, jars of candies and many household articles." Once again, Deckelmayer would have to rebuild his house and business. Neither of his two former cell mates, William Glenn and Michael Geiselman, lost any property as a result of McCausland's torches.[60]

The newly recruited 201st Pennsylvania Infantry was sent to Chambersburg following the devastating fire. With their fine regimental band playing gaily, the soldiers marched out of Camp Curtin in Harrisburg on Tuesday, August 30. They boarded CVRR cars for the trip across the Susquehanna River into the Cumberland Valley. Many were sad at the prospects of leaving their loved ones behind. "Once in the old bridge the boys yelled with a hearty good will, and drove away all traces of sorrow and despondency," Cpl. A. H. Baum reported. "All along the line of the Cumberland Valley railroad we were cheered and greeted with demonstrations of joy; and the regiment, hurried over the rails by two engines, reached Chambersburg at half-past five o'clock. From some cause or other, we lay in this ruined place nearly two hours; and then, after a fatiguing march of four

59 For details on several individual claimants, see *The Franklin County Civil War Damage Claims: Chambersburg Burns* (Franklin County Historical Society, 2014), vol. 1, and/or Damage Claim Applications (Submitted Under Acts Passed 1863-1871), 1871-1879, Record Group 2– Records of the Department of the Auditor General, Pennsylvania State Archives, Harrisburg.

60 Schneck, *The Burning of Chambersburg*, 65; "The Burning of Chambersburg," *Valley Spirit*, August 31, 1864; "The Late Fire," *Valley Spirit*, July 18, 1860. The commissioners later adjusted Deckelmayer's original claim to $1,408.79.

miles—fatiguing became new to most of us." The men wearily pitched their tents at Camp Couch on Slate Hill west of town.[61]

In addition to the sad news of Chambersburg's losses and slow recovery, one of the prevailing topics during the autumn of 1864 in the Cumberland Valley was the upcoming presidential election. Incumbent President Abraham Lincoln faced his former army commander, Maj. Gen. George B. McClellan, the nominee of the Democratic Party. Lincoln, in the wake of the burning of Chambersburg and the mounting casualty counts in Northern Virginia, did not expect to be re-elected. However, as the war results turned more favorable, his chances of victory increased. In an early version of predictive polling, passengers on CVRR trains in and out of Harrisburg could cast their own votes. On October 2, of the twenty-four soldiers on board the "up" train to Carlisle, only one voted for "Little Mac." Four civilians selected Lincoln; one picked McClellan. The next morning on the down train (from Carlisle), Lincoln received 74 votes, McClellan 34, with no soldiers on the train. Later in the day, on the train to Carlisle, 124 riders preferred Lincoln to only 52 for the general. Thirteen draftees were on board; 10 voted for the president and three for McClellan. Across the country, the sentiment seemed to be that Lincoln would receive a second term, following the recent capture of Atlanta.[62]

Politics aside, throughout October, the CVRR continued to carry significant numbers of people who had given up on living in the Cumberland Valley. "Each morning train on the Cumberland Valley Railroad brings a large number of passengers en route for the West," the *Harrisburg Telegraph* commented. "They are principally from Maryland, and the Southern counties of this state—parties who have lost heavily at the hands of the rebels. Many of them owned fine farms, which they have disposed of at a sacrifice, in order to avoid further depredations at the hands of the rebel fiends."[63]

Other "fiends" plied their trade along the line of the Cumberland Valley Railroad—professional slave catchers. Several men, including Jeb Stuart's guide Hugh Logan and his brothers, had made a living before the war hunting fugitive slaves who had crossed the Mason-Dixon Line into southern Pennsylvania. With the CVRR's terminus in Maryland, a slave state, these bounty collectors at times took their captive prizes on a train ride to Hagerstown. From there, they could

---

61 "From the 201st Regiment," *Pennsylvania Daily Telegraph*, September 3, 1864.

62 "A Voice from the Cumberland Valley," *Pennsylvania Daily Telegraph*, October 5, 1864.

63 "Going West," *Harrisburg Daily Telegraph*, October 19, 1864.

return the slave to his or her owner and reap the reward money. Such was the attempt in the case of Martha Jones, "a poor defenceless [sic] female, who had honestly been earning her living in this city some time," the *Harrisburg Telegraph* reported, "and who is regarded by all who know her as a decent and virtuous girl." She and her sister had escaped slavery in Maryland and made their way to Harrisburg, where they each had found gainful employment.

By false pretenses, a woman had enticed Martha to come to her home. She and some friends turned out to be slave catchers, not an occupation commonly associated with females. They confined the frightened girl in a room and awaited the next train to Hagerstown. Martha's sister had learned of the nefarious act when she called at the house where Martha was being held against her will. When the kidnappers thought the way was clear, they escorted the trembling fugitive through the streets of Harrisburg, hoping to arrive at the depot just as the train was scheduled to leave. Martha's sister, however, sprang into action in the meantime. She and several friends went to the depot, where they awaited the arrival of the "negro stealers." When the ladies appeared, dragging Martha with them, her sister stubbornly stood between the party and the platform of the rail car to prevent their passage. The women "fought desperately to force Martha on the train, but as the poor girl struggled, her sister and her friends came gallantly to the rescue, and slavery to-day, in Martha Jones, has one less victim in this land of the free." The reporter covering the case agreed to give up the name of his informant if the authorities wanted to prosecute the women, "and that informant is ready and willing to testify against the ladies who thus stand charged with having violated the fugitive law [Confiscation Act]."[64]

The army continued to have troops stationed outside of Chambersburg, and they helped with the cleanup of the town. However, in at least in one case, their presence turned quite ugly. The railroad lost one of its veteran engineers on Wednesday night, October 26. Jacob Sweitzer, who had piloted many trainloads of Federal and state troops up and down the Cumberland Valley for the past few years, ironically met his death at the hands of soldiers. A group of drunken, disorderly cavalrymen approached Sweitzer's home in Chambersburg near the Catholic church. Claiming he was a bounty-jumper, they demanded admittance, likely using that as a pretext to rob the place. Other accounts suggested they were

---

64 "Late News Items," *Pittsburgh Daily Commercial*, October 25, 1864, citing the *Harrisburg Telegraph*. The 1850 Fugitive Slave Law, which returned slaves to their masters, was repealed in June 1864. The Confiscation Act, enacted in August 1864, barred slaveholders from re-enslaving captured runaways.

actually there to meet "some disreputable females" whom they believed to be at Sweitzer's residence.[65]

When Sweitzer peered outside and ordered the soldiers to go away, they leveled their carbines and threatened to fire into the windows. Sweitzer, described by local newspapers as "a highly respectable citizen, and a man of the most devout piety," emerged from his home and ran to a neighbor's place. While standing at the doorway, one of the cavalrymen suddenly struck him with "a tremendous blow on the back part of the head with some heavy weapon." Sweitzer crumpled to the ground, dying almost instantly. The soldiers standing around the body were quickly arrested. They soon faced a coroner's inquest, but made contradictory statements before the jury about what had happened. Coupled with "some other evidence that seemed to implicate them," the reporter noted, "…the jury seemed warranted in authorizing their commitment to stand their trial for the murder." However, the particular soldier who murdered Sweitzer was never identified, despite intense efforts to do so (under the direction of General Couch), and no one was tried for the crime. The case was dismissed, but some believed that, after this incident, it was no wonder that "a peaceable community considers it a calamity to have a body of troops quartered in there [sic] neighborhood?"[66]

In early November, in his annual report prepared for the stockholders, Frederick Watts rued this third and latest invasion of the Rebels, which had forced his railroad to remove its machinery again from the repair shops in Chambersburg and keep it stored in railcars for almost two full months. Many employees had lost their homes. Buildings destroyed by Jenkins still needed to be replaced, as well as those recently burned. "These disturbing causes tell seriously upon the equipment of the road," he complained. "With the great demand for skilled labor, particularly machinists, and the heavy losses sustained by some of our most valued and efficient men, by the burning of Chambersburg, we have been put to very great inconvenience to keep up the necessary power for the transaction of the heavy and increasing business of the road." The long-time CVRR president praised his employees for their "increased fidelity and industry in their untiring efforts to save the property of the company and promote its interests." Fortunately, the steady increase in passenger and freight revenues offered financial promise, although that

---

65 "Murder," *Newville Star and Enterprise*, October 29, 1864.

66 Cooper, *Recollections of Chambersburg, Pa.,* 61; *Hagerstown Herald of Freedom and Torch Light*, November 2, 1864; *Valley Spirit*, November 2, 1864; *Franklin Repository*, January 4, 1865; *Newville Star and Enterprise*, October 29, 1864. Some accounts suggest a cavalryman smashed a gun into Sweitzer's temple.

had largely precluded using the smaller locomotives and had taxed the machinists' ability to keep the heavier ones in service.[67]

As he looked ahead to the new fiscal year, several challenges remained, all of which would be expensive. A foundation had been laid for the new passenger depot at Chambersburg, but the superstructure had yet to be constructed. The replacement freight house there had not yet been built, nor had the previously planned passenger depot at Shippensburg. Shelters for passengers still needed to be erected at the flag stops in Oakville, Good Hope, Alterton, Middlesex, and Kingston. The temporary bridges at Scotland and Carlisle needed to be replaced with more permanent structures. Too, the railroad had outgrown its freight house in Harrisburg. More space was also needed for passenger service in the capital, which it shared with the Northern Central Railway. "The tracks of our road are entirely inadequate for that purpose," Judge Watts stated. With receipts having increased 34.4 percent over fiscal 1863, the Cumberland Valley Railroad should have the revenues to complete many of the projects, he observed.[68]

Shortly after the CVRR closed the books on fiscal 1864, President Lincoln, buoyed by several recent military successes, defeated General McClellan in the general election, winning a second term to see the war through to its conclusion. He carried Pennsylvania, but lost Franklin County by 38 votes in an area he had won in 1860. There were a number of reasons suggested for the turnaround of Democratic fortunes in Franklin County. Following the burning of Chambersburg, a number of residents had moved away; it is impossible to know how many of them were Republicans, but they had constituted the majority of voters in the previous presidential election. Second, and likely of far more importance, the multiple Confederate invasions and the destruction of Chambersburg had soured many people on the Federal government's ability (or willingness) to protect the border counties.[69]

In mid-November, as the people of Chambersburg continued to try to piece together the remnants of their lives and livelihoods, fresh rumors circulated that the Rebels were coming yet again. The *Valley Spirit* reported on November 16 that three Rebel spies had been captured on the Cumberland Valley Railroad.

67 *Thirtieth Annual Report of the Cumberland Valley Railroad Company, to the Stockholders, Made October 1, 1864* (The Herald Office, 1864), 5-7.

68 Ibid.

69 For a detailed analysis of the war-time politics of Franklin County, driven in part by the rival newspapers, see Matt Bruning, "Disunity in the Union: Franklin County, PA, and the American Civil War," *Western Illinois Historical Review*, vol. II, Spring 2010, 52-63.

Fortunately, no troops appeared, most people stayed put this time, and the nervous residents of Franklin and Cumberland counties could focus on trying to make the best of the holidays they could.[70]

Political passions continued to run deep among Valley residents. Even with the tide of the war by now decidedly in favor of "Mr. Lincoln's army," plenty of Southern sympathizers remained in the region. In Shippensburg on November 24, "Rev. Larnfeldt preached a very pronounced Union patriotic and abolition sermon," a resident wrote in his diary. "Copperheads did not like it."[71]

For a few passengers on the railroad, the Thanksgiving holiday was frightening. The westbound morning train from Harrisburg derailed six miles past Carlisle, not far from Alterton, upsetting and demolishing two or three passenger cars. "It seems almost miraculous that no one was injured," a newsman marveled. It was not until 6:00 p.m. that the debris was removed and the track cleared. The cause was a broken rail, the second in the same day for the CVRR. The other emergency was above Oakville, where, that morning, the engine of the train from Hagerstown blew off its smoke stack. It certainly had been a strange day for the railroad company, but none of the Thanksgiving passengers had been hurt in any of the incidents.[72]

The CVRR was back in the news in early December when a long, bitter dispute between the railroad company and a conductor who was injured on the job finally reached a settlement. Nicholas Meyers, back in 1862, had worked as a conductor on the private freight cars of Henderson & Reed, a freight forwarder based in Carlisle. He attempted to cut loose the rear portion of a moving train, but was thrown from the platform and fell under several passing cars. The accident cost him his right foot. He sued the CVRR in 1863 and received a favorable verdict, which carried with it a $1,000 judgment against the railroad. The case ended up in the Pennsylvania Supreme Court, and the justices ruled that a new trial was in order. The case had recently been heard, and the jury rendered a verdict for the plaintiff and awarded him $2,550 in damages.[73]

A couple of weeks later, several newspapers across the Keystone State reported that the South Mountain Iron Company had purchased the venerable Pine Grove Iron Works and associated land holdings in southern Cumberland

70 "Rebels About," *Valley Spirit*, November 16, 1864.

71 "Effects of War News," *Shippensburg* (PA) *Chronicle*, July 17, 1913.

72 "Accidents," *Waynesboro Village Record*, December 2, 1864.

73 "Damages," *Newville Star and Enterprise*, December 3, 1864.

County for $1.5 million, an extraordinary sum for 1864. "This is an extensive and valuable estate," a Waynesboro paper reported, "well wooded and watered, and contains inexhaustible supplies of the purest iron ore." It had only been a year since Judge Watts' son William M. Watts had sold the same establishment for $225,000, which at the time had been considered "a very high price." The new owners planned to invest heavily to upgrade the iron works, and they wanted to construct a private railroad from Pine Grove to connect with the Cumberland Valley Railroad near Carlisle.[74]

Alleged Rebel spies dominated the news for several days in early December 1864. William Williams, William Thompson, and William Fielding had been arrested on a CVRR train in November and held for questioning. They eventually faced a hearing, but the testimony as to their actual identities and relationship with one another was often contradictory and confusing. Although a reporter predicted that Thompson, at least, would be found guilty, no verdict was handed down and the case was continued into the next year. Meanwhile, a Harrisburg detective arrested another accused spy, who gave his name as Joseph Clarke and denied any wrongdoing. Clarke had in his possession almost $800 in various small denominations, half of which were Confederate notes and half greenbacks. He also had some counterfeit gold pieces. The detective examined the suspect's vest and coat pockets, finding several "lucifer" matches that suggested the stranger was a possible arsonist. Clarke faced charges as a spy and would have to appear before a military commission to judge his guilt.[75]

As the residents of the Cumberland Valley celebrated the Christmas season in 1864, they had plenty of cause for optimism. Robert E. Lee's Army of Northern Virginia was penned up in its squalid entrenchments protecting Richmond and Petersburg. In the Western Theater, Atlanta had fallen, John Bell Hood's Confederate army had moved into Tennessee, and Sherman had marched through Georgia to the port city of Savannah. General Sherman symbolically presented Savannah as a Christmas gift to President Lincoln. There were no credible threats of a fourth consecutive year of a Rebel invasion of south-central Pennsylvania. To finish the job of winning the war, in late December, President Lincoln called for 300,000 fresh soldiers to replenish the heavily depleted ranks of the army and navy.

74 "Carlisle, PA," *The Pittsburgh Gazette,* December 16, 1864. The proposed South Mountain Railroad would not become a reality until 1870.

75 "Important from Harrisburg. The Arrest of Another Rebel Spy," *Philadelphia Inquirer,* December 9, 1864.

In the South, despair and gloom, as well as grief, filled many parlors and drawing rooms. Hundreds of thousands of men and boys would never come home. There were few fresh troops to replace them. Many of the surviving soldiers were resolute in their determination and still confident that somehow, some way, the Confederacy might still prevail, or at least negotiate a favorable outcome that would protect Southern rights. In Richmond, John B. Jones, a clerk in the Confederate War Department, reflected on the prevailing mood in the capital as he sat down on the night of December 19 to write in his diary, "There is deep vexation in the city—a general apprehension that our affairs are rapidly approaching a crisis such as has not been experienced before."[76]

The Civil War was by no means over, but the end was in sight.

---

76 J. B. Jones, *A Rebel War Clerk's Diary*, 2 vols. (J. B. Lippincott & Co., 1866), vol. 2, 359.

Chapter 7

1865: The Final Year of the War and the Legacy of the CVRR

As January 1865 began, bad weather exposed the fact that the Cumberland Valley Railroad's rolling stock and motive power was now substandard. Much of it was worn out from hard use by the military during the war. On January 7, the regular evening train from Harrisburg was delayed about eight hours beyond its scheduled arrival in Chambersburg. "The cause of the detention, we learn," according to a *Valley Spirit* reporter, "was the drifted snow on the track, and the worthlessness of the engine. Several good new engines are sadly needed on this road." The editor of a Newville paper was more gracious in his opinion of the reason. The train had run off the track at Bridgeport instead of plowing through the drifts; it took considerable time to get it back in place and on its way. "This was the chief cause of the delay," he noted. Still, there was little doubt in Judge Frederick Watts' mind that the CVRR should invest in new locomotives as the year progressed, and he and the board began planning accordingly.[1]

Within days, the snow gave way to freezing rain that soon became a major ice storm. "Ice on the streets, on the upright walls of the buildings, on the walks, ice on the trees, and fences and rail-roads, ice everywhere," complained a Harrisburg

---

1 "Train Delayed," *Newville Star and Enterprise*, January 14, 1865, quoting the *Valley Spirit*.

reporter on January 10. "In fact the only safe way to get along anywhere is to skate." He went on to comment on another available transportation route, the railroad. "A ride over the Cumberland Valley rail-road to Chambersburg gives one a favorable opportunity to enjoy, so to speak, the perfect gloominess of the day, and the beauty of the ice-bound earth. During the whole route the rain continued to fall just as fast as it could freeze, and everything around was enveloped in a dense cloud through which the train appeared to cut its way, the passengers could not see ten rods from the cars. The whole country was one unbroken sheet of ice, smooth and glassy as ice was ever made." Along the route, icicles covered the fences, houses, and barns, and even dangled from the sheep and cattle in the frozen fields. "The few people that gathered round the stations appeared to be encrusted in ice," the newsman added.

Chambersburg was desolate, in his opinion. Much of the once-thriving county seat was still in ruins from McCausland's torches the previous summer. "Here and there, along the deserted streets," he noted, "may be seen a lone building newly erected, or repaired, or patched up, standing amid the ruins that surround it, while for many rods, and in some cases for whole squares on either side there is naught but piles of blackened bricks, or half demolished walls, or charred timber." Many families were living in or conducting business in crude shanties, poor protection from the bitter weather. "It will be many long years before Chambersburg will all be rebuilt," he predicted.[2]

The forlorn town indeed would never quite be the same. Already, several hastily-built replacement dwellings had been collapsed by the strong winter winds. The *Franklin Repository* later admonished its readers that a good two-story house was better than a poor three-story one. The houses could be rebuilt, but the homes were gone forever. "Will the old trees grow again, the old rose bushes and honeysuckles put forth, the rare old ivy be green, the cedars that grew before the town was in existence, will *these* same ever make us happy to give us shelter or make us swell with pride again?" the editor lamented. "Let the young enjoy themselves, we old folks will meet unostentatiously, and will remind each other of our losses, not of our houses and lands and books and clothing, but of our *associations*, that are gone forever. And as we repeat our Jeremiahs, we cannot even point to a tree 'planted by a forefather's hands.'"[3]

2 "From Harrisburg," *Bradford Reporter* (Tonawanda, PA), January 26, 1865.

3 "Gossip with Our Friends," *Franklin Repository*, May 31, 1865.

Late in January, the case of three men accused of being Rebel spies finally was resolved, with bad news for the prosecution. William Williams, William Thompson, and William Fielding had been captured on the Cumberland Valley Railroad in December 1864 and had been incarcerated for weeks before their hearing in Harrisburg. Scant testimony, however, could be produced, and the Military Commission had no choice but to declare them to be innocent of the charge, which could have brought the death penalty. Instead, the trio was taken, under armed guard, to Fort Delaware near Philadelphia to be held simply as prisoners of war.[4]

More than two years after the fact, the tragic September 1862 head-on collision in the dense fog near Bridgeport that claimed the lives of several soldiers was back in the news. On February 8, 1865, the state legislature approved a special bill granting a lifetime pension of eight dollars a month to William Keller, formerly a private in the 20th Pennsylvania Volunteer Militia, for permanent injuries suffered in the accident. They included severe cuts to his head, a broken right collarbone, and a crushed left breast.[5]

The Cumberland Valley Railroad faced additional negative press that cold, windy February. The state legislature discussed an act "to compel the Cumberland Valley railroad company to guard against accidents along their line of road in the city of Harrisburg." Despite the occasional presence of flagmen at key road crossings, passing trains still occasionally struck or narrowly missed pedestrians and vehicles. It was not a new issue. After being tabled several times, the bill eventually was passed several months later.[6]

J. D. Morrow, the oft-caustic editor of the Shippensburg *Star of the Valley*, repeatedly mocked the railroad company, including advertising for "four stout mules" to haul trains because the CVRR's antebellum locomotives were so poor. In early March, Morrow added, "The afternoon train from Harrisburg arrived on time last Wednesday. Cause,—a strong East wind and the fireman's stealing a bucket of coal from the North[ern] Central Depot." The Chambersburg *Valley Spirit* quickly jumped to the defense of the CVRR, demanding, "Again we ask, what is the matter? Has your free pass been revoked, or are you maliciously

---

4 "The Alleged Rebel Spies," *Newville Star and Enterprise*, January 28, 1865.

5 "Legislative," *Philadelphia Inquirer*, February 9, 1865; Civil War Muster Roll and Related Records, 1861-1866, 20th Regiment Pennsylvania Volunteer Militia, RG-19, Series #19.11, Pennsylvania State Archives.

6 *Daily Legislative Record, For the Session of 1865* (George Bergner, 1865), no. 22, 176; no.79, 625.

disposed towards the fireman on that train?" The war of words continued for some time. Morrow attacked Judge Watts and O. N. Lull for several more years, denigrating the lack of investment in their "one-horse concern." He also sarcastically suggested that the directors take the cowcatchers off the fronts of the locomotives and attach them to the rear of the last car "to prevent the cows from running into the train."[7]

Another longstanding problem returned that March—pickpockets. The CVRR officials had received periodic reports for some time of professional thieves plying their trade on the rail cars, a problem shared by many railroads of the period. William B. Mullin, a long-time papermaker from Mount Holly Springs, Pennsylvania, was robbed of $300 while riding a train bound for Harrisburg. Someone had skillfully extracted his wallet from his pocket. Authorities arrested a suspicious person at the depot upon the train's arrival, but soon discharged him when Mullin could not fully identify the money he had lost. It was not his first financial setback. In late June 1863, Albert Jenkins' Virginia cavalrymen had visited Mullin's paper mill and his nearby competitors, taking their entire inventory of note paper and letter paper to be sent back to Richmond for Confederate usage.[8]

With the end of the long Civil War finally in sight, the CVRR's directors met in Philadelphia on March 16, 1865, for their regularly scheduled business meeting. Citing the increased living expenses over the past three years as the war escalated, and the personal sacrifices made by the senior leaders, the board authorized a special gratuity of $1,000 each for President Frederick Watts, Secretary/Treasurer Edward M. Biddle, and Superintendent O. N. Lull.[9]

The next day, potential trouble loomed at Harrisburg. Swollen by heavy rains, the Susquehanna River flooded, carrying away a few bridges north of Harrisburg in the "greatest rise since 1847," as a reporter in Harrisburg dubbed the dangerous freshet. Thomas's Island all but disappeared under the deluge. "The water is now beating against the timbers of the Cumberland Valley Railroad bridge, which is usually 15 feet above the level of the river," he declared. "Various household articles, and even horses, have been floating down the river all day." Fortunately,

---

7 "What's the Matter?" *Valley Spirit*, March 15, 1865; Westhaeffer, *History of the CVRR*, 115-16.

8 "Robbery on the Cars," *Adams Sentinel* (Gettysburg), March 7, 1865; "Word-of-Mouth News," *Harrisburg Telegraph*, Dec. 2, 1941. Because of several mills located in Mount Holly Springs taking advantage of water power from nearby mountain streams, the village became widely known as "Paper Town."

9 1865 Minute Book of the Cumberland Valley Railroad, Pennsylvania State Archives.

The Franklin Railroad's modest depot in Hagerstown, Maryland in 1872. It was located on Walnut Street near St. Mary's Catholic Church. *Robert L. Williams Collection*

the sturdy stone piers held fast against the swift current and the vital bridge remained intact, although the Harrisburg end warped about twenty inches when the river crested two feet high on the boards of the sidewall. The railroad had to stop sending trains over the bridge for several days until the damage could be repaired.[10]

War news dominated the spring. In Northern Virginia, Ulysses S. Grant began maneuvering to cut off Robert E. Lee's supply lines to the defensive fortifications and trenches that all but surrounded Richmond and Petersburg. His targets included the last open railroads that led into the towns, connecting the Confederate armies with much needed outside supplies. To the south, Maj. Gen.

10 "Great Flood in the Susquehanna," *Baltimore Sun*, March 18, 1865; "Flood in the Susquehanna," *Valley Spirit*, March 22, 1865; "Correspondence," *Bradford Reporter* (Tonawanda, PA), March 23, 1865. Thomas's Island is now known as City Island.

William T. Sherman was advancing through the Carolinas with his western armies, driving the largest remaining Rebel army in front of him. President Lincoln visited General Grant for several days beginning on March 24 to discuss the potential surrender of the enemy forces. General Sherman and Admiral David Dixon Porter attended some of these sessions.

While the people of the Cumberland Valley eagerly awaited the latest positive war news, they also took time to celebrate the return of three of their own. On July 6, 1863, a group of Chambersburg residents had headed east to Gettysburg to lend aid to the wounded. With rumors abounding of an impending battle near Williamsport, the party walked to Middletown on the state line, where they stopped overnight. The next day, they followed the railroad tracks into Hagerstown, not realizing the town was still in Rebel hands. Several of them were captured, although a few managed to find aid at the home of Jacob Keller, a CVRR employee who lived in the building that doubled as a ticket office. Most of the civilians ended up in Rebel prison camps. Three of them—Dr. George R. Kaufman, J. Porter Brown, and David M. Eiker—bribed a guard in mid-February and slipped away from their confinement near Salisbury, North Carolina. They trekked cross-country across the mountains until they reached safety. After resting and recuperating, they made arrangements to return to Pennsylvania.

On April 8, 1865, their Northern Central train crossed the Mason-Dixon Line and then pulled into Harrisburg at 3:00 a.m. They then took the eight o'clock CVRR train that morning to Chambersburg, taking them home after being gone for more than a year and nine months. "In all my wanderings," Eiker later wrote, "I had never become impatient to get on, but could take things as I found them, and make the best out of them I could, but after taking my seat in the familiar Cumberland Valley train, it did seem to get along rather too slowly." Three hours later, the train finally chugged into Chambersburg, arriving where the depot had stood before they left. An "immense crowd," including the town's band, was on hand to welcome them home. As they walked through the burned district, "with the ruins all about me," Eiker reflected, "a feeling of sadness came over me, but meeting the little woman who was waiting for me, I soon regained my cheerfulness."[11]

While D. M. Eiker and his travel companions planned new beginnings, the end came for the Confederate States of America in April. Grant's well-fed and well-supplied Federal armies forced Lee to abandon his entrenchments at

---

11 Hoke, *Historical Reminiscences of the War*, 141-165.

Richmond and Petersburg. He hoped to follow the Richmond-Danville railroad south but found powerful Union forces blocking his path at Amelia Court House. He then led his "ragged rebels" west in the hope of receiving supplies at Appomattox Station on the South Side Railroad. From there, the beloved Confederate commander believed it was possible to head south and join his forces with those of Gen. Joseph E. Johnston in rural North Carolina. On April 9, with no supplies to be found and his further path blocked by strong Union contingents, Lee decided to surrender the depleted, half-starved men of the once-powerful Army of Northern Virginia. He and Grant met in the parlor of the Wilmer McLean house to finalize the terms.[12]

The news of Lee's surrender spread throughout the Cumberland Valley on April 10. "A day of rejoicing long to be remembered in Shippensburg," a resident wrote in his diary that night. "General Lee surrendered to General Grant. The church bells rang, and the manufacturing plants blew their whistles long and loud, and a general handshaking and rejoicing in the old town." The whistles of passing CVRR trains echoed through the Valley.[13]

The joyous celebrations did not last more than a few days before many Cumberland Valley residents broke out their mourning wear. On the evening of Good Friday, April 14, veteran actor John Wilkes Booth mortally wounded Abraham Lincoln during a special benefit performance of the comedy "Our American Cousin" at Ford's Theater in Washington; Lincoln died the next morning. "Our rejoicing thrown into sadness and gloom on the stealthy assassination of our beloved President Abraham Lincoln by the hands of that traitor and Rebel J Wilkes Booth…" the unidentified Shippensburg diarist recorded on Saturday night, April 15. "Strong men weeping, great sorrow over the country. The church and other bells tolling out their mournful sound."[14]

While the North plunged into grief, Federal authorities feverishly hunted for Booth and his reported co-conspirators. They also used the opportunity to crack down on other people suspected of involvement, or of previously threatening the president. They included John D. Reamer, a Hagerstown shopkeeper who had a reputation as an ardent Southern sympathizer. One of his customers swore that about March 1, he had overheard Reamer confidentially inform a friend, William Gabriel, at his dry goods store that one hundred thousand dollars was being raised

12 For more, see Jay Winik, *April 1865: The Month That Saved America* (Harper, 2001).

13 "Effects of War News," *Shippensburg* (PA) *Chronicle*, July 24, 1913.

14 Ibid.

"to secure the assassination of President Lincoln." The assassin, supposedly, was to receive half of the money in advance and the balance after the deed had been accomplished. The murder was to take place before April 12.[15]

On April 16, Reamer, fearing that an angry mob might harm him once word circulated that Lincoln was dead, voluntarily went to the Hagerstown jail on Sunday evening and asked to be locked up as a place of refuge. The following day, April 17, guards moved his entire inventory from his store to the railroad depot and shipped it to Chambersburg, where it was stored in the trackside Oaks & Linn warehouse. United States marshals seized the goods on Tuesday and then conveyed the shaken Reamer on a special train over the Franklin and Cumberland Valley railroads through the Valley to Harrisburg. From there, he was transported south to Washington for interrogation. He faced the inquisition on April 19 and was arrested after several Hagerstown residents came forward to corroborate the claims, as well as to confirm that Reamer had been in Baltimore, where anti-Lincoln feeling was rife, at the time of the assassination. Gabriel was also held behind bars as a material witness. Three months later, on July 5, Secretary of War Edwin M. Stanton released Reamer and Gabriel from the Old Capitol Prison for lack of firm evidence that either was involved in the actual plot. While Reamer was incarcerated, his 16-year-old son died. A two-year-old daughter had perished in early January.[16]

A special train traversed the Cumberland Valley on Saturday, April 22, hauling people north to the Pennsylvania Railroad station in Harrisburg to view the Lincoln funeral train, which had stopped at Harrisburg on its way from Washington, D. C., across the North to take the body to its final resting place in Springfield, Illinois. Mourners stood in a driving rain for hours to enter the Capitol building and see the body as it lay in state. Many of them, however, were still in line when the funeral train departed for Philadelphia.[17]

While Lincoln's remains crisscrossed the North, the war that the president had prosecuted was winding down. On April 26, Confederate General Joseph E. Johnston capitulated to General Sherman, surrendering the largest Confederate

15 William C. Edwards and Edward Steers, Jr., eds., *The Lincoln Assassination: The Evidence* (University of Illinois Press, 2009), 1085-88.

16 "In Trouble," *Valley Spirit*, April 26, 1865; *Hagerstown Herald of Freedom and Torch Light*, April 19 and June 15, 1865. Reamer, his health and spirit broken, died less than a year later in Hagerstown. His widow lived until 1905, when she and a friend were asphyxiated by a faulty gas stove.

17 "Effect of War News," *Shippensburg (PA) Chronicle*, July 24, 1913.

army in the field at Bennett Place near Durham, North Carolina. It was Johnston who, back in the summer of 1861, had been the primary reason for so many then starry-eyed Union recruits to mass at Camp Slifer in Chambersburg in order to march on Harpers Ferry. Now, Johnston joined Robert E. Lee in laying down his arms. Other Rebel armies soon also laid down their arms, effectively ending the Civil War.[18]

Within weeks after the Rebel capitulation, the CVRR began transporting Union soldiers back to their Cumberland Valley homes. In June, to accommodate "the large and constantly increasing travel through the Cumberland Valley," the company added a third daily train between Harrisburg and Hagerstown. In July and August 1865 alone, the line carried nearly 50,000 passengers. In November, it transported an unprecedented 93,740 passengers.[19]

On May 31, 1865, Judge Watts finally accomplished one of his long-term goals, the formal consolidation of the Franklin Railroad into the Cumberland Valley Railroad after acquiring the remaining stock. "The Franklin had never since its construction paid a dividend to its Stockholders, and was in arrears for the payment of interest upon its bonds," he wrote. "It was manifestly the interests of both companies that they should be made one." Four shares of Franklin Railroad stock could be redeemed for one share of CVRR stock. Interruptions of the war and the yearly visits of Rebel raiders had postponed the consummation of the consolidation, but it was now time. With the threat of Southern saddle soldiers now behind them, the board of directors focused on expanding freight and passenger service, planning to add twenty new eight-wheel freight cars and two new freight engines. The replacement depot at Chambersburg would be open by the winter. An iron bridge now spanned the Conococheague Creek at Scotland at a cost of $7,100. Of promise for the future, "extensive deposits of iron ore have been lately developed near the line of our road, at points near to Chambersburg and Carlisle," Watts reported. The mine owners were constructing lateral roads to

18 For more, see Jay Winik, *April 1865: The Month That Saved America* (New York: Harper, 2001) and Mark A. Smith and Wade Sokolosky, *"No Such Army Since the Days of Julius Caesar": Sherman's Carolinas Campaign from Fayetteville to Averasboro, March 1865* (Savas Beatie, 2017).

19 "Three Trains," *Waynesboro Viillage Record*, June 23, 1865; *Thirty-first Annual Report of the Cumberland Valley Railroad Company, to the Stockholders, Made October 1, 1865* (The Herald Office, 1865), 11; *Thirty-second Annual Report of the Cumberland Valley Railroad Company, to the Stockholders, Made October 1, 1866* (The Herald Office, 1866), 11.

reach the railroad terminals so as to ship the crushed ore to foundries near Harrisburg.[20]

For Frederick Watts and the officials of the CVRR, it was a relief to run their railroad without government interference or the fear of armed Rebel soldiers invading the Cumberland Valley and disrupting passenger and freight service as they had each of the previous three years. As the first war-free summer in several years approached, the company invested in its infrastructure and much needed modern, heavy-duty motive power. On July 19, local newspapers announced that the CVRR was in the process of acquiring two new locomotives from the firm of Danforth, Cooke, and Co., of Paterson, New Jersey, increasing the number of engines from 12 to 14. The first engine, named *General Grant*, had already arrived while the second, *General Sherman*, was expected later in the week. Like much of the North, the regional railroad was already commemorating the chief Union leaders of the late war. The *General Grant* made its inaugural run on July 27, 1865.[21]

In Chambersburg, workers were busily dressing stones for the new, larger CVRR depot to replace the one the Rebels had destroyed. "This structure will be commodious," a reporter mentioned, "of modern style, and the finest building on the line of the road." Several hundred masons and carpenters had flocked to the town to work on the station and other new structures. "There's a better day coming," the newsman opined, "and in a few years Chambersburg will be the most beautiful town in [the] Cumberland Valley, far surpassing in grandeur the old place of the same name."[22]

Not losing a step, in October 1865 Watts outlined an ambitious program for the CVRR. Touting the successful rebuild of the Chambersburg warehouse "which was destroyed by the rebels," he declared: "We want one at Hagerstown, Greencastle, Shippensburg, Newville and Mechanicsburg, and preparations are now being made to supply these wants as speedily as possible." True to his word, the CVRR added a stationmaster's house in Mechanicsburg in 1866 and a depot the following year. However, J. D. Morrow, Watts' editorial nemesis at the Shippensburg *Star of the Valley*, lambasted the lack of energy and insufficient

---

20 *Thirty-first Annual Report*, 5-7.

21 "Local and Personal—New Engines," *Valley Spirit*, July 19, 1865; *The Commercial and Financial Chronicle* (William B. Dana & Company), vol. 3, July 21, 1866, 71; "Effects of War News," *Shippensburg* (PA) *Chronicle*, July 24, 1913. The CVRR also added three new passage cars and a baggage car, as well as 18 freight cars, bringing that total to 100.

22 "Chambersburg," *Newville Star and Enterprise*, July 29, 1865, citing the *Harrisburg Telegraph*.

re-investment in the railroad, including the poor ability to remove snow drifts that occasionally stranded trains.[23]

Valley residents did not hesitate to add their own input. A Chambersburg editor complained that residents in the lower half of the valley "can make no fast trains, and in returning they must take slow trains also or lose time waiting at Harrisburg." He hoped that "fast" service already extended to Carlisle could be stretched to Chambersburg, assuring any CVRR officials who may have read his editorial that such an improvement would pay for itself. It would enable Chambersburg residents to leave Baltimore or Philadelphia at noon and reach home by seven o'clock in the evening, or leave Washington, DC, at 8:30 a.m. and be home the same day.[24]

With peace restored, without the threat of invasion, commerce burgeoned. "[O]ur receipts and expenditures have been considerably increased," Watts proudly reported in October 1867. While the number of passengers remained relatively stable, the revenue from the increased amount of freight hauled rose $50,000 from 1866-1867.[25] The new situation demanded, in Watts' judgement, additional freight cars and a new locomotive, as well as better facilities at Bridgeport, now home to the busiest section of road.[26]

In the decade following the war's end, such repairs and renovations irrevocably changed the face of the CVRR. Between 1865-1873, the road underwent "an almost complete rebuilding," repairing damage caused by Confederates while also modernizing to meet new demands of freight transport. Many of the leading personalities associated with the CVRR during the war years remained with the company. Philadelphia businessman Edward Biddle continued to serve the company for several years after the war as its secretary and treasurer. O. N. Lull remained as general superintendent and then chief engineer and superintendent of motive power before retiring in 1882. His daughter married W. Blair Gilmore, the young Atlantic and Ohio telegrapher at Chambersburg who had given so much invaluable service to the government during the Rebel raids and incursions. At the close of the war, the grateful citizens of Chambersburg

23 *Thirty-First Annual Report*, 5-6; Westhaeffer, *History of the CVRR*, 116.

24 "Local Items," *Franklin Repository*, November 22, 1865.

25 *Thirty-Second Annual Report*, 11; *Thirty-Third Annual Report of the Cumberland Valley Railroad Company, to the Stockholders, Made October 1, 1867* (The Herald Office, 1867), 14.

26 *Thirty-Third Annual Report*, 6; Westhaeffer, *History of the CVRR*, 85.

presented Gilmore with a commemorative set of silver plate tableware as a token of their appreciation. He later served on the town council.[27]

The Civil War had brought about reconciliation and a spirit of cooperation among many rail lines. In the war effort, pre-war competitors had worked together, often to mutual benefit. The ease of long-distance hauls without time-consuming transfers from one rail line's cars to those of another enticed many companies to merge, or purchase smaller lines. The PRR began to absorb both the NCRY and CVRR as subsidiary lines through slow acquisition of their outstanding stock.[28]

After serving for 32 years as president of the Cumberland Valley Railroad, Frederick Watts in October 1873 declined re-election but agreed to serve on the board of directors. Board members for some time had wanted him to retire and "the management of the Company placed in younger and more active hands." New Jersey native Thomas B. Kennedy, affiliated with the CVRR since 1852 as its legal counsel and later as a director and then vice-president, assumed the presidency. He was one of the men the Confederates had held hostage in July 1864 during the burning of Chambersburg. Judge Watts continued his political, educational, and agricultural interests for the remainder of his life. He died at his home in Carlisle on August 17, 1889.[29]

Kennedy, with his personal magnetism, strong business acumen, and personal interest in his employees, proved to be a wise choice. In his capable hands, the CVRR "acquired much valuable real estate, erected suitable shops and station buildings, and, with its roadway, track and equipment brought to and maintained at a standard of excellence equal to that of the Pennsylvania Railroad Company..."[30]

Under Kennedy's capable leadership, the CVRR continued to expand its operations and improve its infrastructure as money became available. The company built a large freight house in Mechanicsburg in 1874, facilitating the railroad's growing dependency on freight hauls up and down the Valley. It was something that the company had been increasing since the mid-1860s. Another

---

27 Westhaeffer, *History of the CVRR*, 85-86; Bates, *History of Franklin County*, 470, 663; B. M. Nead, "Stuart's Raid," in *Kittochtinny Historical Society Papers*, vol. 8, February 1912 to February 1915, 67-70.

28 Eggert, *Harrisburg Industrializes*, 83.

29 *Minutes of the Board of the Cumberland Valley Railroad Company*, February 27, 1873; Westhaeffer, *History of the CVRR*, 117; Wilson, *History of the PRR*, 407.

30 Ibid., 408.

CVRR President Frederick Watts is pictured here in his later years alongside his grandson, John Montgomery Mahon, Jr. *Cumberland County Historical Society*

area of focus was the iron mines and furnaces that dotted South Mountain. Several companies constructed feeder lines that connected to the CVRR tracks. Over time, the Cumberland Valley Railroad absorbed three of these branch lines when their parent entities collapsed into insolvency.

Kennedy and the board, including Judge Watts, were strong proponents of leisure travel, long a hallmark of the CVRR since the days of the special excursions to Mumma's Grove. Following the 1873 national financial reversal, the railroad built several recreational parks along these branch lines to attract passengers to attend special events, concerts, and a day of leisure in the cool mountain shade. Perhaps the most popular, and enduring, of these parks was Williams Grove, first established in 1850 as a small picnic grove in Monroe Township east of Carlisle. The CVRR leased the 28 acres from the Williams family in 1873 along the Yellow Breeches Creek and turned it into a resort destination. The Grange, a national farmers' advocacy organization, for years held its annual convention there, drawing large crowds from across the eastern part of the country. Many of them rode special excursion trains to reach the venue. Its tree-shaded avenues offered "a cooling and inviting aspect to hot and travel-stained tourists," a popular travel guide stated in 1899.[31]

Periodically, the CVRR transported Civil War veterans to various reunions and gatherings. On September 16, 1886, the Col. H. I. Zinn Post of the Grand Army of the Republic, of Mechanicsburg, hosted a "grand reunion of veterans" at Williams Grove. An express train brought excursionists from Harrisburg up the Valley to the venue to listen to patriotic speeches, eat meals together, and reminisce. That night, the CVRR provided at its expense electric lights to illuminate the gathering place. A special train departed the picnic grounds at 9:00 to start the veterans on their way home. *The National Tribune*, a leading newspaper for former Union soldiers, advertised the event, saying "All old soldiers, whether members of the Grand Army of not, are most cordially invited to participate in the Reunion."[32]

---

31 CVRR files, Mechanicsburg Museum Association; Ralph D. Paine, *The Greater America* (The Outing Press), July-August 1899; Joseph D. Cress, "Grangers at the Grove: Annual Farmers Exhibition Ended Nearly a Century Ago," *The Sentinel,* September 5, 2015. Http://cumberlink. com/news/local/communities/mechanicsburg/grangers-at-the-grove-annual-farmers-exhibi tion-ended-nearly-a/article_af28d0f4-f081-5c1f-97d2-f5cf24771ed6.html, accessed January 17, 2018.

32 "The Grand Army" *The National Tribune,* September 16, 1886.

Thomas B. Kennedy capped off his long career with the Cumberland Valley Railroad by serving as its president from 1873-1905. *Mike Marotte*

A recently constructed railroad with an intersection to the CVRR near Carlisle allowed veterans and other passengers to ride down to Gettysburg to tour the battlefield. J. Howard Wert, the principal of Harrisburg's boys high school and a

Typical round-trip ticket issued by the CVRR in the post-war years; this example dates from 1885. *Robert L. Williams Collection*

former army lieutenant, grew up in Gettysburg and boasted an extensive collection of relics and artifacts he had collected in the years following the battle. He was also an author, and wrote a guidebook to the monuments on the battlegrounds. "From Harrisburg there is a first-class route with through trains leaving every few hours via Carlisle to Gettysburg," Wert penned in his introduction. "This route is over the Cumberland Valley R. R., which passed through one of the finest agricultural regions of the worlds, to Carlisle, famed for its Indian School; and thence, over the Gettysburg and Harrisburg R. R., world-famed for its wild, picturesque and magnificent mountain scenery, the time being about two hours." He went on to say, "The line of the Cumberland Valley R. R. is noted for the number of its attractive pleasure resorts. Prominent among these are Williams' Grove on the Dillsburg branch, Pine Grove on the Gettysburg and Harrisburg line, and Mont Alto in Franklin county. All of these are celebrated for their fine scenery, excellent location and varied attractions."[33]

During the 1880s, the Pennsylvania Railroad began buying more stock and exerting more direct influence over the affairs of the Cumberland Valley Railroad, including purchasing engines and cars of all sorts designed and built to PRR specifications. Passenger cars built at CVRR's machine shops in Chambersburg

---

33 J. Howard Wert, *A Complete Hand-book of the Monuments and Indications and Guide to the Positions on the Gettysburg Battle-field* (R. M. Sturgeon & Co., 1886), introduction.

also had to comply to the PRR standards. By 1902, the PRR had expanded its gradual takeover of the CVRR, echoing Judge Watts' mechanism in the 1860s to acquire control of the Franklin Railroad slowly. The PRR integrated the CVRR operations into a larger route to transport coal from the mountains of West Virginia eastward to a company-owned dock in New Jersey that served the port of New York City. The PRR also extended its passenger service from Harrisburg to Martinsburg, West Virginia, through Hagerstown. At its peak, at least 24 trains a day passed up and down the Valley, with as little as 20 minutes in between them. Many were long, slow coal trains.[34]

Thomas B. Kennedy, who oversaw the Cumberland Valley Railroad Company for three decades with competence and compassion following Judge Watts' resignation, fell seriously ill in the spring of 1905. He never recovered, dying on June 19 of that year at his home in Chambersburg. To honor his memory, all CVRR trains were draped in black and stopped wherever they were at 6:30 p.m. on June 22 for a full two minutes of relative silence as a sign of respect. His son, Morehead C. Kennedy, born in March 1862 just a few months before Jeb Stuart's raid on Chambersburg, became the president in 1913.[35]

That same year, more than 53,000 Civil War veterans congregated at Gettysburg for the 50th anniversary of the famed battle that had claimed or changed forever so many lives. Hundreds of old soldiers in the Cumberland Valley attended the commemoration, which included speeches, monument dedications, and other special events from June 29 to July 4. The CVRR carried 249 men, who subsequently traveled from Carlisle over the Gettysburg and the Harrisburg Railway, a subsidiary of the Reading Railroad since 1891. After arriving at the Gettysburg depot, they were taken in carriages to a sprawling tent city at Gettysburg that provided shelter for the aged ex-soldiers during their stay. President Woodrow Wilson, the special guest speaker on July 4, praised the country's reconciliation and reunion, and challenged the audience to never forget the "splendid valor" of the men who fought there in 1863. The Pennsylvania Fiftieth Anniversary of the Battle of Gettysburg Committee paid the CVRR a total of $574.14 for the tickets, which were distributed to the veterans free of charge.

---

34 CVRR files, Mechanicsburg Museum Association.

35 M. L. "Mike" Marotte III, "Train Men: The Kennedys of the Cumberland Valley Railroad," *Chambersburg Public Opinion*, October 27, 2016. See www.publicopiniononline.com/story/life/2016/10/27/train-men-kennedys-cumberland-valley-railroad/92663594/, accessed January 17, 2018.

Almost 10,000 men used the services of the Pennsylvania Railroad and another 4,000 took Philadelphia and Reading trains.[36]

The Federal government had taken over the CVRR and other railroads at times during the Civil War. With the United States' entry into World War I in the spring of 1917, the government again assumed control of private railroads to use them to move troops, munitions, and supplies to eastern ports. With the war's end, control passed back to the railroad companies. The Cumberland Valley Railroad's days as an independent legal entity ended in 1919 when the Pennsylvania Railroad completed its slow acquisition. The following year, the PRR fully integrated the CVRR into its local operations as the Cumberland Valley Division with Morehead Kennedy as the vice-president, based at Broad Street Station in Philadelphia.[37]

Regularly scheduled passenger service for Cumberland Valley residents ended in 1952. The Penn Central (the consolidation of the old Pennsylvania Railroad and the New York Central) shuttered the Chambersburg railroad facilities in 1972, drawing to a close the town's 130 years as the hub of the Cumberland Valley Railroad and its successor, the Cumberland Valley Division. Today, the Norfolk Southern Railway is the Valley's current major railroad line, still using many of the original CVRR's right of ways.

The once-vibrant Cumberland Valley Railroad is long gone, but its history as one of the Civil War's most bitterly contested Northern railroads lives on. They truly were "targeted tracks."

---

36 Lewis E. Beitler, ed. and compiler, *Fiftieth Anniversary of the Battle of Gettysburg Report of the Pennsylvania Commission* (Wm. Stanley Ray, State Printer, 1913), 31.

37 Marotte, "Train Men," *Chambersburg Public Opinion*.

Appendix 1

Stations and Flag Stops on the
CVRR During the Civil War

Station distances from Hagerstown

Morganstown: 4
State Line: 6
Greencastle: 11
Marion: 16
Chambersburg: 22
Scotland: 27
Shippensburg: 33
Oakville: 40
Newville: 43
Alterton: 48
Woodhope: 51
Carlisle: 56
Middlesex: 59
Kingston: 61
Mechanicsburg: 65
Shiremanstown: 69
Bridgeport: 73
Harrisburg:74

Source: *Detroit Free Press*, June 28, 1863.

Appendix 2

The CVRR's Growth During the Civil War

	Fiscal 1862-63	Fiscal 1863-64	Fiscal 1864-65
Locomotives	12	12	14
Passenger cars	8	9	12
Baggage, mail, and express cars	4	4	5
Freight cars	79	82	100
Mileage of engines	165,712	173,001	175,889
No. of passengers	256,926	309,950	326,914
Tons of freight	106,722	144,390	123,781
Gross earnings: passengers	$125,222	$185,646	$215,137
Gross earnings: freight	$124,943	$154,604	$183,280
Gross earnings: mail (fixed contract)	$5,200	$5,200	$5,200
Gross receipts*	$363,051	$484,349	$522,812
Operating expenses	$158,044	$201,052	$320,981
Net profits from operations	$97,321	$144,398	$83,052

* Includes revenues from the Cumberland Valley Railroad and Franklin Railroad, as well as dividends from securities held by the company.

Source: Adapted from CVRR data reported in *The Commercial and Financial Chronicle* (New York: William B. Dana & Company), vol. 3, July 21, 1866, 71.

CVRR Engine Roster During the Civil War

Engine Name	Wheel Arrangement	Builder	Date Service Began	Primary Wartime Use
Nicolas Biddle	4-2-0	William Norris	1838	Passenger
William Penn	4-4-0	Wilmarth	1850	Freight
Robert Morris	4-4-0	Wilmarth	1850	Freight
Tiger	4-4-0	Wilmarth	1850	Freight until late 1862; then Susquehanna Bridge service
Leopard	4-4-0	Wilmarth	1850	Extra passenger, freight
Pioneer	2-2-2T	Wilmarth	1851	Passenger
Jenny Lind	2-2-2T	Wilmarth	1851	Passenger
Utility	0-4-0T	Wilmarth	1854	Bridge service until Sept. 1862 crash; then yard switcher in Chambersburg
Boston	2-2-4T	Wilmarth	Early 1855	Passenger
Enterprise	2-2-4T	Wilmarth	Early 1855	Passenger
Judge Watts	4-4-0	Lancaster Locomotive Works	July 1857	Freight

Engine Name	Wheel Arrangement	Builder	Date Service Began	Primary Wartime Use
Col. Gehr	4-4-0	Danforth, Cooke	1861	Freight
T. B. Kennedy	4-4-0	Danforth, Cooke	1862	Freight

Source: Westhaeffer, *History of the CVRR*, 298-303.

The terms 4-4-0, 4-2-0, 0-4-0T, 2-2-2T and 2-2-4T refer to the postwar Whyte notation of wheel arrangement: the number of leading wheels, the number of driving wheels, and the number of trailing wheels. The T refers to a "tank engine," which carried its own water supply on board in one or more tanks, as opposed to a 4-4-0 or 4-2-0 engine, which used auxiliary tenders located immediately behind the locomotive.

Bibliography

PRIMARY SOURCES

Newspapers

Baltimore American
Baltimore Sun
Bradford Reporter (Tonawanda, PA)
Carlisle (PA) *Volunteer*
Carlisle (PA) *Weekly Herald*
Chambersburg (PA) *Semi-Weekly Dispatch*
Columbia (PA) *Spy*
Evening Star (Washington, D. C.)
Franklin Repository (Chambersburg, PA)
Greencastle (PA) *Pilot*
Hagerstown (MD) *Herald of Freedom and Torch Light*
Hagerstown (MD) *Mail*
Harrisburg Patriot and Union
Harrisburg Telegraph
Maryland Free Press (Hagerstown, MD)
National Daily Intelligencer (Washington, D. C.)
National Tribune (Washington, D. C.)
New York Herald
New York Times
New York Tribune
Newville (PA) *Valley Star*
Philadelphia Age
Philadelphia Evening Bulletin
Philadelphia Inquirer
Philadelphia Press
Pittsburgh Daily Post

Pittsburgh Gazette
Richmond Daily Dispatch
Shippensburg (PA) *Chronicle*
Shippensburg (PA) *News*
Shippensburg (PA) *Star of the Valley*
Valley Spirit (Chambersburg, PA)
Waynesboro (PA) *Village Record*

PERSONAL PAPERS, LETTERS, DIARIES, JOURNALS

Cumberland County Historical Society, Hamilton Library, Carlisle, PA
    Brooks-Bigler Family Papers
Dickinson College, Archives & Special Collections, Waidner-Spahr Library, Carlisle, PA
    Jacob Bretz Letters
    George D. Chenoweth Letters
    Charles F. Himes Papers
    Eli Slifer Papers
Franklin & Marshall College, Lancaster, PA
    Eleanor Reynolds Scrapbook
Franklin County Historical Society, Chambersburg, PA
    Cumberland Valley Railroad Files
    Emma Ritner Roberts, "Recollections of John Brown"
    Agnes Wolfe Papers
Gettysburg National Military Park, Gettysburg, PA
    Sarah Broadhead Diary
Historical Society of Dauphin County, Alexander Family Library, Harrisburg, PA
    Caspar Dull Papers
Historical Society of Pennsylvania, Philadelphia
    Joseph Boggs Beale Papers
Maryland Historical Society, H. Furlong Baldwin Library, Baltimore
    Shriver Family Papers
Montana State Univ. Lib., Merrill G. Burlingame Special Collections, Bozeman, MT
    William Minor Roberts Papers
Pennsylvania State Archives, Harrisburg
        Cumberland Valley RR files, Penn Central RR Collection, Manuscript Gr. 286
        Records of Transportation and Telegraph Department, 1861-1869,
            Military Dispatches Received and Sent, Pennsylvania Military Telegraph
            Department, RG 19 Subgroup B
        John S. Witmer Papers, MG-7
        Warren J. Harder Collection, MG-214
Railroad Museum of Pennsylvania, Strasburg, PA
    Cumberland Valley Railroad files
Simpson Public Library, Mechanicsburg, PA
    H. H. Snavely, "Personal War Sketch," Col. H. I. Zinn Post No. 415 Papers
United States Army Heritage and Education Center, Carlisle, PA
    J. C. Altick Diary, Civil War Times Illustrated Collection

Henry A. Bilighous Diary, Boyer Collection
Bond-Martin Papers
Henry F. Charles Memoir, Boyer Collection
Robert J. Forrest Diary, Harrisburg Civil War Round Table Collection
Isaac Harris Diary, Civil War Documents Collection
William Robinson Diary, Civil War Miscellaneous Collection
John Stumbaugh Papers, Harrisburg Civil War Round Table Collection
University of Iowa Library, Ames
Joseph F. Culver Papers
Univ. of North Carolina, Louis Round Wilson Special Collections Library, Chapel Hill
Charles Edward Lippitt Diary and Medical Record Book
Thomas Ware Diary
J. Kelly Bennette Papers
University of Virginia, Alderman Library, Charlottesville
Washington Hands Civil War Memoirs
Virginia Military Institute, Lexington
John McCausland Letters and Papers

ARTICLES

"Cumberland Valley Railroad Company." in *American Railroad Journal*, January 11, 1862.

Donavin, S. K., "The Invasion: Rebel Occupancy of Carlisle, 1863." *Cumberland County History*, vol. 15, no. 1, Summer 1998.

Hazard, Samuel, "Cumberland Valley Railroad." *Hazard's Register of Pennsylvania*, vol. XVII, no. 20, November 14, 1835.

Jones, Ephraim N. and Richard H. Steinmetz, "A Civil War Adventure." *Railroad Stories*, vol. XV, no. 3, October 1934.

Livermore, Thomas L., and Theodore F. Dwight, ed. "Patterson's Shenandoah Valley Campaign," in *Papers of the Military Historical Society of Massachusetts*. Volume 1, Campaigns in Virginia 1861-1862. Boston and New York: Houghton, Mifflin and Company, 1895.

McClure, A. K., "An Episode of John Brown's Raid." *Lippincott's Magazine of Popular Literature and Science*, vol. 32, September 1883.

"Sanitary Commission No. 48." *Documents of the United States Sanitary Commission*, vol. 1, Numbers 1 to 60 inclusive. New York: United States Sanitary Commission, 1866.

Schuricht, Hermann, "Jenkins' Brigade in the Gettysburg Campaign." *Southern Historical Society Papers*, vol. 24, 1896.

Slingluff, Fielder C., "Burning of Chambersburg—Retaliatory." *Confederate Veteran*, vol. XVII, no. 11, November 1909.

"Stated Meeting, March 18, 1864." *Proceedings of the American Philosophical Society*, vol. 9, no. 70, June 1863.

Stone, Jane Dice, ed., "Dairy of William Heyser." *Papers Read Before the Kittochtinny Historical Society*, vol. 16. Mercersburg, PA: Mercersburg Printing, 1978.

Stouffer, Amos and William Garrett Piston, ed., "'The Rebs Are Yet Thick About Us': The Civil War Diary of Amos Stouffer of Chambersburg." *Civil War History*, vol. 38, no. 3, September 1992.

Taylor, Charles H., "The Burning of Chambersburg." *Thomas L. Wilson's Sufferings Endured for a Free Government: A History of the Cruelties and Atrocities of the Rebellion Philadelphia*. King & Baird, 1865.

BOOKS AND PERIODICALS

Anderson, Osborne P. *A Voice from Harper's Ferry: A Narrative of Events at Harper's Ferry; with Incidents Prior and Subsequent to its Capture by Captain Brown and His Men.* Boston: Printed for the Author, 1861.

Carman, Ezra A., Thomas G. Clemens (ed.). *The Maryland Campaign of September 1862: Vol. 1: South Mountain.* New York and California: Savas Beatie, LLC, 2010.

Committee on the Joint Conduct of the War, *Report of the Joint Committee on the Conduct of the War,* in Three Parts. Washington: Government Printing Office, 1863.

Cooper, John M. *Recollections of Chambersburg, Pa.: Chiefly Between the Years 1830-1850.* Chambersburg, PA: A. Nevin Pomeroy, 1900.

Cormany, Rachel and Samuel, James C. Mohr, ed. *The Cormany Diaries: A Northern Family in the Civil War* (Pittsburgh: University of Pittsburgh Press, 1982.

Cumberland Valley Railroad, *Annual Reports of the Cumberland Valley Railroad Company, to the Stockholders.* Carlisle, PA: Printed by the Herald Office, 1838-1865.

Dyer, Frederick H. *A Compendium of the War of the Rebellion Compiled and Arranged from Official Records of the Federal and Confederate Armies, Reports of the Adjutant Generals of the Several States, the Army Registers, and Other Reliable Documents and Sources* (Des Moines, IA: The Dyer Publishing Company, 1908).

Francis, Augustus Theodore (compiler), George Edward Lowen (ed.). *History of the 71st Regiment, N.G., N.Y., American Guard.* New York: The Eastman Publishing Company, 1919.

Green, Helen Binkley, ed. *Pages from a Diary, 1843-1880: Excerpts from the Diaries of Jacob Stouffer and Eliza Rider Stouffer.* Hagerstown, MD: s. n., 1966.

Haupt, Herman and Frank A. Flower. *Reminiscences of General Herman Haupt.* Milwaukee: Wright & Joys, 1901.

Hoke, Jacob, *The Great Invasion of 1863: Or, General Lee in Pennsylvania.* Dayton, OH: W. J. Shuey, 1887.

————. *Reminiscences of the War; or, Incidents Which Transpired in and about Chambersburg, during the War of the Rebellion.* Chambersburg, PA: M. A. Foltz, 1884.

Jacobs, Michael. *Notes on the Rebel Invasion of Maryland and Pennsylvania and the Battle of Gettysburg.* Philadelphia: J. B. Lippincott, 1864.

Johnston, David E. *The Story of a Confederate Boy in the Civil War.* Portland, OR: Glass & Prudhomme, 1914.

Leon, Louis. *Diary of a Tar Heel Confederate Soldier.* Charlotte: Stone Publishing Company, 1913.

Lockwood, John. *Our Campaign Around Gettysburg.* Brooklyn: A.H. Rome & Brothers, 1864.

McClellan, H. B. *I Rode with Jeb Stuart: The Life and Campaigns of Major General J.E.B. Stuart.* Bloomington, IN: Indiana University Press, 1958.

McClure, Alexander K. *Old Time Notes of Pennsylvania,* 2 vols. Philadelphia: John C. Winston Co., 1905.

Patterson, Robert. *A Narrative of the Campaign in the Valley of the Shenandoah, 1861.* Philadelphia: John Campbell, 1865.

Poor, Henry V. *American Railroad Journal.* New York: J. H. Schultz & Co., 1850-1865.

Richards, Louis. *Eleven Days in the Militia During the War of the Rebellion; Being a Journal of the "Emergency" Campaign of 1862.* Philadelphia: Collins, 1883.

Roberts, William Milnor. *Report of William Milnor Roberts, Chief Engineer of the Cumberland Valley Rail Road Company, Made to the Board, on the 23d Oct. 1835.* Philadelphia: John C. Clark, 1835.

—————. *Second Report of William Milnor Roberts, Chief Engineer of the Cumberland Valley Rail Road Company, Made to the Board, on the 29th of December 1836.* Chambersburg, PA: Hickok & Blood, 1836.

—————. *Third Annual Report of William Milnor Roberts, Chief Engineer of the Cumberland Valley Rail Road Company, Made to the Board, on the 28th of December, 1837.* Chambersburg, PA: Hickok & Blood, 1837.

Schneck, Rev. B. S. *The Burning of Chambersburg, Pennsylvania.* Philadelphia: Lindsay & Blakiston, 1864.

Schwarz, J. R., and J. Zeamer. *The Cumberland Blue Book: A Compendium of Information of Lower Cumberland County.* Camp Hill, PA: J. Robley Schwartz, 1903.

Stillé, Charles J. *History of the United States Sanitary Commission.* Philadelphia: J. B. Lippincott & Co., 1866.

Sullivan, James W. *Boyhood Memories of the Civil War, 1861-'65: Invasion of Carlisle.* Carlisle, PA: Hamilton Library Association, 1933.

The War of the Rebellion. *A Compilation of the Official Records of the Union and Confederate Armies,* 128 vols. Washington, D. C.: United States Government Printing Office, 1880-1901.

Whittemore, Henry. *History of the Seventy-First Regiment, N.G.S.N.Y.* New York: W. McDonald & Co., 1886.

Wilson, William Bender. *A Few Acts and Actors in the Tragedy of the Civil War in the United States.* Philadelphia, s. n., 1892.

—————. *From the Hudson to the Ohio.* Philadelphia: Kensington Press, 1902.

—————. *History of the Pennsylvania Railroad Co.* Philadelphia: Henry T. Coates, 1895.

SECONDARY SOURCES

Articles

Alexander, Ted, "A Regular Slave Hunt," *North & South*, Vol. 4, No. 7 (2001), 82-88.

Billett, Glenn E., "The Department of the Susquehanna," *Journal of the Lancaster County Historical Society*, Vol. 66, No. 1 (1962), 1-64.

Brubaker, Jack, "Defending the Susquehanna," *Civil War Times*, vol. 42, no. 2, 2003.

Brumbaugh, Frederick D., "A History of the Cumberland Valley Railroad: 1831-1837," *Papers Read Before the Kittochtinny Historical Society*, vol. 16, March 1971-1978.

Bruning, Matt, "Disunity in the Union: Franklin County, PA, and the American Civil War," *Western Illinois Historical Review*, vol. II, Spring 2010.

Conrad, William P., "The Burning of Chambersburg," *Papers Read Before the Kittochtinny Historical Society*, vol. 15, May 1963-February 1979.

Cree, John G., "John Brown at Chambersburg: Written in 1906 by James W. Cree," *Papers Read Before the Kittochtinny Historical Society*, vol. 14, October 1957-April 1963.

Crist, Robert Grant, "Highwater 1863: The Confederate Approach to Harrisburg," *Pennsylvania History*, vol. XXX, no. 2, April 1963.

Ent, Uzal, "Rebels in Pennsylvania," *Civil War Times, Illustrated*, vol. 37, no. 4, 998.

Fisher, Charles E., "The United States Military Railroads," *Railway and Locomotive Historical Society Bulletin*, No. 59, 1942.

Gherst, Col. Milton A., "Military Situation and Burning of Chambersburg," *Papers Read Before the Kittochtinny Historical Society*, vol. 8, March 1912-February 1915.

Kennedy, J. H., ed., "The Railroad Men of America: Joseph D. Potts," in *Magazine of Western History Illustrated*, vol. IX, 1889.

Landis, Merkel, "Civil War Times in Carlisle: An Address Delivered at Hamilton Library, Carlisle, Pa., February 12th, 1931," *Carlisle in the Civil War*. Carlisle, PA: Hamilton Library and Historical Association, n. d.

Osmond, Thornton, "Hon. Frederick Watts," in *Paper read before the Hamilton Library and Historical Association of Cumberland County*, February 28, 1930, Cumberland County Historical Society, Carlisle, PA.

Podvia, Mark W., "Canals, Railroads, Philadelphia, and the Struggle for Internal Improvement in the Cumberland Valley, 1825-1837," *Cumberland County History*, vol. 21, no. 1, Summer 2004.

————, "The Honorable Frederick Watts: Carlisle's Agricultural Reformer," *Penn State Environmental Law Review*, 299, 2009.

Price, Channing, "Stuart's Chambersburg Raid: An Eyewitness Account," in *Civil War Times, Illustrated*, vol. 4, no. 9, January 1966.

Riddle, H. A., "A Few Facts About the C.V.R.R.," *Papers Read Before the Kittochtinny Historical Society*, vol. 11, February 1928-June 1939.

Savukas, Elaine M., "Bibliography of the Confederate Invasions of Chambersburg," *Papers Read Before the Kittochtinny Historical Society*, vol. 16, 1971-1978.

————, "The Confederate Invasions of Chambersburg, Pennsylvania: A Historical Research Paper," Department of History, Millersville State College, copy in the collection of the Franklin County Historical Society, Chambersburg, PA.

Van Dolsen, Nancy, "Transportation, Competition, and the Growth of a Town: Carlisle, 1750-1860," *Cumberland County History*, vol. 14, no. 1, Summer 1997.

White, John H., "The 'Pioneer': Light Passenger Locomotive of 1851 in the Museum of History and Technology," *Smithsonian Institution*, United States National Museum, Bulletin 240, Contributions from the Museum of History and Technology, Paper 42, 1966.

BOOKS

Alexander, Ted, Jim Neitzel, Virginia Stake, and William P. Conrad. *Southern Revenge! Civil War History of Chambersburg, Pa*. Greater Chambersburg Chamber of Commerce, 1989.

Annual Reports of the Cumberland Valley Railroad. 1840-1865, Chambersburg, PA.

Ayres, Edward L. *In the Presence of Mine Enemies: War in the Heartland of America, 1859-1863*. New York and London: W. W. Norton & Company, 2003.

Baird, Matthew, et. al. *Baldwin Locomotive Works: Illustrated Catalogue of Locomotives*. Philadelphia: J. B. Lippincott & Co.

Bates, Samuel P. *History of Franklin County, Pennsylvania*. Chicago: Warner, Beers & Co., 1887.

Bianculli, Anthony J. *Trains and Technology: The American Railroad in the Nineteenth Century*. Volume 2, Cars. Newark, DE: The University of Delaware Press, 2002.

Bockmiller, Stephen R. *Hagerstown in the Civil War*. Charleston, SC: Arcadia, 2011.

Burkhart, William H., ed. *Shippensburg Historical Society, Shippensburg, Pennsylvania, in the Civil War*. Shippensburg, PA: Burd Street Press, 2003.

Churella, Albert J. *The Pennsylvania Railroad, Volume 1: Building an Empire, 1846-1917*. Philadelphia: University of Pennsylvania Press, 2012.

Clark, John E., Jr. *Railroads in the Civil War: The Impact of Management on Victory or Defeat*. Baton Rouge: Louisiana State University Press, 2001.

Coddington, Edwin B. *The Gettysburg Campaign: A Study in Command*. New York: Charles Scribner's Sons, 1968.

Colwell, David G. *The Bitter Fruits: The Civil War Comes to a Small Town in Pennsylvania*. Carlisle, PA: Cumberland County Historical Society, 1998.

Conrad, W. P., and Ted Alexander. *When War Passed This Way*. Greencastle, PA: Greencastle Bicentennial Publication/Lilian S. Besore Memorial Library, 2002.

Donehoo, George P. *A History of the Cumberland Valley in Pennsylvania*. Harrisburg: Susquehanna History Association, 1930.

Durant, Pliny A. *History of Cumberland and Adams Counties, Pennsylvania*. Chicago: Warner, Beers & Co., 1886.

Eicher, John H., and David J. Eicher. *Civil War High Commands*. Palo Alto, CA: Stanford University Press, 2001.

Egle, William H. *Life and Times of Andrew Gregg Curtin*. Philadelphia: The Thompson Publishing Co., 1896.

The Franklin County Civil War Damage Claims: Chambersburg Burns. Chambersburg, PA: Franklin County Historical Society, 2014.

Hinton, Richard J. *John Brown and His Men*. New York and London: Funk & Wagnalls, 1894.

Hunt, Roger D. *Colonels in Blue: Union Army Colonels of the Civil War: The Mid-Atlantic States…* Mechanicsburg PA: Stackpole Books, 2007.

Kamm, Samuel R. *The Civil War Career of Thomas A. Scott*. Philadelphia: University of Pennsylvania Press, 1940.

Leavy, Michael. *Railroads of the Civil War*. Yardley, PA: Westholme, 2010.

Majewski, John. *A House Dividing: Economic Development in Pennsylvania and Virginia Before the Civil War*. New York: Cambridge University Press, 2000.

McCauley, I. H. *Historical Sketch of Franklin County, Pennsylvania: Prepared for the Centennial Celebration, Held at Chambersburg, Pa., July, 1876*. Harrisburg: Patriot Printing Company, 1876.

Mingus, Scott L. *Flames Beyond Gettysburg: The Confederate Expedition to the Susquehanna River, June 1863*. El Dorado Hills, CA: Savas Beatie, LLC, 2011.

———. *Soldiers, Spies & Steam: A History of the Northern Central Railway in the Civil War*, York, PA: Amazon CreateSpace, 2016.

———. *"This Trying Hour": The Philadelphia, Wilmington and Baltimore Railroad in the Civil War*. York, PA: Amazon CreateSpace, 2017.

Nevin, Alfred. *Men of Mark of Cumberland Valley, Pa. 1776-1876*. Philadelphia: Fulton Publishing, 1876.

Nye, Wilbur Sturtevant. *Here Come the Rebels!* Dayton, OH: Morningside Bookshop, 1988.

Rosenberger, Francis C. *The Cumberland Valley of Pennsylvania in the 1860s*. Rose Hill, PA: Rose Hill Seminar, 1963.

Scharf, J. Thomas. *History of Western Maryland*, 2 vols. Philadelphia: L. H. Leverts, 1882.

Steinmetz, Richard H. *The Cumberland Valley Railroad*. s. n., 1938.

Stewart, Harriet Wylie. *History of the Cumberland Valley*. Pennsylvania. s. n., 1918.

Stoner, Jacob H. *Historical Papers: Franklin County and the Cumberland Valley, Pennsylvania*. Chambersburg, PA: The Craft Press, 1947.

Thompson, D. W., ed. *Two Hundred Years in Cumberland County*. Carlisle, PA: Hamilton Library & Historical Association of Cumberland County, 1951.

Thompson, John W. *Horses, Hostages, and Apple Cider: J.E.B. Stuart's 1862 Pennsylvania Raid*. Mercersburg, PA: s. n., 2002.

Toomey, Daniel Carroll. *The Civil War in Maryland*. Baltimore: Toomey Press, 2000.

———. *The War Came by Train: The Baltimore and Ohio Railroad During the Civil War*. Baltimore: B&O Railroad Museum, 2013.

Trout, Robert J., ed. *Memoirs of the Stuart Horse Artillery Battalion: Moorman's and Hart's Batteries*. Knoxville: University of Tennessee Press, 2008.

———. *With Pen and Saber: The Letters and Diaries of J. E. B. Stuart's Staff Officers*. Mechanicsburg, PA: Stackpole Books, 1995.

Turner, George Edgar. *Victory Rode the Rails: The Strategic Place of Railroads in the Civil War*. Lincoln: University of Nebraska Press, 1992.

Warner, Ezra J. *Generals in Blue: Lives of the Union Commanders*. Baton Rouge: LSU Press, 1964.

Watts, Randy. *Mainline Railroads:1828 to 1993, Railroads of the Cumberland Valley*. Book 5. Carlisle, PA: Keystone Computer Services, 1993.

Weber, Thomas. *The Northern Railroads in the Civil War*. Bloomington: Indiana University Press, 1999.

Westhaeffer, Paul J. *History of the Cumberland Valley Railroad, 1835-1919*. Falls Church, VA: Washington Chapter, National Railway Historical Society, 1979.

Williams, W. *Appleton's Railroad and Steamboat Companion, Being a Travellers' Guide through the United States of America, Canada, New Brunswick, and Nova Scotia*. New York: D. Appleton & Company, 1848-1865.

Wingert, Cooper H. *The Confederate Approach on Harrisburg: The Gettysburg Campaign's Northernmost Reaches*. Charleston, SC: The History Press, 2012.

WEBSITES

Baer, Christopher T. "A General Chronology of the Pennsylvania Railroad Company, Its Predecessors and Its Historical Context." www.prrths.com/Hagley

Dr. William H. Boyle to Isaac McCauley, July 5, 1863, Gilder Lehrman Collection. www.gilderlehrman.org/content/civilian-describes-pillaging-near-gettysburg-1863

"Chronicling America: Historic American Newspapers," Library of Congress. Https://chroniclingamerica.loc.gov/lccn/sn84026707/

Lawrence, Gordon Boyer, "The Burning and Reconstruction of Chambersburg, Pennsylvania 1864-1870," Master's theses no. 1228, 2008, http://scholarship.richmond.edu/masters-theses/1228

Mechanicsburg (PA) Museum Association, "The Cumberland Valley Railroad & Mechanicsburg." www.mechanicsburgmuseum.org/cvrr.html

NewspaperArchive, www.newspaperarchive.com/

Newspapers.com, https://www.newspapers.com/

Penn State University Libraries, "Civil War Newspaper Collection," http://digitalnewspapers.libraries.psu.edu/Olive/APA/CivilWar/

University of Virginia, "The Valley of the Shadow: Two Communities in the American Civil War," http://valley.lib.virginia.edu/

Index

About the Authors

Scott Mingus, a scientist and consultant in the global pulp & paper industry, holds patents in self-adhesive postage stamps and bar code labels. The Ohio native graduated from the Paper Science & Engineering program at Miami University. He has written or co-authored nineteen Civil War and Underground Railroad books. His books include *Flames Beyond Gettysburg: The Confederate Expedition to the Susquehanna River, June 1863* (2011), *The Second Battle of Winchester: The Confederate Victory That Opened the Door to Gettysburg June 13-15, 1863* (2016), and *Confederate General William "Extra Billy" Smith: From Virginia's Statehouse to Gettysburg Scapegoat* (2013), the latter of which won multiple awards including the Dr. James I. Robertson, Jr. Literary Award for Confederate history. Scott has also written many articles for many publications including for *Gettysburg Magazine*.

Cooper Wingert is the author of a dozen books and numerous articles on slavery and the American Civil War. His book *The Confederate Approach on Harrisburg* won the 2012 Dr. James I. Robertson, Jr. Literary Award for Confederate history. His other works include *Slavery and the Underground Railroad in South Central Pennsylvania* (2016), *Abolitionists of South Central Pennsylvania* (2018), and *Harrisburg and the Civil War* (2013). He has also written articles for *Gettysburg Magazine* and has appeared on C-SPAN Book TV and Pennsylvania Cable Network. Cooper received the Camp Curtin Historical Society's inaugural General Joseph F. Knipe Award in recognition for his research on the Harrisburg area during the Civil War. A Pennsylvania native, he is currently a student at Dickinson College in Carlisle, Pennsylvania.